THE GREAT CHIEFS

THE GREAT CHIEFS

By the Editors of

TIME-LIFE BOOKS

with text by

Benjamin Capps

TIME-LIFE BOOKS / ALEXANDRIA, VIRGINIA

Time-Life Books Inc.
is a wholly owned subsidiary of

TIME INCORPORATED

Founder: Henry R. Luce 1898-1967

Editor-in-Chief: Henry Anatole Grunwald
President: J. Richard Munro
Chairman of the Board: Ralph P. Davidson
Executive Vice President: Clifford J. Grum
Chairman, Executive Committee: James R. Shepley
Editorial Director: Ralph Graves
Group Vice President, Books: Joan D. Manley
Vice Chairman: Arthur Temple

TIME-LIFE BOOKS INC.

Editor: George Constable
Executive Editor: George Daniels
Board of Editors: Dale M. Brown, Thomas H. Flaherty Jr.,
William Frankel, Thomas A. Lewis, Martin Mann, Philip W.
Payne, John Paul Porter, Gerry Schremp, Gerald Simons,
Nakanori Tashiro, Kit van Tulleken
Art Director: Tom Suzuki
 Assistant: Arnold C. Holeywell
Director of Administration: David L. Harrison
Director of Operations: Gennaro C. Esposito
Director of Research: Carolyn L. Sackett
 Assistant: Phyllis K. Wise
Director of Photography: Dolores Allen Littles

President: Carl G. Jaeger
Executive Vice Presidents: John Steven Maxwell,
David J. Walsh
Vice Presidents: George Artandi, Stephen L. Bair,
Peter G. Barnes, Nicholas Benton, John L. Canova,
Beatrice T. Dobie, Carol Flaumenhaft, James L. Mercer,
Herbert Sorkin, Paul R. Stewart

THE OLD WEST

Editor: George Constable
EDITORIAL STAFF FOR "THE GREAT CHIEFS"
Assistant Editor: Joan Mebane
Picture Editor: Mary Y. Steinbauer
Text Editor: Valerie Moolman
Designer: Herbert H. Quarmby
Staff Writers: Lee Greene, Sam Halper, Kirk Landers,
Robert Tschirky, Eve Wengler
Chief Researcher: June O. Goldberg
Researchers: John Conrad Weiser, Loretta Britten,
Jane Coughran, Mary Leverty, Donna Lucey,
Michael Luftman, Archer Mayor, Nancy Miller,
Mary Kay Moran, Vivian Stephens
Design Assistant: Faye Eng
Copy Coordinators: Barbara H. Fuller, Gregory Weed
Picture Coordinator: Susan Spiller
Editorial Assistant: Lisa Berger

EDITORIAL OPERATIONS
Production Director: Feliciano Madrid
 Assistants: Peter A. Inchauteguiz, Karen A. Meyerson
Copy Processing: Gordon E. Buck
Quality Control Director: Robert L. Young
 Assistant: James J. Cox
 Associates: Daniel J. McSweeney, Michael G. Wight
Art Coordinator: Anne B. Landry
Copy Room Director: Susan Galloway Goldberg
 Assistants: Celia Beattie, Ricki Tarlow

THE AUTHOR: Benjamin Capps, a freelancer who makes his home in Grand Prairie, Texas, has written nine books dealing with the Great Plains in the 19th Century, including *The Indians* for TIME-LIFE BOOKS. Shortly before undertaking *The Great Chiefs* he completed *The Warren Wagontrain Raid*, a study of an 1871 episode that marked a high point of Kiowa resistance against encroaching Texans.

THE COVER: This portrait of Crow chief He Who Jumps over Every One, astride a war pony whose feather plumage matches his own, was created by artist George Catlin in the 1830s. At the time, the leaders of the Western tribes were barely aware of the stirrings of a white horde on the margins of their dominion. By the end of the 19th Century, the threat had swept them to ruin and only elegies remained—none more masterful than E. S. Curtis' frontispiece photograph of Chief Red Hawk. The Sioux leader had helped vanquish Custer at the Little Bighorn in 1876 and lived to see his tribe suffer a countermassacre at Wounded Knee in 1890.

CORRESPONDENTS: Elisabeth Kraemer (Bonn); Margot Hapgood, Dorothy Bacon, Lesley Coleman (London); Susan Jonas, Lucy T. Voulgaris (New York); Maria Vincenza Aloisi, Josephine du Brusle (Paris); Ann Natanson (Rome). Valuable assistance was also provided by: Judy Aspinall, Karin B. Pearce (London); Carolyn T. Chubet, Miriam Hsia, Christina Lieberman (New York); Mimi Murphy (Rome).

This volume is one of a series that chronicles the history of the American West from the early 16th Century to the end of the 19th Century.

For information about any Time-Life book, please write:
Reader Information
Time-Life Books
541 North Fairbanks Court
Chicago, Illinois 60611

Library of Congress Cataloguing in Publication Data
Time-Life Books
 The great chiefs/by the editors of Time-Life Books; with text
by Benjamin Capps.—New York: Time-Life Books, c1975.
 240 p.: ill. (some col.); 28 cm.—(The Old West)
 Bibliography: p. 236-237.
 Includes index.
 1. Indians of North America—The West—Biography.
 2. Indians of North America—The West—Wars.
 3. The West—Biography. I. Capps, Benjamin, 1922-
 II. Title. III. Series: The Old West (Alexandria, Va.)
 E78.W5T55 1975   970'.004'97   75-744
 ISBN 0-8094-1494-5
 ISBN 0-8094-1493-7 (lib. bdg.)
 ISBN 0-8094-1492-9 (retail ed.)

©1975 Time-Life Books Inc. All rights reserved.
No part of this book may be reproduced in any form or by any electronic or mechanical means, including information storage and retrieval devices or systems, without prior written permission from the publisher, except that brief passages may be quoted for reviews.
Sixth printing. Revised 1982. Printed in U.S.A.
Published simultaneously in Canada.

TIME-LIFE is a trademark of Time Incorporated U.S.A.

CONTENTS

1 | An assembly of eagles

Proud, joyously combative, free as the wind—these were the chiefs of the Old West at the beginning of the 19th Century, when the buffalo ran 30 million strong and the white frontier had barely vaulted the Appalachians.

Popular imagination saw them as powerful feudal lords, reigning over multitudes of bloodthirsty but obedient subjects. In fact, there were neither monarchs nor multitudes between the Mississippi and the far side of the Rockies. The 200,000 Indians of that region were fragmented into bands and tribes ranging in size from a few dozen members to several thousand. Each group regulated its affairs by a system of leadership that was as supple as the Indians' nomadic life style itself.

The relationship of Western tribesmen to their chiefs was recognized as early as 1805 in the journals of the explorers Meriwether Lewis and William Clark: "Each individual is his own master, and the only control to which his conduct is subjected is the advice of a chief, supported by his influence over the rest of the tribe." The chief's power was anything but absolute: "His commands have no effect on those who incline to disobey."

Only by earning the respect of his peers could a man become chief. Ambitious warriors strove to emulate the eagle, the high-flying predator whose feathers were prized symbols of bold exploits. The warrior who amassed feathers enough to sport a trailing war bonnet was well on his way to attaining a chieftainship.

Despite their limited authority, the chiefs were able to provide remarkably resourceful leadership when called upon to face the inexorable tide of white invasion. Some resisted with uncompromising ferocity, like Geronimo of the Apaches, who battled settlers and soldiers for more than 30 years. Others, like Washakie of the Shoshonis, invested all their hopes in cooperation, earning less fame than those who resisted to the bitter end yet leaving a deep imprint on history. Still others were fervent idealists: Chief Joseph of the Nez Percés attempted desperately to avoid war with the white man, but when a long list of injustices culminated in a ruthless attack by the United States Army, he fought until his band was nearly destroyed. Even then he cried out for peace and understanding: "I hope that no more groans of wounded men and women will ever go to the ear of the Great Spirit above, and that all people may be one people."

No artist ever captured the essence of Indian leaders more sensitively than George Catlin, a Pennsylvania-born portraitist who set out in 1830 to preserve a memory of the customs and character of "the noble races of red men, melting away at the approach of civilization." During the course of a six-year Western odyssey, Catlin visited 146 tribes and painted the portraits of scores of chiefs, including those depicted here. In their raiment of feathers and buffalo robes they appeared indomitable, but already they were beset with tribulations that no chief could long withstand. "To use their own very beautiful expression," Catlin observed, "they are fast traveling to the shades of their fathers, towards the setting sun."

BLACK ROCK, BAND CHIEF OF THE TETON SIOUX
The majestic leader of the Neecoweegee band, which roamed the upper reaches of the
Missouri, was painted by Catlin with "the battles of his life emblazoned on his robe."

SMOKE, HEAD CHIEF OF THE PONCAS
"A noble specimen of native dignity and philosophy" was Catlin's description of the
Ponca leader, whose people lived near the union of the Missouri and Niobrara rivers.

CLERMONT, HEAD CHIEF OF THE OSAGES
Seated on a rock throne, the chief of the Osages — a small tribe on the southern plains
— cradles a war club rendered more lethal by a metal blade obtained from white traders.

WOLF CHIEF, HEAD CHIEF OF THE MANDANS
"A haughty, austere, and overbearing man," said Catlin of this tribal leader, whose
people lived along the upper Missouri in lodges constructed of earth-covered logs.

MOLE IN THE FOREHEAD, BAND CHIEF OF THE PAWNEES
Named, as many Indians were, for a physical trait, this "very distinguished warrior"
headed a Pawnee contingent whose lands lay between the Platte and Kansas rivers.

CHARGER, HEAD CHIEF OF THE YANKTON SIOUX
An exemplar of valor in a northern plains tribe that Catlin called "one of the most
numerous and powerful" he had seen, Charger suffered nine gunshot wounds in battle.

EAGLE'S RIBS, WAR CHIEF OF THE PIEGAN BLACKFEET
War leader of a band living by the mouth of the Yellowstone River, Eagle's Ribs boasted to a startled Catlin of "eight scalps taken from the heads of trappers and traders."

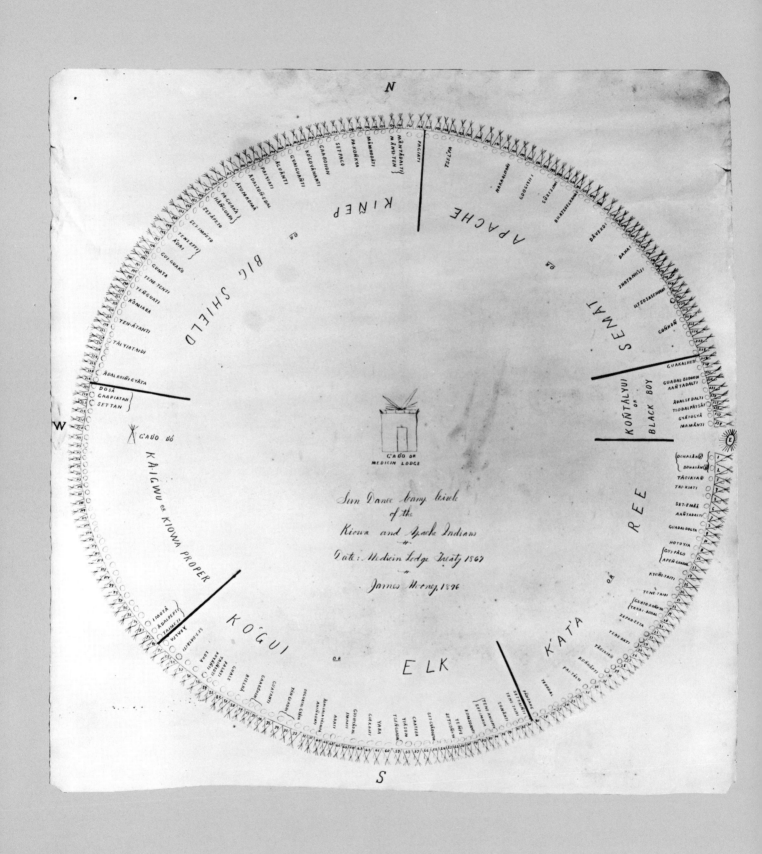

Sun Dance Camp Circle
of the
Kiowa and Apache Indians
"
Date: Medicin Lodge Treaty 1867
"
James Mooney, 1896

The Kiowas' star-crossed aristocracy

For the past 10 months, the Kiowas of the southern plains had been separated into small bands, each going its own way to find buffalo-hunting grounds and good grazing for their horses. But now, obeying custom, the whole tribe of some 2,000 souls was gathered in a single great camp under their principal chief, Islandman, to confer on matters that concerned them all—future military actions against enemy tribes, and the staging of the annual summer sun dance, the religious ceremony that they believed would ensure the continued fecundity of the earth.

It was the beginning of the spring moon the Kiowas called *Pai Aganti*—the time of hot-weather-soon—in the year 1833 by the white man's calendar. During this moon would occur a tragedy that not only precipitated a crisis of leadership in the tribe but coincided with the start of nearly half a century of grievous trial for the Kiowas and other Indians of the West.

The Kiowas were a smallish tribe, only about a tenth the size of their powerful neighbors, the Comanches, for instance. But they possessed a full measure of the horseback panache and exultant fighting spirit that, in time, would make Plains tribes seem the model of the American Indian. And their saga epitomized the story of chieftainship in a time of unparalleled turbulence, when an unknown force came out of an unknown place to challenge Indian suzerainty and even Indian existence. An array of vigorous Kiowa chiefs would grapple with this challenge in many ways to find themselves hopelessly overmatched by the new enemy.

This spring their world was still wild, free and vast. The Kiowas' traditional range extended from north of the Arkansas River to south of the Red, and it included parts of Texas and those regions that would someday be known as Kansas, New Mexico, Colorado and Oklahoma. They had come together at the very heart of their domain, amid the timber-clad granite knobs of the Wichita Mountains. Almost as far as the eye could see, buffalo-hide tipis were sprawled along the banks of Rainy Mountain Creek—so named because a cloudburst occurred almost every time they pitched camp there. In the valleys nearby, antelope and buffalo grazed amid patches of red, brown and gold wild flowers, called gaillardias, or Indian blankets.

The camp basked in well-being. Reunited friends were exchanging visits. Women were cooking meat in brass buckets obtained through barter with the Pawnees of the north, who in turn had procured them from white traders. Old men sat in the sunshine and contemplatively smoked the aromatic mixture of tobacco leaves and bark they called *kinnikinick*. A singular personage among these retired warriors was the keeper of the sacred medicine idol, called the *taime*—a vital element in the sun-dance ritual. No doubt he and the other men who were past their prime felt pangs of envy when nearly all the men of fighting age rode off one morning to raid against the Utes, whose domain lay to the northwest. The war party intended to return with scalps, horses and other plunder in time for the sun dance. While they were gone, the rest of the tribe would remain in the vicinity of their campsite, moving only a few miles in one direction or another in order to find fresh grazing and hunting.

Some days after the warriors departed, a group of hunters left Islandman's camp to seek buffalo to the north. They came upon the carcass of a buffalo with an

In a white scholar's diagram of a Kiowa encampment at a religious ceremony, hundreds of tipis—many identified by the owner's name—form a circle encompassing the tribe's six divisions. Although separated most of the year, all divisions acknowledged the primacy of the one principal chief.

15

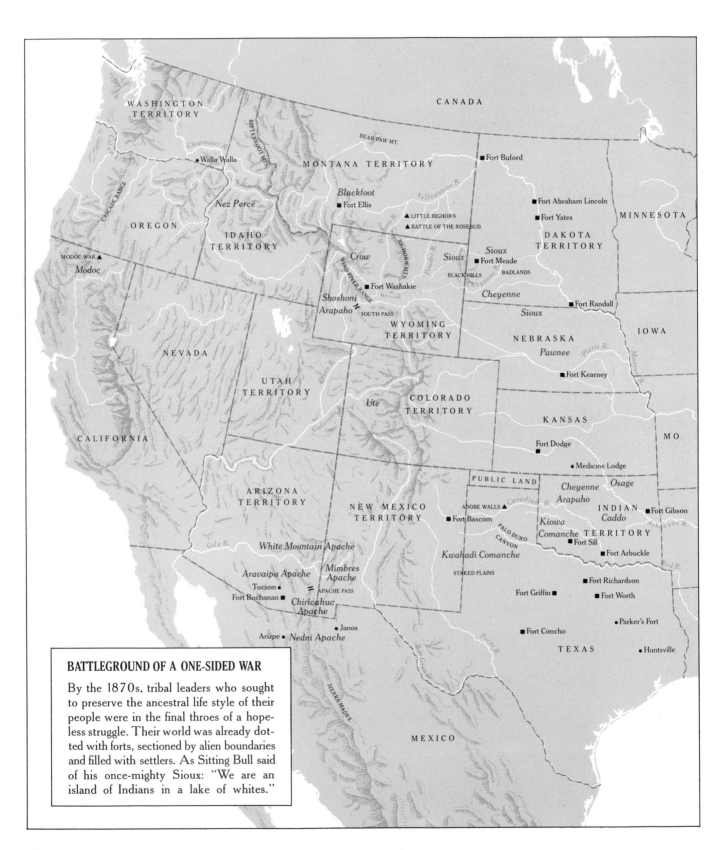

CANADA

WASHINGTON TERRITORY

Clearwater R.

BEAR PAW MT.

■ Fort Buford

MONTANA TERRITORY

Yellowstone R.

BITTERROOT MTS.

● Walla Walla

Salmon R.

Blackfoot
■ Fort Ellis

■ Fort Abraham Lincoln

MINNESOTA

Nez Percé

OREGON

▲ LITTLE BIGHORN
▲ BATTLE OF THE ROSEBUD

■ Fort Yates

Powder R.

IDAHO TERRITORY

Crow

BIGHORN MTS.

Sioux

Sioux
■ Fort Meade

DAKOTA TERRITORY

MODOC WAR ▲

Modoc

Snake R.

WIND RIVER RANGE

■ Fort Washakie

Cheyenne R.

BLACK HILLS   BADLANDS

Shoshoni
Arapaho   SOUTH PASS

Cheyenne

■ Fort Randall

CASCADE RANGE

Columbia R.

WYOMING TERRITORY

Sioux

IOWA

NEVADA

Green R.

UTAH TERRITORY

Ute

COLORADO TERRITORY

NEBRASKA

Pawnee   *Platte R.*

Missouri R.

■ Fort Kearney

KANSAS

MO.

CALIFORNIA

Colorado R.

■ Fort Dodge

● Medicine Lodge

PUBLIC LAND

Cheyenne   *Osage*
Arapaho

INDIAN
Caddo   ■ Fort Gibson

Arkansas R.

ARIZONA TERRITORY

NEW MEXICO TERRITORY

ADOBE WALLS ▲   *Canadian R.*

■ Fort Bascom

Kiowa
Comanche   TERRITORY
■ Fort Sill

Gila R.

White Mountain Apache

PALO DURO CANYON

■ Fort Arbuckle

Red R.

Aravaipa Apache

Mimbres Apache

Kwahadi Comanche

STAKED PLAINS

■ Fort Richardson

Tucson ●

APACHE PASS ■

■ Fort Griffin

■ Fort Worth

Fort Buchanan ■   *Chiricahua Apache*

● Parker's Fort

● Janos

■ Fort Concho

Arizpe ●   *Nedni Apache*

TEXAS

● Huntsville

SIERRA MADRE

Pecos R.

Rio Grande

MEXICO

BATTLEGROUND OF A ONE-SIDED WAR

By the 1870s, tribal leaders who sought to preserve the ancestral life style of their people were in the final throes of a hopeless struggle. Their world was already dotted with forts, sectioned by alien boundaries and filled with settlers. As Sitting Bull said of his once-mighty Sioux: "We are an island of Indians in a lake of whites."

arrow sunk deep into its flesh—not an arrow of their own, but one whose shaft bore the markings of the Osages, another long-time enemy. Their presence so near the Kiowa camp was ominous. The hunters galloped back to warn their principal chief. All revelry ceased at once. Islandman posted sentries and supervised the building of adobe breastworks for defense.

Days passed and no attack came. Finally the Kiowas began to breathe more easily. What they had feared to be hostiles in force was, they concluded, a handful of Osage hunters prowling the plains for meat.

By now the grass near the camp had been nibbled low by the herd of Kiowa mounts, and there was need to move. Islandman took council with the few leaders who had not gone off with the raiding party and agreed to permit the tribe to split into several groups. The buffalo hunters again set off on their own. Another group headed for a known range of wild horses; there they would hobble their brood mares in the path of stallions too wild to be captured, and thus breed up the hardiness of the Kiowas' domestic herds. Islandman himself led another contingent—comprised mainly of old men and women, young mothers and children—through a mountain gap to a green valley on Otter Creek.

Late in the afternoon of the day that Islandman pitched his new camp, some girls went to the creek for water. As they cupped their hands to drink from a still pool, a pebble dropped from the rocks above. They looked up: no one was there. But when the ripples smoothed away, a girl bending toward the water saw, to her horror, not only her own reflection but also the wavering image of a strange warrior.

Trying to act as though nothing was amiss, the girls went quietly back to camp to spread the alarm. On hearing their report, Islandman and the other old men smiled and dismissed the incident as a prank played by some of the boys to exploit the girls' fears after the scare caused by the Osage arrow.

Early the next morning a youth left the camp to lead his family's ponies to pasture. Something moved behind a rock; as his eyes followed the movement into the gloom, he was appalled to see the shaved head of an Osage. He ran back, screaming, to wake the others.

Stumbling half-dressed from their tipis, Islandman's people found their camp already aswarm with Osages. "To the rocks! To the rocks!" yelled Islandman as he

himself ran in that direction. His panic-stricken people tried to follow. Some ran headlong into the enemy, who slashed and stabbed with long knives, mercilessly ripping the throats of young and old. There were individual acts of heroism, but very few. As the keeper of the *taime* scuttled for safety, leaving the sacred idol tied to a tipi pole, his wife tried to rescue it and was butchered. Sensing its value, the Osages tore the *taime* from her dying hands.

Without their warriors and without effective leadership, the Kiowas were routed in a shameful defeat. While many women and children were slaughtered, only five of the men lost their lives. Islandman escaped with a minor wound. Not a single one of the attackers died—and this in the camp of the Kiowas' principal chief.

When the killing was done, the Osages cut off the heads of the dead and placed them in the Kiowas' own brass cooking buckets. They then carefully arranged the buckets in rows amidst the devastation of the camp and left them there as a greeting for the returning Kiowa warriors. After that, they fired the tipis and left, taking with them the *taime* and two captive children.

The Kiowa fighting men came back from the land of the Utes expecting a joyous reception, for they had fared well. Instead, they found a scene of unbridled grief. The surviving women were mourning the dead by slashing their faces and bodies until the blood flowed as it had on the day of the massacre. And on the grim face of every man could be read the same thought: that Islandman was not worthy of being their principal chief. It was an issue that had to be aired in council.

Summoned by a camp crier, every man who had any claim to importance in the tribe—as orator, warrior, hunter or healer—came together around a fire, smoked a ceremonial pipe in silence and prepared to discuss the dereliction of the chief and the consequent necessity of choosing a successor. One of the older men, respected by all for his wisdom, arose and spoke first.

Islandman, he said, had failed utterly in his responsibility to the tribe. Not only had he exercised poor judgment in permitting the reduced camp at Rainy Mountain Creek to break up into several smaller groups, not only had he neglected to take the minimal precaution of posting sentries when Osages were about, but he had even failed to make a stand and inspire others by his personal example. It had been his duty to place the welfare of his tribe above all else, including his own life, yet he had fled in terror before the enemy. This having been bluntly said, and unanimously agreed to, the council members spoke of Islandman no more, nor would they ever heed his voice again. There would be no formal punishment for him: he would simply slip into obscurity and become an ordinary tribesman, a man who had for all time forfeited his influence and following. Far more important now than Islandman was the question of replacement.

Members of the council who wished to make statements rose to do so in an order befitting their years and experience. There was no rigidly prescribed sequence, but always the older men spoke first and then the men of middle years. Even a young warrior might, after his elders had spoken, ask and receive permission to express his views if he had some bold deeds and a measure of eloquence to his credit.

Each man was heard with the utmost courtesy for as long as he wished to speak, and each viewpoint was solemnly considered, for the art of persuasion was the essence of such meetings and a man was entitled to his chance to persuade. No orator was interrupted and no council member was permitted to leave the session until consensus declared it recessed. This was custom in most of the tribes that roamed the Western plains. In one such meeting a council member suffered a severe nosebleed and could do nothing but stop up his nostrils and choke down the blood, almost suffocating in the process, until the meeting was over.

The Kiowa council dwelt at length on the requirements for the office of principal chief and on the qualities desired in the man named to fulfill it. To begin with, he must have a record of outstanding accomplishment in war; although in his new role he would not himself be a tactical leader, he would be expected to set an example of courage if circumstance brought war to his people, as it had to Islandman. He must possess a compelling personality that would draw others to him and inspire their loyalty and respect. Indeed, respect was his sole source of power, and to be truly effective he must be a man of great wealth—the owner of many horses obtained by leading raids. Moreover, he must have demonstrated his generosity by giving feasts and providing food, horses and buffalo hides to those who

An Indian family treks through the Wichita Mountains in this painting of the Kiowa heartland by soldier-artist Hermann Stieffel. Driven from the northern plains by the Sioux in the early 19th Century, the Kiowas reasserted their power in a range extending from central Kansas into Texas.

After ambushing the Kiowas in 1833 and sending their chief into disgraceful flight, Osage warriors filled this bucket and dozens like it with the heads of their victims —possibly as an offering to their deities.

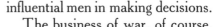

were less fortunate than he was.

Finally, he must be energetic, equable of temper, receptive to the opinions of others, deliberate in reaching judgments and gifted with an eloquent tongue. These traits would be indispensable in carrying out his primary duties: suggesting the division of hunting assignments when the tribe separated again, acting as spokesman in meetings with other tribes, mediating factional and personal disputes within the tribe, and at all times encouraging the unity of his people.

As speaker after speaker vividly expressed his point of view, more and more council members were swayed into accepting the man who appeared to be the popular preference. It was the basis of tribal decision-making that agreement in all matters of importance had to be unanimous or very nearly so. After much slow, reflective talk, the choice of the council fell upon a man named Little Mountain, who was selected not by vote but by the weight of opinion as expressed in orations. It was agreed that Little Mountain had all the requisite qualities in abundance. He was acclaimed as the first voice of the tribe. It turned out that he would retain that role for fully 33 years.

The Kiowa organization of which Little Mountain had become principal chief was formal but flexible. The tribe was made up of six divisions or subtribes. Each subtribe was semiautonomous and led by a chief who had emerged as a natural leader by virtue of accomplishments and qualities that were similar to those of Little Mountain. Some of these subtribes had grown too large to live together the year round, and they had divided into two or more bands to hunt their own meat, gather their own wild prairie turnips and plums, collect their own firewood and seek their own pasturage. Every band had its own leader, who usually arrived at his position by being the head of the wealthiest family in the group. Like Little Mountain, both the subtribe chiefs and the band chiefs dealt with the day-to-day peacetime life of their people. Their duties were to keep order, supervise camp activities, determine the band's movements, negotiate with traders when the opportunity arose and always—without fail—consult with other influential men in making decisions.

The business of war, of course, required leadership too. Every male, in the course of his life, rode with war parties—to gain plunder, to revenge an attack by the foe or simply for the zest of combat. It was a triumph to return from a raid with horses or scalps; but the greatest glory was achieved by riding into battle and striking the foe with a hand or a stick—whether or not the warrior went on to kill the man. This feat, considered the ultimate proof of courage, was known as counting coup.

With a good coup count and a fair number of stolen horses to his credit, any young warrior could rally others to set off on a raid. Continuing successes, coupled with his own eloquent accounts of his deeds, could earn him permanent recognition as a war chief—a man able to lead scores or hundreds of men on combat missions. During an expedition, a war chief selected the camping sites, posted the watch, sent out scouts, delegated men to locate water supplies and tend horses, and devised strategy. His authority was suspended between raids, but if he showed a capacity to win men's loyalty in peace as well as war, he might aspire to the principal chieftainship itself.

The Kiowas had many words to differentiate the various levels and categories of leadership. Regrettably, people of other cultures who attempted to interpret the Kiowa tongue could not precisely translate these words, for which there were no equivalents in other languages; nor did they fully understand tribal organization. Therefore, making no distinction between civil and military duties, and none among principal chief, subtribe chief and band chief, interpreters indiscriminately applied the one word "chief" to all roles and ranks having anything to do with leadership. So far as the Kiowas were concerned, the word was a hopeless oversimplification of an intricate leadership system.

The attributes and responsibilities of chiefs, on whatever level, varied little across the West. However, the ways in which the various tribes were organized varied considerably. The Mandans of the northern plains, for example, had two principal chiefs—a civil and a military chief acting in concert. The Cheyennes had a governing

Captured by the Osages, the sacred *taime,*
shown in replica, was the Kiowas' bitterest
loss. Without the idol — made of stone, and
adorned with eagle down and deerskin —
they could not hold their annual sun dance.

body of 44 chiefs: four principal chiefs and four from
each of the 10 bands of their tribe. The Apaches had
no principal chief at all; their component bands were
completely autonomous.

While the chiefs of some tribes inherited the position
from their fathers, chieftainship among the Plains tribes
usually was nonhereditary. As in other societies, it was
no disadvantage for a would-be leader to come of
wealthy, influential stock; nevertheless, he had to earn
his position by his own qualities and accomplishments.
In all tribes, it was essentially the man who made the office. Individuals of deep convictions, forceful character
and proven ability stood out and were recognized as
great chiefs. These were the men who were going to
have to come to grips with a challenge that had no precedent: a devastating confrontation with a people far
more powerful, numerous and cohesive than they.

At the time Little Mountain assumed the principal
chieftainship of the Kiowas, his people's contact with
white men had been infrequent and not always friendly.
Wagon freighters with goods bound for the Mexican
city of Santa Fe had begun traveling an 800-mile trail
from Franklin, Missouri, as early as 1821, and Kiowa
raiding parties had sporadically launched fierce attacks
upon these caravans, making off with much booty. Only
the year before, in 1832, the Kiowas had fallen upon
an American pack train and captured— among more useful goods— a large number of silver dollars. Not knowing the purpose of money, they had made hair ornaments
of the silver.

Yet, even if they had no real understanding of white
civilization, it had already done much to shape their
own. The horse, upon which their nomadic way of life
depended, had been introduced to the American continent two centuries earlier by the Spaniards, and had
been acquired in vast numbers by the Plains Indians
through trade and theft. The Indians' iron tools — hatch-
ets, lance blades, arrow points, butcher knives — all had
been supplied to them by enterprising white traders.

Disease had also come. As early as 1816, smallpox,
possibly contracted on raiding expeditions into Mexico,
had infected first one tribe and then another. Both the
Kiowas and the Comanches, who had been their friends
and allies since 1790, had suffered a dreadful toll since
they possessed no natural resistance. Thus, although

21

Destined to lead the Kiowas for more than three decades, Little Mountain strikes a pose of stolid confidence for artist George Catlin in 1834, a year after rising to power in the wake of the massacre by the Osages.

the Indians' lands were still unfenced and unplowed, their life was not unchanged, and the pace of change would quicken with every passing year.

In the summer of 1834, a force of U.S. dragoons under Colonel Henry Dodge rode through the lands of the Kiowas, Comanches, Cherokees, Creeks, Osages and Wichitas to establish friendly relations with these tribes, whose hostilities had been interfering with white trade and travel on the plains. At a Wichita village Dodge met a visiting contingent of Kiowas, led by Little Mountain, and in the face of their initial suspicion he quickly explained that the government wished to establish a lasting peace with them. Little Mountain greeted the strangers with affable dignity. Although he had never before encountered American troops and considered them decidedly bizarre in appearance, he was prepared to deal with them as he would with a peaceful delegation from a neighboring tribe.

In a grand council, the colonel offered the Kiowas generous trading privileges in return for the safe passage of U.S. citizens traveling the Santa Fe Trail. To sweeten the proposition he bestowed an unexpected gift: a Kiowa girl who had been taken captive by the Osages during the massacre of the previous year. The soldiers had ransomed her for the purpose of bringing about a friendly meeting with Kiowa leaders.

Little Mountain was extremely gratified. "White men and brethren," he said, "this day is the most interesting period of our existence. The Great Spirit has caused a light to shine all around us so that we can see each other. The Great Spirit has sent us to see these white men and brothers. Kiowas, take them by the hand and use them well. They are your friends; they have brought home your lost relation."

In this atmosphere of brotherhood and trust it was not difficult for Dodge to persuade Little Mountain and 14 other Kiowa chiefs to accompany the dragoon force to Fort Gibson some 200 miles to the east. There the Kiowas received presents of food and clothing, and promised to cease their depredations along the Santa Fe Trail. There, too, they held peace talks with representatives of the Cherokee, Creek, Choctaw and Osage tribes, whose lands lay to the east—close enough to the frontier so that whites were desirous of avoiding intertribal disturbances. Little Mountain was able to make a most felicitous exchange with a chief of the Osages:

one fine Kiowa horse in return for the priceless *taime*.

For well over a decade the Kiowas kept their promise to the white men and let travelers pass unmolested along the great trail. But they did not hesitate to swoop down into Texas on raiding expeditions against the hated white men there who seemed intent upon thrusting their way up into Kiowa-Comanche territory.

Life continued much as before until gold was discovered in California in 1848. Thereafter, seemingly endless trains of covered wagons came rolling across the Kiowa range, bringing a devastating cholera epidemic and laying waste the grasslands alongside the Santa Fe Trail. Smaller strikes elsewhere in the West maintained the cavalcade of fortune hunters through the middle of the 1850s. Then, in 1858, gold was found in large quantities in the Pikes Peak region of Colorado.

With that, the trek across the plains developed into a stampede. Within one year some 100,000 white adventurers of every stripe swarmed unchecked across the Kiowas' hunting grounds, despoiling the Earth Mother with a recklessness that the Indians found appalling. They chopped down trees and wasted precious wood along the trails. Their horses, mules and oxen gnawed bare the good grazing land. Hunters shot buffalo and antelope from their wagons, and when there was nothing left in sight to shoot they ranged far afield in search of game. When they killed too much, as often they did, they left the unwanted carcasses to rot and moved on, killing more. Some travelers gave up their quest for gold and set up farms, ranches and even fledgling towns on the tribe's accustomed range.

The Kiowas, enraged by the intrusions and devastation, fell upon settlers and travelers alike—and also picked up the tempo and ferocity of their raids into Texas. Late in 1858, at a Kiowa encampment on the Arkansas River, a government-appointed Indian agent named Robert Miller delivered a warning to Little Mountain. Unless the Kiowas and their allies ceased their depredations, Miller threatened, the government would send troops to punish them.

For the first time, Little Mountain spoke hostile words to a white official. Admitting his warriors' raids only indirectly, he said scornfully: "The white chief is a fool. He is a coward. When my young men, to keep their women and children from starving, take a cup of sugar or coffee from the white men passing through our

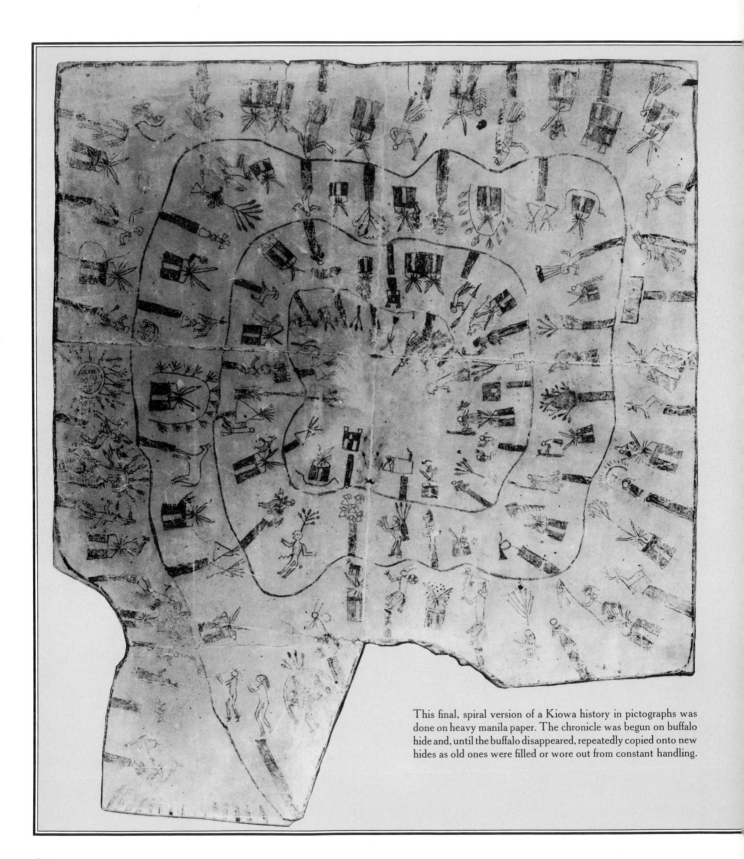

This final, spiral version of a Kiowa history in pictographs was done on heavy manila paper. The chronicle was begun on buffalo hide and, until the buffalo disappeared, repeatedly copied onto new hides as old ones were filled or wore out from constant handling.

A sixty-year picture history of a valiant people

Through good times and bad, the Kiowas were keenly interested in keeping track of their history to reinforce a sense of tribal identity. Since they lacked a written language, they recorded important events in cumulative chronicles like the one opposite, which expresses almost 60 years of Kiowa history in an ingenious visual shorthand. It was started in 1833 by Little Mountain, soon to be principal chief. After his death in 1866, the record was continued by his nephew, who made a final copy in spiral form, beginning at the lower left and ending in the center.

Each year in the long saga is represented by two images—one recalling an event of the winter, the other showing a summer incident. Wintertime entries were drawn above a black bar symbolizing a dead blade of grass. Summer occurrences were usually depicted above an image of the sacred lodge *(below, far right)* in which the annual sun dance was held.

A few of the entries, such as the one second from right below, reflect the personal concerns of the chronicler, but mostly they document vicissitudes of great moment to the whole tribe—a victory over an enemy, for instance, or the death of a chief. During the long nights in winter camp, the chronicler would call to other men, "Come and smoke"; a pipe would be passed, and each warrior present would elaborate on the circumstances surrounding a particular pictograph, thus bringing the past to life again.

In the chronicle the destructive effect of an alien culture is registered only indirectly — by the disappearance of the sun dance symbol near the end. Its absence reflects the banning of the ceremony by reservation authorities — a bitter blow to the tribesmen.

In 1892, Little Mountain's nephew turned the chronicle over to the United States Army, so the power that had subjugated his tribe might at least preserve the memory of what the Kiowas had been in times gone by.

ENTRIES FROM THE KIOWA CHRONICLE

A butcher knife circled by severed heads represents the 1833 massacre of Kiowa women and children by the Osages. The disaster—at a site in the Wichita Mountains later known to the tribe as Cutthroat Gap—was the second entry on the chronicle.

The Kiowa girl memorialized by this pictograph returned to her people in 1834, a year after she was taken captive by the Osages. The joyous reunion was brought about by Colonel Henry Dodge, who ransomed the girl to facilitate peace parleys with the tribe.

Placed over a dead blade of grass indicating a winter entry, a knife-wielding warrior symbolizes an incident of 1843, when a man stabbed his wife for riding behind Little Mountain in a procession. The woman, who had acted at the chief's invitation, survived.

An auspicious manifestation of the spirits in 1858 is marked by a sun dance lodge with a forked stick protruding from it. The stick was left in the ground following the previous year's sun dance, and when the Kiowas returned, they found that it had taken root.

country, killing and driving away our buffalo, the white chief is angry and threatens to send his soldiers. I have looked for them a long time, but they have not come. His heart is a woman's. I have spoken."

So the Kiowas continued their attacks. No reprisal came, for much of the white army was occupied with the Civil War. By the summer of 1864, drivers of freight wagons were afraid to cross the plains, and the Denver area began running short of food. Mail service to Santa Fe was stopped because of Kiowa strikes against stage stations and coaches.

In July, Kiowa war chief White Bear and a party of warriors attacked a ranch a few miles from Fort Lyon, Colorado, then moved on to a nearby stage station where they killed four men. A few days later White Bear led a raid into a settlement near Menard, Texas, and killed several residents. That same month, another war party of Kiowas attacked a wagon train in Kansas and killed 10 teamsters. In October, growing ever more audacious, Kiowa raiders joined a force of Comanches and ravaged a series of settlements on Elm Creek near Fort Belknap, Texas, this time killing 11 people and capturing seven others.

If the raiders thought themselves secure from retaliation, they were mistaken. It came from Colonel Kit Carson—the famed trapper and scout—who was serving in the Southwest with the New Mexico Volunteers, organized to protect frontiersmen against Indian depredations. In the fall of 1864 Carson was ordered by his commanding officer, General James H. Carleton, to launch a slashing punitive attack on the marauders.

By November most of the Indians were in their winter camps, no longer raiding because their horses, subsisting on paltry winter grass and cottonwood bark, were too weak for spirited action. Early that month Carson rode east from Cimarron, New Mexico, with a regiment made up of 14 officers, 321 cavalrymen and 72 Indian scouts—Utes and Jicarilla Apaches who had no love for Kiowas but understood their thinking and tactics. Entirely unaware of their approach, Little Mountain was encamped, along with some Comanches, on the Canadian River in the Texas Panhandle.

When Carson's force struck early one cold morning, Little Mountain—unlike Islandman in his moment of crisis—swiftly organized his warriors into an orderly retreat, protecting the women and children, and sent a

courier galloping downriver to call for help from neighboring Kiowa and Comanche camps. He himself had his horse shot out from under him while leading the defense, but he continued to rally his warriors as reinforcements arrived from one camp after another.

The battle raged all day over the river bottoms and surrounding hills. At intervals the white soldiers blew bugle calls as signals to each other; a Kiowa warrior who had become the owner of a bugle captured in previous hostilities responded by blowing contradictory calls until the soldiers were totally confused.

Carson's troops might well have been overrun had they not brought along two 12-pound howitzers that fired explosive shells and were horribly effective in breaking up concentrations of warriors. The Kiowas scattered, circled the whites' position, and re-entered the village they had fled. There they succeeded in saving their precious horse herd; but the soldiers again put them to flight with the deadly howitzers. After the withdrawal of the Indian forces, Carson set fire to the 176 lodges of their camp, burned all their dried meat and other winter provisions, and all their buffalo robes and clothes. This done, the soldiers retired in good order. Three of Carson's men were killed in the engagement and 15 wounded. The Kiowa-Comanche forces, by Carson's count, lost 60 killed and 150 wounded.

It was a stunning blow to Little Mountain. He knew that the white attack would have been repelled if it had not been for the devastating howitzers. But against these terrible weapons there was no defense. What was a man to do in the face of such unthinkable force?

In 1865, Little Mountain recommended to his council that there be another peace meeting with the United States. At Bluff Creek near the mouth of the Little Arkansas River, the Kiowas and their Comanche allies met in October with a U.S. delegation headed by Colonel Jesse Leavenworth. Little Mountain and other tribal leaders listened with grave skepticism as government spokesmen tried to explain that it would be in the best interests of all parties for the Kiowas to confine themselves to certain areas distant from the main travel routes: specifically, lands south of the Canadian River and north of the Red.

Little Mountain protested. How could the whites parcel out lands that did not belong to them? Nevertheless, in the interests of peace with such a powerful people, he and six other Kiowa leaders signed the treaty on the government's terms, giving up all claims to western Texas, southwestern Kansas, eastern New Mexico and southeastern Colorado. The pact left them with the southwestern part of Oklahoma—then called Indian Territory—and most of the Texas Panhandle, which fortunately included the best of their traditional buffalo-hunting grounds. In return for their acceptance of limits on their roving and their promise of future docility, they were to be given annual presents of hunting rifles, staple foods, utensils and tools, seeds for planting, blankets and—of all things—suits.

They left the meeting not realizing the nature of the bargain they had made. After all, they still had their best buffalo range, and the presents of foodstuffs and other items would help to see them through hard times. The hints of the peace commissioners that they settle down, farm and become educated in white men's ways registered only dimly. In their innocence, with only the vaguest understanding of the terms of the treaty, they had committed themselves to life on a reservation.

The placing of troublesome—or inconveniently located—Indians on reservations was a long-standing U.S. policy. Between 1790 and 1834, Congress had passed a series of laws called the Indian Trade and Intercourse Acts, aimed at guaranteeing the Indians a safe homeland and gradually narrowing the gulf between the two cultures. Under the legislation, reservation-bound Indians were to be subject to their own laws rather than those of the United States, and an agent—appointed by the President—would serve as liaison with the tribe. His duties included dispensing provisions—called annuities—arresting traffickers in liquor, evicting trespassers attempting to settle on the reservations and arranging consultations between Indian tribes or between Indian chiefs and government representatives. Working under the agent's supervision—when the system functioned according to plan—were teachers, carpenters, blacksmiths and farmers, whose task was to abet the Indians in the various arts of civilization.

This was all very well in theory, but the handouts of food and other goods tended to drain the initiative of the Indians. Nor could the people of the Plains tribes reasonably be expected to take up farming. Such drudgery was anathema to horseborne knights who gloried in combat; and in any case, the lands allotted to them were often too arid for cultivation by the techniques they were taught. And as for the supposedly iron-clad guarantee of reservation lands, it was a fiction. Time and time again, the government found ways to induce the Indians to give up territory that had been described to them as a permanent homeland.

This was the system to which Little Mountain and his fellow chiefs had unwittingly committed the Kiowas. Perhaps it was fortunate for their principal chief that he died a natural death the following year. For more than three decades he had served his people honorably and bravely. He had kept his tribe unified, even if the world into which he had been born was no longer intact. White Bear said of Little Mountain: "He did all he could to make peace, and kept talking and talking, but the white man kept doing something bad to him, and he was in so much misery that he died."

For months after Little Mountain's death uncertainty about a successor persisted in Kiowa council meetings. The tribe had many strong personalities who made their voices heard, but they could not agree even after many council sessions. Two factions emerged, and their differences ran deep: Was it to be peace, or was it to be war? Should they become copies of white men, with schools and houses and the planting and plowing of fields? Or should they ignore the treaty that had been signed and pursue the life of their forefathers, raiding wherever and whenever they pleased?

Tacit in all their discussions was a recognition that white influence would loom large in the future. The only real question was how to cope with it—or, more specifically, what sort of leader was best suited to cope with it. If the future course was to resist the whites and all that they stood for, perhaps the great war chief Sitting Bear could best unite them. He was the leader of the Society of the Ten Bravest, the Kiowas' most elite military organization, and his courage was legendary. But, though deeply respected, Sitting Bear was in his sixties—and it was agreed that he was too old to take on the principal chieftainship of a troubled tribe.

White Bear, about 45, was a more likely choice. In some ways he was like Little Mountain: a capable man, jovial and outgoing, a noted warrior—but more complex and flamboyant. For important occasions, such

Meeting with government delegates at Medicine Lodge Creek, Kansas, in 1867, Kiowa dignitaries reluctantly accept a plan to concentrate the tribe on a reservation in Indian Territory—later Oklahoma. If the Indians had not acquiesced, the government intended to "conquer a peace."

as peace meetings and wars, he liked to paint his entire body flaming red. His tipi, too, was painted red, with streamers of red cloth tied to the protruding poles. In April 1864, a government physician who had come among the Plains tribes to vaccinate them against smallpox met White Bear and found him most friendly — indeed, impressive in every respect. "He is a fine-looking Indian," the visiting physician reported, "very energetic, and as sharp as a brier. I ate my meals three times a day with him in his lodge. He puts on a great deal of style, spreads a carpet for his guests to sit on."

But for all his hospitality and cordial contacts with Indian agents, traders and Army personnel stationed in the forts along the Arkansas River, White Bear was, in white terms, inconsistent. He knew the importance of getting along with the intruders and participated enthusiastically in all peace meetings, but he did so with the full intention of getting whatever he could out of them while continuing to raid and plunder. "I take hold of that part of the white man's road represented by the breech-loading gun," he said, "but I do not like the ration of corn; it hurts my teeth. The good Indian, he that listens to the white man, gets nothing. The independent Indian is the only one rewarded."

This attitude made him unacceptable as principal chief to the more peace-oriented Kiowas, whose preference was Kicking Bird. Born in 1835, Kicking Bird, like all other Kiowa leaders, had made his mark as a warrior. Nonetheless he held a belief that would have been inconceivable only three decades before and was still unacceptable to the older men of the tribe: that the future of the Kiowas lay in cooperation with the whites.

Both White Bear and Kicking Bird commanded great influence in the tribe, and the factions behind them were unalterably opposed. Finally, the council compromised and chose Lone Wolf, a slightly built but fearless warrior a few years older than White Bear. His main recommendations were that he was less vociferous in his commitment to either peace or war than White Bear and Kicking Bird and that he had in fact been Chief Little Mountain's own preference as successor.

But compromise, which never before had been the Kiowas' way, did not make for unity. Lone Wolf could not impose solidarity on a tribe that was so deeply split. White Bear and Kicking Bird held to their separate paths as if they had no principal chief, one continuing

to raid in forbidden areas, the other counseling peace.

And the white pioneers kept coming, all the while clamoring for government protection and a tougher policy toward the Indian menace. Many humanitarians back East — far from the line of battle — argued for moderation and understanding, but an 1867 editorial in the *Cincinnati Gazette* spoke for the majority: "The facts are obvious and men are either idiots or knaves who do not see that nothing short of the strong arm of the government will subdue these demons of the Plains."

As a result of this pressure, a government commission was sent west that year to hold a peace council at an encampment on Medicine Lodge Creek in southern Kansas. Kiowas, Comanches, Cheyennes and Arapahos flocked to it, lured by the promise of gifts.

Leading the huge Kiowa contingent were Sitting Bear, White Bear, Kicking Bird and Lone Wolf, each accompanied by his own following. Kicking Bird created something of a minor sensation by appearing in a breechcloth and a tall silk hat which had been given to him by one of the peace commissioners. But White Bear, who spoke five languages — four Indian tongues and Spanish — fluently and often at considerable length, was the center of attention. Henry M. Stanley, later to track down Dr. David Livingstone in Africa but at the time working as a correspondent for the *Missouri Democrat,* met White Bear at Medicine Lodge and wrote of him: "He has won a great name for reckless daring all the way from the Arkansas to the Rio Grande. His name is on every lip and his praises are sounded by the young damsels of his tribe as the greatest chief and warrior of the red man."

White Bear's eloquence quickly inspired newsmen to dub him "Orator of the Plains." Many of them first heard him when he bitterly protested the wanton shooting of buffalo along the line of march by soldiers accompanying the peace commissioners. One reporter noted with admiration: "White Bear, never backward in speech, resented in strong terms the shooting of his game on his own ground. Said he, while his eyes flashed and his lips curled with scorn: 'Has the white man become a child, that he should recklessly kill and not eat? When the red men slay game, they do so that they may live and not starve.'"

His point was well taken. The killing was quickly stopped, and the guilty were reprimanded. However

Seeking a site for a military post on the new reservation shared by Kiowas and Comanches, Army scouts arrive at Medicine Bluff Creek in southwestern Indian Territory—a locale where warriors held religious vigils. Fort Sill was established nearby in 1869.

33

White Bear was by no means finished. In a later speech, he described himself as the white man's friend, yet he added: "All the land south of the Arkansas belongs to the Kiowas and Comanches, and I don't want to give away any of it. I love the land and the buffalo, and will not part with it. I don't want any of the medicine lodges"—he meant schools and churches—"within the country. I want the children raised as I was. I don't want to settle. I love to roam over the prairies. There I feel free and happy, but when we settle down we grow pale and die. A long time ago this land belonged to our fathers; but when I go up the river I see camps of soldiers on its banks. These soldiers cut down my timber; they kill my buffalo; and when I see that, my heart feels like bursting."

Nevertheless he signed the treaty proposed by the peace commission. Kicking Bird signed too, and so did dour old Sitting Bear. Lone Wolf, perhaps because of growing antipathy toward the whites, did not.

Under the terms of this latest treaty the Kiowas and Comanches were squeezed farther south and into a shrunken area bounded on the north by the Washita River, on the south and west by the Red River and its North Fork, and on the east by the 98th meridian. For its part, the government guaranteed to supply the Kiowas and Comanches annually, for a period of 30 years, with $25,000 for the purchase of "such articles as may seem proper to the condition and necessities of the Indians." Also, they were to retain hunting privileges north of the Washita.

The latter concession, however, was soon to be withdrawn. In September of 1868, General William Tecumseh Sherman, military commander of the Division of the Missouri, announced that Indians would no longer be permitted outside their reservation for hunting —not even when the migrating buffalo herds failed to move through their territory and they were desperate for meat. "We have now selected and provided reservations for all, off the great road," announced Sherman. "All who cling to their old hunting grounds are hostile and will remain so till killed off."

Ulysses S. Grant, General of the Army, was in total agreement. In October, *The New York Times* reported him as saying that "the settlers and emigrants must be protected, even if the extermination of every Indian tribe is necessary to procure such a result." By the following year, Grant had been elected President, and he enthusiastically provided the authorization for the Army to clear away—by whatever means—all the Indians who lingered outside the boundaries the white man had set. Furthermore, he decreed that Indians were now to be subject to the laws of the United States. Thus the wild tribes were corralled, hamstrung, dependent on capricious masters and handouts that often did not come in time to appease their hunger.

Sparks of friction flew in the Kiowa camps and produced a white heat of division. White Bear was openly rebellious. Kicking Bird called eloquently for patience, but as a member of a fighting tribe he was at a disadvantage. Had he forgotten that he was a warrior? His influence began to wane and finally, in 1870, at the sun dance held on the North Fork of the Red River, he was openly accused of cowardice. It was a challenge he had to face, an accusation that he must prove untrue or he would have no more power as a leader.

He passed the pipe for war. The object: go down to Texas, lure out the cavalry from Fort Richardson, and fight—just to show the stuff Kiowas were made of. The sheer brazenness of the plan appealed to the hotbloods of the tribe. A hundred of them smoked the pipe, painted their faces and bodies, decorated themselves in their finest regalia and mounted their most spirited horses.

Kicking Bird led them south across the Red River and through the hot, sparsely populated Texas grasslands. A few warriors separated from the main party and attacked a stage station, killing the attendants and seizing whatever took their fancy. This impulsive and bloody action alerted Fort Richardson.

Captain Curwen McClellan of the 6th Cavalry rode northwest out of the fort to track down the attackers,

Performing brilliantly in off-reservation for-
ays, Big Tree *(left)* won the stature of a
war chief by 1870, though he was still in
his early twenties. Fellow militant White
Bear *(right)* actually boasted to the reservation agent of leading raids into Texas.

Chained to the wheel of a burning wagon, a teamster faces a grisly end as Kiowas ravage a freighting caravan in Texas in 1871. The raid, led by Sitting Bear, Big Tree and White Bear, cost seven white lives.

taking with him 53 troopers and one scout. Six days later, in mid-morning, he finally sighted them. But Kicking Bird was ready for him and sent out flanking groups to right and left. Already almost within the claws of the attack, McClellan dismounted his men; he realized that the Indians' horses were more lightly loaded than his own and that the Indians were the better riders, and he thought his troops—using their own horses as shields—would have a better chance on foot.

Then Kicking Bird crouched low on his horse and led a charge straight into the soldiers, personally impaling a trooper on his lance. After that spectacular feat of arms, McClellan had no doubt of the proper strategy: retreat. For eight hours under the July sun he slowly moved backward. Kicking Bird alternated his attacks. When the troops were prepared to defend the front, he struck one of the flanks; and when they swung to protect the flank, he bore into the front. Three of McClellan's men had been killed, 12 wounded, and 18

mounts lost by the time a party of 20 well-armed cowboys happened unexpectedly upon the scene. Kicking Bird pulled his forces away into the darkness and headed north to Kiowa country.

No one ever called him a coward again. Indeed, respecting him more than ever, the tribesmen listened attentively to his arguments for peace. Although other chiefs and their warriors continued to leave the reservation and raid into Texas, Kicking Bird remained close to the Kiowa-Comanche agency near Fort Sill, on the eastern edge of the Wichita Mountains.

In May of 1871, White Bear put together a war party for a large expedition. He wanted spoils, he wanted to keep pressure on the spreading white settlements, and he wanted action for its own sake. More than 100 warriors followed him, including Sitting Bear, Sky Walker—a noted warrior thought to have prophetic powers—and Big Tree, a daring young war chief in his own right. They passed the spot where Kicking Bird had fought the year before and went on to a point on the old Butterfield stage route between Fort Richardson and abandoned Fort Belknap. Here White Bear spied a small group of traveling soldiers: a few officers riding in an open coach, with a mounted escort of 17 men. Not much promise of plunder here, it seemed; and when Sky Walker prophesied that another and much richer caravan would soon present itself, White Bear decided to let the little group pass unmolested. In fact, there had been an exceedingly rich prize in the coach heading for Fort Richardson—General William Tecumseh Sherman, nemesis of the Plains Indians, on an inspection tour of the frontier.

The next day, true to Sky Walker's prophecy, the war party spotted a wagon train approximately 20 miles from Fort Richardson. White Bear's forces fell upon the hapless freight haulers, killed seven men, and mutilated the living and the dead. The warriors chained one teamster to his wagon, cut out his tongue, and burned him to death. Then they helped themselves to guns, camping equipment and 41 mules before heading back to the reservation.

About a week later Sitting Bear, White Bear and Big Tree came to the agency to draw rations of coffee, sugar, flour and bacon. The agent, a firm but fair Quaker named Lawrie Tatum, called them into his office and asked if they knew anything about the wagon-train attack in Texas. White Bear spoke out proudly: "Yes, I led in that raid. I have repeatedly asked for arms and ammunition, which have not been furnished. I have made many other requests which have not been granted." He went on to list a number of other Kiowa grievances: annuities were being delayed, goods due to the Indians were being stolen, the whites were planning to build a railroad through the reservation. He then described the raid in detail, giving due credit to those who had gone with him, and concluded: "If any other Indian claims the honor of leading that party he will be lying to you. I led it myself."

After the Indians left, the stunned agent notified the commanding officer of Fort Sill, who in turn reported the proud confession to Sherman. The general ordered the Kiowa chiefs to be arrested and sent back to Texas to be tried for murder.

When the soldiers started south with the three handcuffed prisoners, White Bear and Big Tree were in one open wagon and Sitting Bear in another, guarded by a corporal and two privates carrying carbines. Neither the guards nor the cavalrymen riding alongside paid any attention when Sitting Bear began to chant and periodically duck his head beneath a blanket. Perhaps they took his song for some Indian expression of despair. But it was in fact the death song of the Society of the Ten Bravest; beneath the blanket, the old warrior was gnawing the flesh of his hands until he could slide the cuffs over them. Furthermore, beneath that blanket he held a butcher knife, which had probably been slipped to him by another warrior, although the Kiowas later said that he made it appear by magic.

He was determined not to die in the drab indignity of a white man's jail, but in his own time and his own way. Leaping up for his last battle, he slashed at his guards with the butcher knife and grabbed a carbine to aim at the cavalrymen. They cut him down with a volley of bullets, as he had wanted them to do.

In July 1871, White Bear and Big Tree were tried for first-degree murder in the frontier town of Jacksboro, Texas. Their fate was to be determined by nothing resembling a jury of their peers. The men in the jury box were cowboys with pistols in their belts. Feeling in the courtroom ran high. Many of the townspeople, including some of the jurors, had lost kin or friends to Indians, and even those not moved by vengeance were ready to make examples of these chiefs. White Bear was permitted to give a brief speech. "I am an important chief among my people," he informed the court, "and have great influence among the warriors of my tribe; they know my voice and will hear my word. If you let me go back to my people I will withdraw all warriors from Texas. I will wash out the spots of blood and make it a white land and there shall be peace. But if you kill me, it will be like a spark on the prairie. It will make a big fire—a terrible fire!" In spite of this warning, he and Big Tree were quickly found guilty and sentenced to death by hanging.

Immediately, humanitarian groups in the East protested the harshness of the sentences. Even the judge who had presided at the trial wrote to Texas Governor Edmund Davis suggesting that Davis commute the sentences to life imprisonment at hard labor. The Governor did so, and in November the Army delivered

An experiment in friendly persuasion

Wearing the gold watch and chain that was his only indulgence, Lawrie Tatum sits with Mexican boys he rescued from Indian raiders.

In 1869, shortly after the Kiowas, together with the Comanches, were settled on a 5,000-square-mile reservation, President Ulysses S. Grant appointed a 47-year-old Iowa farmer named Lawrie Tatum as their agent —an unenviable post that entailed teaching agriculture to the Indians, distributing provisions and protecting them from land-grabbers. Tatum possessed one special qualification: he was a Quaker. It was Grant's avowed hope that he and other agents drawn from the pacifist denomination could "make Quakers out of the Indians; it will take all the fight out of them."

But the Quaker policy of friendly persuasion seemed ill-suited to handle the Kiowas. As a show of trust, Tatum refused to let soldiers at the Fort Sill agency guard provisions held for distribution. This merely convinced the Kiowas that he was weak, and they not only stole supplies but also launched raids into Texas.

Tatum thereupon showed a surprising streak of toughness. He put the supplies under guard and withheld rations from marauders. And he took a hard line on retrieving white children captured on raids. Whereas other agents paid the Indians ransom for captives, Tatum realized that this was an incentive for further depredations, and would have no part of such bargains. He managed to pry loose 26 captives by threats and moral persuasion. But he never could quench the Kiowas' ardor for war. Disillusioned, he resigned in 1873, concluding that "nothing less than military authority, with perhaps some punishment by troops, will bring them into such subjection as to again render the services of a civil agent of benefit to them."

White Bear and Big Tree to the state prison at Huntsville in east Texas.

That winter a writer from *Scribner's Monthly* visited the prison and found Big Tree diligently making furniture while his fellow inmate was sedulously avoiding the slightest semblance of labor. The writer described White Bear as a "finely formed man, princely in carriage, on whom even the prison garb seemed elegant." Even in jail, he had not lost his pride and dignity. Nevertheless, both Kiowa leaders found life in the Texas prison intolerable. The climate was humid, the food strange, the clothes uncomfortable, the cell air stale. Worst of all was the inaction after the vigorous life of the open plains.

Meanwhile, Kicking Bird was working tirelessly on the reservation to convince the Kiowas that they must adapt to changing conditions. Even Lone Wolf, who in the absence of White Bear had emerged as leader of the more hostile faction, made some effort to hold his young men back from raiding. Both chiefs promised to keep the peace if the prisoners were freed.

The incarceration of the two great Kiowa chiefs became a cause célèbre. The Indian Bureau favored their release on the grounds that they had committed an act of war rather than murder. Petitions for their freedom poured into Washington. Finally pressure from the public and the government brought about their conditional release in the fall of 1873 after two years of imprisonment. Governor Davis emphatically warned them that a single step off the reservation would send them back to prison.

General Sherman was livid. He wrote to the Governor: "I now say to you that I believe White Bear and Big Tree will have their revenge and that if they are to have scalps, yours is the first that should be taken."

The tide of events was now sweeping rapidly toward its inevitable end. As the settlers came closer and closer to the Kiowa-Comanche reservation, fewer and fewer buffalo migrated through the Indian lands. White buffalo hunters were swarming across the plains, stripping off hides and leaving carcasses to rot. Between 1872 and 1874 nearly four million buffalo were killed, less than 5 per cent of them by Indians. Though the mainstay of their way of life was being wantonly destroyed, their complaints continued to go unheeded. It seemed,

once more, that they had no choice but to fight.

In the first six months of 1874 war parties of Plains Indians—mixed groups of Kiowas, Comanches, Cheyennes and Arapahos—raided through Texas, Kansas, eastern Colorado, New Mexico and even the territory occupied by their Indian neighbors to the east. They struck isolated ranches, hunters' camps, surveying parties, whiskey peddlers, traders, soldiers and any other white men they happened upon.

By mid-July, General Sherman, now General of the Army, advised President Grant that drastic steps were necessary, and promptly received Presidential permission to take them. The Army was to pursue and punish all hostile Indians within as well as outside their reservations. Every Indian capable of bearing arms must answer roll call at the reservation agency once a week —on Thursday—or be declared hostile. Hostile bands would be run down relentlessly, starved out, attacked, their horses killed, their camps burned. The ringleaders among the raiders, when caught, would be shipped off to exile at Fort Marion in Florida.

To carry out the plan, Sherman sent some 3,000 troops into the field in a five-pronged force from Fort Dodge in Kansas, Fort Sill in the Kiowa-Comanche reservation, Forts Richardson and Concho in Texas and Fort Bascom in New Mexico Territory. The Indians of the southern plains had been doomed from the start, but this was to be the end.

White Bear and Big Tree left the reservation and eventually headed north. Lone Wolf and Sky Walker hid out on the plains of the Texas Panhandle. Kicking Bird stayed in his own camp near Fort Sill. The weather was hot and dry as autumn came on. A plague of grasshoppers descended, stripping the leaves from the trees along the water courses. Violent thunderstorms ripped across the prairie.

For the Kiowa renegades it was a time of skirmishes and of flight. Bands and even families scattered and ran. There was no opportunity for rest and regrouping, no sanctuary for fighting men, no respite during which a war chief could rally them. Kicking Bird alone exercised his capacity for leadership. Many times he, too, had been deeply discouraged by the white man's arrogance and broken promises, but he held fast to his vision of a better way of life. Continuing to urge peace with all the eloquence and logic at his command, he per-

Following the death of Little Mountain, Kicking Bird, seen here in 1868, emerged among the Kiowas as the spokesman for peace. Immediately after listing militants for exile in 1875, he died — possibly by poison.

suaded many Kiowas to camp with him near Fort Sill and stay out of the hostilities. So strong was his influence with the tribe that he kept at least three quarters of the Kiowas from going on the warpath.

Government authorities decided to use him as a liaison to persuade hostiles to give themselves up. Accepting the charge, Kicking Bird rode out on the plains and began talking them back to Fort Sill. Most of them came out of hiding and returned with him. But he could not find White Bear or Big Tree.

These two parolees were encamped in the Red Hills of the Cheyenne reservation to the north. On September 29, Big Tree rode up to the Cheyenne agency and said that White Bear wished to surrender. A group of friendly Indians was sent to White Bear's camp to encourage him to come in. He did so, on October 3, bringing with him his following of 35 warriors, 106 women and children, and two old men. In reply to the agent's questions, he insisted that he and Big Tree had left the Kiowa reservation only to visit friends.

But the fact remained that they had broken the terms of their parole. They were promptly arrested and taken to Fort Sill. Big Tree was confined on the spot. White Bear — presumed to be the worse offender, although he bitterly proclaimed his innocence — was sent back to the Texas state prison at Huntsville to serve a life sentence. Finally, late in February 1875, the last of the recalcitrants hiding in the Texas Panhandle, Lone Wolf and Sky Walker, rode into the reservation and, with 200 followers, gave themselves up.

Kicking Bird now faced a difficult and delicate task. He was asked by the whites to decide which of the fighting Kiowas were to be sent to exile in Fort Marion. These were supposed to be the most incorrigible militants. He selected 26, among them Lone Wolf, Sky Walker and four other particularly intransigent war chiefs. But for the most part he picked nobodies, young warriors of little reputation in the tribe who would be no great loss. He took pains to spare men he thought would use their influence for the future welfare of the Kiowas. He had done his best, according to his lights. His people and their children would go to war no more. They would have settled homes and schooling in the skills of civilized living.

While the soldiers were loading the prisoners in the wagons to begin the unhappy journey to Florida on an April day in 1875, Kicking Bird rode up proudly on a spirited gray horse given to him by an Army officer. In his parting speech he addressed the men in chains as "brothers," saying that he was sorry he had failed to keep them out of trouble but that he would work for their release.

"You think you have done well, Kicking Bird," Sky Walker said, staring at him balefully. "You remain free, a big man with the whites. But you will not live long."

Kiowas afterward reported that on the second night after they left Fort Sill, Sky Walker prayed for the death of Kicking Bird, who now ranked as the most powerful man in the tribe, but who had not come by this position in the time-honored way of the Kiowas. Circumstance and the white man, rather than solemn council, had made him what he was. Less than a week later Kicking Bird was seized by painful and mysterious cramps. He died before the end of the day. The post surgeon asserted that he had been poisoned by strychnine; but who had done it, no one would ever say. Sky Walker, the prophesier, himself died shortly after reaching prison in Florida.

How quickly it had all happened, once it started. In 1865, these lordly tribesmen of the southern plains had made their first land concession to white men. Only 10 years had passed; and in that time they had lost much of their land and most of their leaders.

Big Tree, daring young chief of great potential, persuaded his captors of his rehabilitation and was released from Fort Sill in that year of 1875, when all came to an end. He gathered his band and established his camp in the beautiful land alongside Rainy Mountain Creek, where principal chief Islandman had camped many years before. In that country where the Wichita Mountains scatter their granite knobs and knolls across the plains, Baptists came to establish a mission not far from the scene of the long-ago massacre by the Osages. And Big Tree, who had sat in council with Kiowa chiefs through the most turbulent of times and fought for the war honors that could someday have made him principal chief, became a deacon and a Sunday school teacher in the Rainy Mountain Baptist Church.

Perhaps sometimes he thought to pray for White Bear who, having entered the Huntsville prison hospital in a depressed state, killed himself in October 1878 by jumping — headfirst — from a second-story balcony.

An era of fierce suzerainty over the southern plains came to an end in 1875 as these Kiowa, Comanche, Cheyenne and Arapaho militants arrived in St. Augustine, Florida, sentenced to an indefinite stay in a military prison 1,000 miles from their homeland.

Tired of trying to elude the Army after leaving the reservation, a band of Kiowa raiders surrenders near Fort Sill in 1875.

Record of a bitter journey into exile

On April 28, 1875, 72 Kiowas and allied tribesmen—identified as ringleaders in recent raids against whites—looked upon their families at Fort Sill for what they thought would be the last time. Then, guarded by troops, they set forth on a 24-day journey by wagon and railroad to Fort Marion, a decaying, Spanish-built strong point in St. Augustine, Florida.

They expected to be executed there. Instead, they learned that their sentence was indefinite imprisonment. The difference seemed slight—until they became acquainted with the Army officer who was in charge of them. Lieutenant Richard Henry Pratt was like no white soldier in their experience. Although he had fought against the Kiowas, he perceived that the task at hand was to educate, not punish.

Pratt quickly had the Indians moved out of Fort Marion's humid dungeons and into barracks they built themselves. He put them to work as bakers, sailors, fishermen and field laborers—for pay—and he enlisted the help of white women to teach them to read and write English. Nor did he insist that they forswear their past entirely. With his encouragement, the younger warriors began to draw pictures narrating and explaining Indian life. One young Kiowa named Zotom chose a subject of particular immediacy—the deportation to Florida, shown here and on the following pages.

Three years after the Kiowa exile began, Pratt persuaded his superiors that the prisoners were firmly converted to the white man's road, and they were granted freedom. Most returned to the reservation, but a few of the once-fierce raiders chose to stay in the East. Wrote one: "I good boy now."

As a guard detachment stands by, authorities at Fort Sill ask the defeated Indians the identity of their war leaders. There was much covering up. Only the most notorious raiders were named for deportation and some deportees were later found to be obscure tribesmen or Mexican captives.

At a campsite on the way to the railroad that would take them to Fort Marion, the prisoners bathe in the Blue River in Indian Territory. The tents were reserved for their 4th Cavalry escort; the warriors were forced to sleep on the bare ground, shackled together with a continuous chain.

49

An excited crowd gathers at the Indianapolis railroad station to gawk at the warriors — a scene repeated in every city along the way. Riding on a train terrified the Indians, and some kept their blankets over their heads. Near the journey's end, one chief was shot to death attempting to escape.

The day after reaching St. Augustine, the Indians are brought to the parapet of Fort Marion to view the Atlantic Ocean. During the first few weeks of confinement in sweltering cells that lacked exterior windows, one warrior died of natural causes and a chief starved himself to death.

2 | Guerrilla fighters in a rugged domain

When Americans began to settle the Southwest in the middle of the 19th Century, they found themselves confronting an estimated 7,000 Apaches who had already made the Spaniards and Mexicans pay a steep price for trespassing. Of the dozen or so autonomous Apache bands, the most formidable turned out to be the Chiricahuas.

Led by Cochise, they struck ranches, mining outposts, stages and wagon trains, then slipped back to mountain strongholds where, as a frustrated cavalryman noted in 1857, "You could as well catch a wild chamois."

Another observer likened Apaches to man-eating tigers—a metaphor that seemed even more apt when Geronimo rose to a position of leadership among the Chiricahuas following the death of Cochise. Pitted against impossible odds, he continued to maraud in the timeless way of the Apaches, long after most Western tribes had been forced onto reservations. In the process he earned for himself undying fame—and infamy—in the history of the West.

Outlined against a darkening desert sky, members of a nomadic Apache band pause to rest their horses on a ridge overlooking the camp.

55

Fantastic rock formations in the Dragoon Mountains of southeastern Arizona conceal the entranceway to a narrow, six-mile-long canyon — the only access to a 40-acre valley where Cochise's Chiricahua warriors could find water, grass and near-perfect security after one of their raids.

A warrior finds a receptive audience as he spins out a tale, using a stick as a narrative aid. Storytelling was a favorite pastime of the Indians; many of their yarns were in praise of tribesmen who excelled in the Apache virtues of stealing without being caught and killing without being killed.

58

Only a few months of the traditional life of hunting and raiding remained to Geronimo's renegade group when this picture was taken during an unsuccessful peace parley in 1886. Several warriors wear the distinctive Apache boot, which could be pulled over the knee as protection against cactus.

COSTUMES MEXICAINS.
Cacique Apache
des bords du Rio Colorado dans la Californie.

Apache warlords: Cochise and Geronimo

One spring shortly before the midpoint of the 19th Century (the exact year remains uncertain) the leaders of the Mimbres Apache band assembled in council to consider their future dealings with the Mexican state of Chihuahua, which lay on the southern fringe of their traditional range. Included in the council was a young warrior named Gokhlayeh (One Who Yawns). Although he was entitled to speak his mind, his opinions were not likely to carry much weight; he was still in his twenties and not yet a man of much importance in a group dominated by the great chief, Mangas Coloradas. But a decision reached at the meeting proved fateful for Gokhlayeh. The chain of events begun that day would ultimately earn him a new identity that became a war cry recognized all over the world: Geronimo. Along with his fellow Apache, Cochise, the man known as Geronimo would be responsible for some of the bloodiest, bitterest and most unremitting fighting ever waged by Indian against white.

Ironically, the issue at hand was whether or not to accept a peace bribe. For 200 years, the Apaches had preyed on the villages, the haciendas, the herds and pack trains of Mexico; in return, they were warred upon by Mexican soldiery. In no man's memory had there been a time when Mexicans and Apaches had not hated each other. To the Mexicans, the Apaches were a scourge and a curse. To the pragmatic Apaches, the Mexicans, once assigned the role of unwilling suppliers, were worthy of nothing but contempt. Even so, the Indians did not scorn taking Mexican women—if comely —as wives to bear and rear sons who would kill more Mexican men. (Mangas Coloradas, whose name was Spanish for Red Sleeves, himself had a Mexican wife.)

Now the government of Chihuahua was willing to give up bloodlessly what the Apaches would otherwise have seized in violence. In one of their rare peaceful contacts with the Indians, the Mexicans let it be known that, at certain stations four times a year, the Apaches would be welcomed and issued supplies of blankets, cloth, meal and other necessities—and mescal, the fiery distilled essence of the agave plant, for which Apache men suffered a powerful thirst.

This was indeed a tempting proposition. Nevertheless, the Apaches were under no illusion that genuine brotherhood waited in Chihuahua. Since 1837, the state had been paying a bounty of 100 pesos for a male Apache scalp, 50 for a woman's, 25 for a child's. Although Chihuahua was now offering to suspend the bounty system, deep animosities surely lingered. Perhaps killing was a habit too deeply rooted to be easily changed by government order. In any case, the Apaches knew that whatever Chihuahua did, the adjoining state of Sonora would continue to pay scalp money.

After weighing the dangers against the potential gains, Mangas Coloradas recommended that a party set forth to receive the tribute, and most of the other men at the council agreed with him. Gokhlayeh was free to stand aloof, for no Apache warrior owed blind allegiance to a chief. He decided to go. It was an important venture for his people—and possibly it would present opportunities to assert himself as a leader.

If Gokhlayeh sometimes felt that he had a greater right than most men to a role of leadership, that was only natural. Chieftainship was hereditary among the Apaches, and his grandfather had been the chief of the Nedni Apaches, a band that roved the wilds of northern Mexico. However, his father had forfeited his—and his future son's—inheritance when he left his own peo-

---

An Apache chief, as envisioned by Italian artist Claudio Linati in 1828, conjures up the image of Genghis Khan. Linati was attempting to interpret the Apaches' legendary ferocity for a book about Mexico.

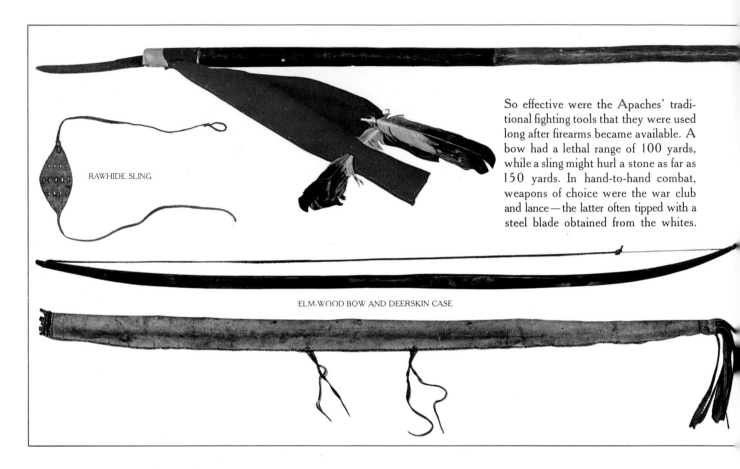

RAWHIDE SLING

So effective were the Apaches' traditional fighting tools that they were used long after firearms became available. A bow had a lethal range of 100 yards, while a sling might hurl a stone as far as 150 yards. In hand-to-hand combat, weapons of choice were the war club and lance—the latter often tipped with a steel blade obtained from the whites.

ELM-WOOD BOW AND DEERSKIN CASE

ple to marry into the Mimbres. Thus Gokhlayeh's ambitions were focused on a second route to prestige—through war and pillage. By showing himself to be an exceptional fighter, he might win respect equaling or even surpassing that of a hereditary chief. And that would be honor indeed, for the Apaches could not conceive of a people more powerful than themselves.

At a time faded from memory they had come into this land as conquerors. Speaking a dialect of the Athapascan tongue, once heard all across the northwestern part of the continent, they first appeared in the north of what would become New Mexico and Arizona. They pushed onto the Mogollon Rim, that gigantic upthrust of rock bearing the mighty canyon scar of the Colorado River. From the rim they looked southward across the hot desert waste toward the majestic peaks of the Sierra Madre in Mexico.

All this became theirs. Moving against the cliff-dwelling Zunis in the center, the Comanches to the east and the Yumans to the west, the invaders carved out a range that measured 500 miles across and as much north to south. Here, sheltering in frail hovels of sticks and brush called wickiups, they lived as nomadic hunters, uninterested in farming except for an occasional garden patch of maize.

The vast territory was divided among a loose-knit confederation of bands that mostly went their separate ways and sometimes even warred on one another. But if their unity was tenuous, the various peoples with whom they came in conflict saw them as a single foe. Indeed the name Apache was apparently derived from the Zuni word *apachu,* "enemy." Passed on to Spaniard, to Mexican, to American, the word never lost its validity. Each successive pretender to the Apaches' terrain discovered them to be an antagonist who expected and gave no quarter.

Gokhlayeh, like every Apache male, had been drilled from boyhood in the cardinal virtues of cunning and toughness—the twin sources of his people's strength. He was taught that trickery ranked above pure courage:

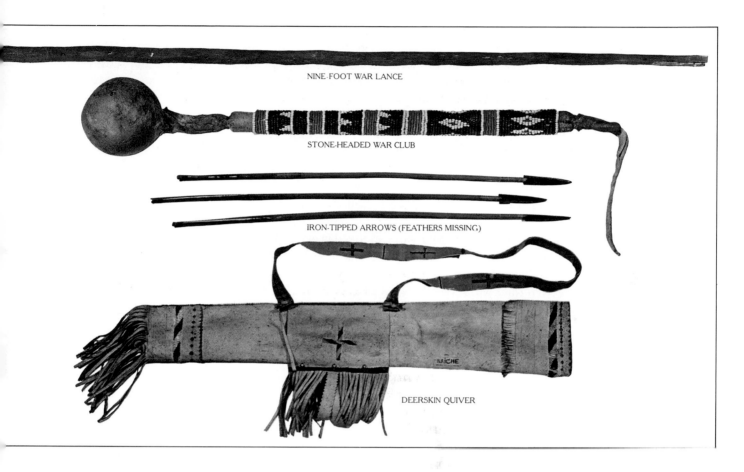

NINE-FOOT WAR LANCE

STONE-HEADED WAR CLUB

IRON-TIPPED ARROWS (FEATHERS MISSING)

DEERSKIN QUIVER

raiders who could quietly make off with a few horses or cattle from a Mexican ranch were more esteemed than those who won a bigger haul but suffered losses in the process. He was made to stay awake for long periods to learn how to deal with exhaustion. He trained as a long-distance runner, traversing four-mile courses through rough country, carrying a mouthful of water all the way without swallowing it or spitting it out. (A mature Apache warrior had to be able to cover 70 miles a day on foot, in the most forbidding terrain.) With arrows or rocks flung from slings, he fought scarcely mock battles against other acolytes. To survive, the boys relied only on hide shields and agility.

Out of such strenuous apprenticeship emerged a youth who was uniquely equipped to fight or flee in his environment of desert, mesquite, grassy valley or crag and canyon. By the time of the conference on Chihuahua's tempting offer, Gokhlayeh had been well blooded. He had grown to be a man of medium height —five feet seven inches or so—big chested, with a fierce

countenance of overhung brows, outthrust cheekbones, and a hawk's-beak nose above a straight, thin mouth. Later one of his eight battle wounds caused the right corner of his mouth to droop in a permanent sneer.

At that council to consider the Chihuahua offer, it was decided to include women and children in the peace party, for women would be needed as burden bearers to fetch home the tribute. Gokhlayeh took his young wife, Alope, their three young children and his aged mother. The party moved out of the Apache stronghold in the Mogollon Mountains in the southwestern portion of present-day New Mexico and started south. Their destination, the distribution point for tribute, was the village of Janos, about 60 miles into Mexico, in the foothills of the Sierra Madre.

The Apache party had no way of knowing that a man as warlike as themselves also had Janos much on his mind. He was the military governor of Sonora, General José Maria Carrasco. Several years later, Carrasco met Major John Cremony of the U.S. Army—then engaged in surveying the Mexican-American border — and related that he had been aware of the impending peace bribe and had resented it. "Not being able to comprehend the virtues of a policy which feeds Indians in one state that they might prey upon and destroy the citizens of another, I concluded that it was my duty to destroy the enemy wherever I could find him," he said. And so, while Gokhlayeh and his fellow tribesmen moved southward toward Chihuahua, General Carrasco, with two troops of Mexican cavalry, moved westward from Sonora by forced night marches, heading for the same place.

The Indians arrived at Janos first. With inbred caution, they pitched their main camp well outside the town. Against the possibility of trouble, they also chose a rendezvous area in protective thickets beside the Janos River. Then the headmen and a few warriors approached the town to test the temperature of their welcome. Their reception was as open-handed and guileless as they could have wished, and they returned to camp laden with blankets, bright cloth, trade trinkets and armloads of bottled goods. That night there was feasting and a grand spree. The second day was even better, and the warriors detailed to remain and guard the camp were solaced by drink.

General Carrasco's cavalry struck on the third day. The blow was swift and merciless. The general withheld the order to open fire until the camp was entirely surrounded. The first volley cut down women over the cooking fires, killed infants at the breast, killed warriors sleeping off a hangover. Then Carrasco's men charged with club and bayonet. In a few minutes, the screams and moans died away as the cavalrymen finished off the wounded. The few survivors who had bolted through the Mexican lines crept into the brush. "We killed 130 and took about 90 prisoners, principally women and children," General Carrasco was to tell Major Cremony, adding in annoyed tones: "Colonel Medina, commanding the state of Chihuahua, was so enraged at my action that he made formal complaint to the Supreme Government which, however, after some unnecessary delay, approved of my course."

Mangas Coloradas and Gokhlayeh were among the warriors who, returning at dusk after collecting tribute, were met and warned by fugitive survivors. Slowly the remnants of the group assembled at the rendezvous.

Scouts were sent to spy on the ruined camp, and when they reported the place completely occupied by Mexicans, the Apaches knew they could not retrieve their dead or try to rescue the captives. They counted those who had reached the rendezvous. Gokhlayeh's wife, mother and children were not present.

The murder of his family affected Gokhlayeh deeply. When he and the other survivors slipped back across the border and into their mountain fastness a few days later, Gokhlayeh gave in to intense grief. Tribal custom called for him to mourn his wife by burning her possessions; but he went further, burning his wickiup and the toys of his children as well. Fellow tribesmen began to discern profound changes in him. They had known him to be an affectionate husband and indulgent father, but now he turned bitter, quarrelsome and prone to unpredictable outbursts of wild violence. Many warriors came to fear and dislike him.

Over the next year, the Mimbres gradually recovered strength, fashioning new bows, lances and war clubs, and augmenting these weapons with a few guns taken in raids. Meanwhile, Gokhlayeh's lust for Mexican blood grew almost obsessive. And so it was a particular joy to him when Mangas Coloradas decided the time had come to summon a council to consider revenge. Mangas Coloradas was a giant among the Apaches, both figuratively and in body; he stood six feet, six inches tall, and he was brilliant. Just a few years earlier the Mexican government had mobilized fully 1,000 soldiers in a futile effort to run him down. Now he was almost 60, but his reputation for ferocity in war was undiminished.

The Mimbres chief decided that Gokhlayeh was the proper messenger to recruit warriors from other Apache bands. He sent first to Cochise of the Chiricahuas. Commissioning a man of Gokhlayeh's modest attainments to approach Cochise as an equal was a signal honor for the former, almost an impertinence toward the latter. Cochise was recognized by all the scattered Apaches as a chief of Mangas Coloradas' caliber. Only a few years older than Gokhlayeh, Cochise had inherited from his father the leadership of the Chiricahuas, who commanded the region of the Dragoon and Chiricahua mountains in southeastern Arizona. Building on this legacy, he proved himself shrewd in war, sagacious in council, and deeply concerned for his people's welfare—all the qualities that evoked Apache loyalty.

As the Americans came to know him, they agreed in many ways with the Indian estimate of Cochise. Although they learned to fear him and tried hard to kill him, they recognized that he was a leader of rare presence and poise. Captain John Gregory Bourke, who at different times both pursued and talked peace with him, wrote: "Cochise is a fine-looking Indian, straight as a rush—six feet in stature, deep-chested and roman-nosed. A kindly and even somewhat melancholy expression tempers the determined look of his countenance. There was neither in speech or action any of the bluster characteristic of his race." (By contrast, Bourke would later say of Gokhlayeh: "He and his warriors were certainly as fine-looking a lot of pirates as ever cut a throat or scuttled a ship.")

Cochise consenting, Gokhlayeh addressed the Chiricahuas. "Kinsmen," Gokhlayeh told them, according to his own later account, "you have heard what the Mexicans have done without cause. We are men the same as the Mexicans are—we can do to them what they have done to us. Let us go forward—we will attack them in their homes. Will you come? It is well —you will all come."

With the Chiricahua agreement in hand, Gokhlayeh next was sent into the Sierra Madre to make contact with his father's original people, the Nednis, now under Chief Juh. They, too, agreed to join in the chastisement of Mexico. The chiefs chose as a target the rich agricultural town of Arizpe in Sonora, 120 miles south of Tucson. Arizpe was selected for sound strategic reasons. It was situated at the head of a narrow canyon, it would be difficult to reinforce, and the escape route back home lay through thinly populated farmland.

In the summer of the year following the massacre at Janos, a great war party gathered and, as the sun set, began a nightlong war dance around a huge bonfire. To the throb of drums and the chanting of seated warriors, four dancers came out abreast, circled the fire four times, separated into pairs and danced south and north of the flames. Four times more they repeated the routine. (The number four and the cardinal points of the compass were sacred to the Apaches and found a place in most tribal rituals.) As the drums beat on, the moment came for individuals to declare their intention. A warrior who pledged to fight could signify the fact merely by walking around the fire; the more demonstrative leaped forward and, with prancing legs and gesticulating arms, enacted the ways in which they would kill. At dawn, the dance ended and the war party moved out afoot. It was no time to be encumbered by animals.

The Apaches made their final approach from the east, coming down through precipitous defiles of the Sierra Madre. Just outside Arizpe and across the Sonora River, the warriors—carefully staying out of sight—arrayed themselves in a great half circle, with the open side toward the town. Then a few of them moved into the open and waited for Arizpe to react. Response came quickly; eight horsemen bearing a flag of truce crossed the river, entered the semicircle and approached the handful of visible warriors. When they came within reach, more Apaches leaped from their concealed positions and killed them, leaving Arizpe in no doubt of its peril. In full view of the frightened town, the Indians scalped these first dead, a gesture to remind the Mexicans of their own scalp-bounty system.

At last a Mexican commander marched out on the attack with two companies of infantry, bringing along a pack train laden with ammunition and rations. In vengeful joy, Gokhlayeh believed he recognized the soldiers as the same unit that had killed his family. The fighting lasted all that first day. The Indians kept covetous eyes on the mule train and its valuable packs, realizing that, if they could seize it, they would be greatly strengthened. Just at dusk, they saw their chance. A sudden swoop out of the concealed flank and the train was in their hands. Dismayed, the Mexicans pulled back to the barricaded town.

The next morning the Mexican commander came out with his entire force, the infantry now backed by two cavalry companies. The Indians waited until the soldiers were within the semicircle and then charged. The Mexican line broke and the battle fell into wild confusion. Now the fighting was all over the field, without order on either side—bayonet against lance, saber against war club.

Gokhlayeh was everywhere—reckless, almost berserk. Probably he did not know how many men he killed that day; long afterward he was to say that Mexicans "were not worth counting. We kill Mexicans with rocks." Before the day ended he ceased to be Gokhlayeh. Somewhere in the melee, watching him in

Inheriting a leadership role because of his parental training, Mangas became chief of the Mimbres Apaches in 1863, when his father, Mangas Coloradas, died. However, since he never matched his father's prowess in battle, he was not as influential.

awe, an unknown Mexican, for an unknown reason, shouted "Geronimo!" Others took up the cry and ever after, to Indian and white alike, Gokhlayeh was Geronimo. The connotation is beyond explaining; in Spanish the word is the equivalent of "Jerome."

When the two sides separated after three hours of fighting, the field was littered with far more Mexican dead than Apache. Six men still held the field: Geronimo, three other Indians and two Mexican cavalrymen. The Mexicans fired, bringing down two of the warriors. Geronimo and the other Apache, weaponless except for knives in the leggings of their moccasins, sprinted for their own lines. One Mexican with a saber caught up with and brought down Geronimo's last companion. Geronimo ran on, seized a lance from another Apache, then turned back and killed his pursuer. Taking the slain man's saber, he went for the remaining Mexican. They grappled and fell. As they struggled, Geronimo dropped the saber, got one hand on the haft of his knife and killed his last enemy of the day.

Laden with booty and honor, blood lust requited, the war party moved back across the border. Gokhlayeh had been a man of minor consequence; nobody could say the same of Geronimo, then or thereafter.

But his hour of greatest renown—such as it was—still lay far in the future. For the moment, he left the Mimbres band, took a Chiricahua wife, and placed himself under the leadership of Cochise. It proved a satisfactory shift to a man who lived to wage war on whites, for Cochise was destined to become to the Americans what Mangas Coloradas was to the Mexicans: a source of dread.

The United States took over Mexico's claim to much of the Apaches' range by the Treaty of Guadalupe Hidalgo, which formally concluded the war between the two nations in 1846, and by the Gadsden Purchase of 1853, a $10 million transaction involving some 30,000 square miles of land south of the Gila River. At first, the new claimants seemed uninterested in occupying the land, aside from establishing a handful of mining outposts in Mangas Coloradas' territory during the mid-1850s. They didn't bother the old chief; he was willing to tolerate a few prospectors.

Cochise faced a more significant incursion in 1858 when the route for a transcontinental stage line, the Butterfield Overland, was laid out across his land. In the heart of his stronghold he commanded a strategic passage and fresh water springs at Apache Pass, between the Dragoon and Chiricahua mountains. However, when Butterfield representatives sought permission to build a stage station there, Cochise granted it, realizing that useful knowledge might be gained from the newcomers. He stipulated only that the buildings must stand back several hundred yards from the springs, a precaution to ensure that these new neighbors, should they take such a notion, could not monopolize the precious water. By 1860 he was on terms good enough to negotiate what was probably the first formal commercial deal ever made by an Apache: a contract to cut firewood for the station.

But these fragile beginnings of friendship were soon shattered. At the time the firewood agreement was concluded, a ne'er-do-well white man, John Ward, was living with his mistress, a Mexican woman named Jesusa Martinez, on a nondescript ranch near the new Fort Buchanan, west of Apache Pass. With them was Felix, their 10- or 11-year-old son. During the summer some warriors of the Pinal Apache band raided the Ward place, drove off some cattle and abducted young Felix.

Ward reported the kidnapping to Fort Buchanan, but the fort was shorthanded and for months nothing was done. Meanwhile, Ward somehow conceived the notion (now known to be mistaken) that the kidnappers must be Cochise's men. The Army accepted his view. In January 1861, George N. Bascom, a young second lieutenant fresh to the West and eager to make a name, was dispatched to Apache Pass with 54 men — and Ward. At the stage station, Bascom paused long enough to plant a falsehood with James Wallace, a driver and personal friend of the Chiricahua leader. The soldiers, said the officer, were on a routine patrol toward the Rio Grande; then he continued on his way and camped in the canyon nearby.

Cochise soon appeared at the station and inquired about the intentions of such a large body of troops. Reassured, he decided to pay a formal call on the Army detachment. He took along his brother Naretena, his wife Nahlekadeya, his young son Nachise, and two warrior nephews. At the camp, the Apaches were bidden to enter Bascom's tent. When they sat down for polite dis-

69

Adorned with health symbols, the yard-high painting was done in vegetable dyes on doeskin.

A warrior's portrayal of a puberty dance

Like other Indians of the West, the Apaches were a deeply religious people who constantly propitiated the spirits believed to dwell everywhere in the natural world. Most of their ceremonies were private affairs. For instance, a warrior would sing a prayer over his weapons to strengthen them against the enemy (Geronimo was said to have a powerful rite of this kind).

Of the few public ceremonies, the most important was staged when a girl attained puberty. Scattered members of a band came together to thank the spirits for seeing her safe to child-bearing age and, by extension, for looking after their future. Thus when Naiche, a son of Cochise, decided in the 1890s to depict Apache customs, he chose this joyous ritual as his subject.

In the painting, shown in its entirety above and with its center enlarged at right, tribesmen dance facing a ceremonial fire, while seven girls — each paired under a blanket with an older woman who acted as a protector — dance off to the sides. They are joined by four masked warriors (top) wearing bizarre headdresses that identify them as mountain spirits, and by two small boys, serving as messengers between performers and onlookers (bottom). The ceremony lasted more than four days and its completion marked the promise of prosperity and long life.

Custom called for every girl to be so honored. But when the Apaches were placed on reservations, their white supervisors decided the rites were too time-consuming. They decreed that all the girls who came of age each year had to receive a single ceremony — to be held at the time the Americans were celebrating the Fourth of July.

course, Ward slipped out and told Bascom's men to surround the tent.

Inside, without preliminary, the eager shavetail accused Cochise of the raid and demanded return of the stock and the boy. Astounded, Cochise asked: What stock? What boy? Nettled, Bascom repeated his charge. When Cochise finally understood what the officer was talking about, he promised to inquire among other Apaches and use his influence to free the boy, if he could be found. Taking Cochise's attitude as deceitful, Bascom grew abusive and finally laid down an ultimatum: until the boy and stock were produced, Cochise and his people were prisoners. Cochise instantly sprang to his feet, drew a knife from his moccasin legging, slashed the wall of the tent, plunged through and disappeared into the canyon rocks. His family had no chance to follow him.

Cochise, furious, was certain he had been betrayed — and he leaped to the conclusion that the villain was the stage driver James Wallace. The chief collected a few of his men, advanced on the stage station and called the occupants out. Unaware of what had taken place in the canyon, Wallace came to meet Cochise, accompanied by Charles Culver, the station agent, and a hostler named Walsh. The Indians seized all three, but Culver and Walsh broke loose and ran for the station. Culver was shot at the door by the Apaches, and Walsh was killed by a soldier who mistook him for an Indian. Wallace was held by Cochise as a hostage.

The situation even yet might have been saved from exploding into full-scale war, since Cochise was determined to win the freedom of his kinsmen and apparently was willing to make a deal. Nevertheless, he remained bitterly angry. Partly in fury, partly to build up his negotiating position, he raided a wagon train the same day. He took two Americans prisoner — and he tied eight Mexican drovers to wheels of their wagons and set the torch to them.

Shortly afterward, he reappeared near the station, now occupied by Bascom's force. He was leading Wallace on a lariat tether. Approaching within shouting distance, he offered to trade his captives for the soldiers', but despite the anguished pleas of Wallace, Bascom refused, demanding the kidnapped boy as well.

At that point, Cochise concluded that negotiation was futile, and he dragged Wallace out of sight to mete

out justice in his own fashion. Its nature was discovered a few days later by dragoons who were searching the area for some sign of the Apaches. One of them related: "In a small valley on the western side of the Chiricahua range, we came upon three bodies, one of which, upon examination, I knew to be that of Wallace by the gold filling of some of his teeth, and the other two could be no others than his fellow prisoners. They had been tortured to death. All the bodies were littered with lance holes." Bascom and another officer promptly ordered Cochise's brother and two nephews hanged from an oak tree near the place where the corpses of the three whites had been found.

The chief's wife and son were allowed to go free, but if this gesture was designed to appease Cochise, it failed. He embarked on a campaign to drive the treacherous Americans from his land forever. Ranging forth from their mountain strongholds, his warriors attacked wagon trains, stagecoaches, mines, ranches, even small settlements. Settlers throughout the region fled for their lives. According to one estimate, Cochise and his Chiricahuas killed 150 whites within two months of the hanging of his kinfolk.

Shortly after Cochise took to the warpath, Mangas Coloradas' wary tolerance toward the Americans was similarly replaced by bitter grievance. In 1860 and 1861, the aging chief had grown increasingly uneasy about American prospectors flocking into the gold-mining town of Pinos Altos in his traditional range in New Mexico. He himself saw no value in gold, but he knew the Americans were strangely mad about the useless "yellow iron." Thinking to lure them elsewhere, he had approached several miners separately, telling each that he could lead them to gold in abundance. When the miners cautiously talked among themselves, they were enraged to learn that he had made the offer to so many. They seized the chief, bound him and flogged him unconscious, using a bull whip. Humiliated, he turned to Cochise in the spring of 1862, seeking help to drive the miners out. Cochise asked him to delay his vengeance. First, he told the Mimbres chief, there was more imperative work to be done.

Ironically, the task Cochise had at hand was a byproduct of a nationwide quarrel between Americans, rather than white man against Indian. The Civil War had begun the year before. Now, in 1862, the Confederates had penetrated New Mexico and Arizona, and that summer the Union sent 1,800 California Volunteers to beat them back. By July the Confederates were in retreat and the Union was consolidating its hold. General James Carleton of the Volunteers dispatched Captain Thomas Roberts with 126 soldiers to cross Arizona and take possession of New Mexico. They had to penetrate Apache Pass.

Through his scouts, Cochise knew they were coming. Together with Mangas Coloradas and Geronimo, he assembled 700 fighting men, the largest single combat unit the Apaches ever had. The Indians mounted an ambush on both rocky walls of the pass. Concentrating the forces above the vital springs, Cochise set his men to something new in Apache warfare: building breastworks of rock with firing slits in between. By now, many of the Apaches were armed with white man's guns. The trap should have been deadly.

Captain Roberts entered Apache Pass on July 14, intending to secure the water at the springs. The Apaches let him penetrate, expecting to wipe him out in the narrow defile near the water. They took little note of two strange looking wagons in his train. The first Indian volley produced a scene to gladden Cochise's heart—horses rearing, men dropping from the saddle, others falling out of rank to seek shelter behind rocks. One of the strange wagons capsized as its driver tried to wheel it off the trail.

But it was not to be Cochise's day. Roberts rallied his men, got the upset wagon back on its wheels and turned both vehicles so they faced opposite sides of the canyon. Up among the rocks, Cochise was puzzled at these frantic efforts. Then flame and smoke belched from the vehicles and thunder cracked above the Indians' heads. Roberts' strange wagons carried mountain howitzers and fired 12-pound canister which, bursting above and downward, ripped the Apaches with shrapnel behind their futile breastworks.

The howitzers effectively finished the business. Under their cover, Roberts moved his troops to the station and barricaded himself. Cochise rallied his warriors and tried again that evening. But once more the cannon proved overwhelming.

Even after this defeat, Cochise entertained no thoughts of accommodation with the enemy. But less than a year later, Mangas Coloradas, weary of fighting, ventured to the town of Pinos Altos to talk peace with the miners. Entirely by chance, Brevet General Joseph West happened on the scene and in short order accomplished what 1,000 Mexican troops had failed to do. He seized the chief, accused him of plundering wagon trains and sent him from his tent, telling the guards, "I want him dead or alive tomorrow morning. Understand? I want him dead."

One of the miners, walking about the camp that night, later testified: "About 9 o'clock I noticed the soldiers were doing something to Mangas. I discovered that they were heating their bayonets in the fire and burning his feet and legs. Mangas rose upon his left elbow, angrily protesting that he was no child to be played with." Thereupon, said the witness, the guards killed the chief with four shots. To complete the deed, he was scalped and decapitated.

For 10 years after Mangas Coloradas' death, Cochise fought on, goaded to greater fury than ever by this latest betrayal. After the debacle at Apache Pass, he never again attempted a mass action, but his small war parties were continually in action against travelers, prospectors, and settlers living on remote, unprotected ranches. Troops who went after them returned to their base only to find that the Apaches had hit half a dozen places in the opposite direction; evidently they knew the locations and movements of almost all the civilians and soldiers in their territory. Undoubtedly Geronimo rode on many of these raids, although he occasionally drifted back to live with the Mimbres band or ventured into Mexico to harry his old enemies while Cochise waged war on the Americans.

This was a war that defied statistical accounting. A Cochise raid on an isolated pack train or ranch would claim one or two or a half-dozen lives; but rumor, spread like prairie fire by frantic frontier editors, would count the casualties in dozens or scores. Conversely, a good many transients probably died with no one to mark their deaths but their killers and the vultures. Although hard to pin down, the toll taken by Cochise was indubitably heavy—and a source of deep concern in the highest councils of the nation. In 1870, General Sherman wrote only half-jokingly to the Secretary of War: "We had one war with Mexico to take Arizona, and we should have another to make her take it back." ◉

The demeaning routine of the reservation

For the Apaches, bred to a life of nomadic marauding, confinement to a reservation was an especially oppressive experience. The 5,000 Apaches who were forced onto the San Carlos reservation in southern Arizona by the 1880s, when these scenes were photographed, represented at least eight different bands. Since some of them were long-time antagonists, the mere fact that they were placed in close contact was a source of deep unease.

Even more unnatural than the proximity of enemies was the program for self-improvement imposed on the Indians. The reservation's overseers—at various times either the U.S. Army or the Office of Indian Affairs—expected the Apaches to become self-sufficient farmers. However, the Indians knew little about growing crops, even under the best conditions—and still less about the large-scale irrigation techniques required to make this desert land yield even a modest livelihood. Instead, they subsisted on weekly food rations.

Reservation policy also called for the Apaches to govern themselves. But their own culture had no equivalent to the police force and courts they were required to set up. Nor did they see the worth of the white man's law, which prohibited a wide range of formerly accepted practices, from the brewing of *ti-swin*—a beer made from corn—to slicing off the nose of an unfaithful wife.

Perhaps the greatest hardship was the same boredom that triggered Geronimo's flight in 1878 and sent scores of lesser chiefs off to enlist as scouts for their recent foe, the U.S. Army. Although women and children kept busy gathering bundles of hay at a penny a pound for the cavalry's horses, there was little for the men to do. Restless warriors whiled away the hours gambling, singing and comforting one another with wistful tales of the days when an Apache could pitch his wickiup wherever he chose and measure his worth by the number of horses he stole.

Under the watchful eyes of the Army, Apaches hack out an irrigation ditch—part of a stubbornly resisted effort to turn them to farming.

Families queue up for their weekly rations of flour and beef, which were seldom sufficient for more than four or five days.

Women collect their allotment of firewood, consisting mostly of cottonwood and mesquite, on ration day.

To pass the time on the reservation, Apache men try their hand at an ancient betting game in which a pole was thrust at a rolling hoop.

Met by a cavalry officer and stray dogs, Apache women return from their hay-gathering labors.

A chair, factory-made pails and a canvas-sided wickiup mark a family's acceptance of alien ways.

Unknown to those who feared him, Cochise was a sorely troubled man. Kill as he might, he looked down and saw the white invasion increasing month by month. "We kill ten; a hundred come in their place," he told his warriors. His early strikes had frightened away many settlers, but after Arizona won territorial status in 1863, the government tried hard to promote immigration. By 1870 some 10,000 miners, ranchers, farmers and townsmen had arrived; a decade later, the white population would be 37,000—ten times the Indian population.

Cochise, being a realist, knew that not even desperate courage could turn back the tide. It was this realization—and curiosity at another man's bravery—that moved him not to kill Thomas Jeffords, an extraordinary frontiersman who would finally bring the long vendetta to an end.

Jeffords, born a New Yorker, came west as a Civil War scout in 1862, worked as a stage driver for a time, and in the mid-1860s became a superintendent of U.S. mails. By 1871, he had lost 14 mail drivers to Cochise's warriors and he made up his mind to see the chief in person. Alone, lighting signal fires as he went, he made his way into Chiricahua country, perfectly aware that the Apaches had him under their eyes and at their mercy every foot of the way. Cochise watched him come, valley by valley, ridge by ridge. Amazed, the chief withheld permission to kill the interloper.

In camp, Cochise confronted Jeffords with impassive gravity. Jeffords, who knew the Apache tongue, said, "I want to leave my arms with you or with one of your wives, to be returned to me after I have had a talk with you." Cochise recognized that this was neither impudence nor stupid bravado but the action of a man who was putting incredible courage to the test of serious purpose. He decided to let the man have his say.

Jeffords asked that the mail drivers be given safe passage through the region. Cochise said the request was unreasonable, since they carried military messages against him. Jeffords said no, military messages went by courier. After much thought, concluding that a man as brave as Jeffords must speak with only one tongue, Cochise agreed to let the mail go in peace. It was the beginning of a strange, enduring friendship. "I found him to be a man of great natural ability," Jeffords recounted later. "A splendid specimen of physical manhood with

78

Serving as the eyes of the Army in the labyrinthine terrain of the Southwest, Apache scouts like these broke the resistance of their own people. Yet even their targets accepted the scouts' role as reasonable rather than treasonous — a consequence of intertribal rivalries and reservation boredom.

VICTORIO

NANA

LOCO

CHATO

ALCHESAY

ESKAMINZIN

Apache proponents of peace and war

VICTORIO, who won a leadership role among the Mimbres by ability rather than birth, urged peace until the Army moved his people from a reservation on their original New Mexico lands to bleak San Carlos in 1877. Turning renegade, he led 250 warriors on a rampage that left 400 whites dead before he was killed in 1880.

NANA moved to the forefront of the remaining Mimbres renegades after the death of Victorio and held to the warpath, although he was rheumatic and in his seventies. With hundreds of soldiers in hot pursuit, his group of 40 warriors claimed more than 30 lives in less than two months. He later threw in his lot with Geronimo.

LOCO, an eloquent and widely respected voice for moderation among the Mimbres, was forced at gunpoint by Geronimo to leave the San Carlos reservation in 1882 and join the war on whites. Although he broke away and surrendered the next year, he was placed under military arrest and sent off to a prison in Florida.

CHATO was allied with Geronimo for a time but reformed in 1884 and became an Army scout. In 1886, he received a medal for services against Geronimo; then — just a few days later — the military, under pressure from nervous Arizonans, shipped him to Florida to be confined with the renegades he had helped bring to bay.

ALCHESAY, a chief of the White Mountain Apaches of eastern Arizona, never deviated from the path of friendship with the whites. He proved a peerless scout, received the Congressional Medal of Honor for valor in General George Crook's 1872-1873 campaign in Arizona, and went on to become a prominent cattleman.

ESKAMINZIN, chief of the Aravaipa Apaches of south-central Arizona, favored peace until 1871, when 144 of his people were massacred by Tucson vigilantes avenging raids by other Apaches. He shot his closest white friend, served a jail sentence and became a successful reservation farmer — until some miners took his land.

an eye like an eagle. He respected me; I respected him. He was a man who scorned a liar." A year later, this unlikely friendship would serve to defuse the foremost Apache enemy of the United States.

The end was almost anticlimactic. In 1872, President Grant sent a pious, one-armed Civil War officer to make peace with the Apaches. General Oliver O. Howard sought out Jeffords and asked to be led to the Chiricahua leader. When Cochise and Howard met in the mountains, the onlooking warriors were startled at the general's habit in moments of importance of suddenly dropping on one knee to pray. Assured by Jeffords that Howard was consulting the Almighty and not making bad medicine, they relaxed.

Cochise and Howard spent 11 days in negotiations and finally settled their differences. The Chiricahuas were allowed to keep their weapons, their way of life and their own traditional range; they were granted a reservation that enclosed the Chiricahua and Dragoon mountains where they had lived, hunted and fought time out of mind. At Cochise's insistence, Jeffords was appointed reservation agent. And at Jeffords' insistence, the Interior Department granted the new agent absolute authority to deal with the Chiricahuas and to keep away any white intruder, civilian or military.

"The white man and the Indian are to drink of the same water, eat of the same bread and be at peace," Cochise said when the pact was sealed. He was not privileged to enjoy this new era of coexistence for long. In 1874, in his fifty-first year, he was taken mortally ill. Near the end, he called Jeffords to his blanket.

"Brother, do you think you will ever see me alive again?" Cochise asked.

"No," Jeffords replied, "I think by tomorrow night you will be dead."

"Yes, I think so—about 10 o'clock tomorrow morning. Do you think we will ever meet again?"

"I don't know," Jeffords confessed. "What is your opinion?"

"I believe good friends will meet somewhere," Cochise said.

The chief was dead by the hour he named. That night his warriors painted him in yellow, black and vermilion, shrouded him in a red blanket, propped him on his favorite horse and took him deep into the mountains. They lowered his body and his weapons into a crevice whose location was never afterward revealed.

For two years after the death of Cochise, Jeffords managed to maintain a semblance of peace. But with Cochise gone his task was not easy. Gradually the situation began to slip out of his control. Increasing numbers of warriors, following Geronimo's lead, used the reservation merely as a sanctuary: they raided in Mexico and returned when things got too hot. Often these vacationing marauders brought stolen horses and cattle with them to sell to reservation brethren.

Mexican authorities complained to Jeffords bitterly, and in 1876 Americans, too, gained cause for deep grievance. That March, two stagecoach attendants on the reservation heard that some raiders had returned from Mexico with stolen gold and silver; to get their hands on some of the loot they offered to sell the Apaches whiskey at the equivalent of $10 a bottle. The warriors, swapping booty for booze, became drunk. Soon the liquor was gone and the Indians demanded more. When they were refused, they killed both white men. The next day, continuing their murderous binge, they killed a rancher in the vicinity. Jeffords called in the Army and tracked the offenders into the Dragoon Mountains, but he failed to capture them.

The outcry among Arizonans was immediate and vehement. Governor Anson P. Safford demanded that Washington replace Jeffords. The *Arizona Citizen* of Tucson declared in mid-April: "The kind of war needed for the Chiricahua Apaches is steady, unrelenting, hopeless, and undiscriminating war, slaying men, women and children, until every valley and crest and crag and fastness shall send to high heaven the grateful incense of festering and rotting Chiricahuas."

Washington responded by dissolving the Chiricahua reservation in June 1876 and removing the band—or as many of its members as could be found—to San Carlos, the largest reservation in the Southwest, shared by some 4,000 other Apaches. However, Geronimo, learning of the plan, hastened across the border, along with his family and other recalcitrant Chiricahuas.

In the years to come, Geronimo would earn himself a conspicuous place in Western history as the ultimate holdout, a renegade who was willing to fight for his freedom and the traditional way of life longer and more ferociously than any other Apache leader—or almost any other Indian, for that matter. Although the largest group he ever led numbered a mere 100 followers, he was credited with possessing a fiery, unyielding spirit that no man could break.

Legend oversimplified him. Geronimo was, in fact, something of a paradox: alternately tough-minded and indecisive; a man who sometimes stayed and fought, sometimes cut and ran; a chief who interrupted his career as a holdout to test reservation life, never finding it quite to his taste, but never deciding against it altogether. To the end, he seemed a prisoner of the personality that had emerged after his wife was murdered at Janos long before, given to passions that inspired fear, awe and horror — but that somehow never amounted to more than a mystery.

His first stint as a holdout was short-lived. Late in the winter of 1876-1877, he came out of Mexico into the vicinity of the Warm Springs agency in New Mexico, where the Mimbres Apaches resided. Geronimo's visit was not merely social: he had a herd of stolen cattle to trade or sell. Weeks later, news of his whereabouts reached the agent of San Carlos, a cocky young

Never one to shun publicity, Geronimo (*in front of horse*) lines up his warriors for a Tombstone photographer who crossed the Mexican border to

man named John Clum, who immediately set off on the 400-mile journey to Warm Springs to apprehend him.

In April, Geronimo received word that Clum desired to talk. In no wise intimidated, Geronimo painted himself for war, took up his weapons, summoned a dozen of his leading warriors and rode three miles to the agency. He found Clum sitting on the veranda, surrounded by a half-dozen Indian police, with a few others standing nearby. The San Carlos agent opened proceedings on a characteristically imperious note: "No harm will come to you if you listen with good ears." Geronimo, noting Clum's small force, was not humbled. "Speak with discretion," he advised the agent, "and no harm will come to *you.*" To emphasize the point, he hitched up the rifle in his arms.

At that moment, Clum touched the brim of his hat. It was a signal. The doors of an adjoining commissary building burst open and 80 additional policemen charged out and surrounded Geronimo's party with leveled guns. Geronimo began to thumb back the hammer of his rifle but thought better of it and stood motionless, stolidly watchful. Clum approached him. "I'll take

record peace negotiations with General Crook in 1886. At the time, the renegade group numbered 35 men and 80 women and children.

The departure of cavalry patrols from Fort Bowie was a familiar sight as long as Cochise and Geronimo were at large. The fortress was built in 1862 to control Apache Pass, a vital route through the Chiricahua Mountains that opened the way between Tucson and all points East.

your gun myself," he said and lifted the weapon from Geronimo's arms.

Conveyed to San Carlos under close guard, Geronimo found his people's new home to be even worse than he had feared — a miserable substitute for the mountains they had once roamed. The reservation, established in 1872 by the one-armed General Howard, was a tract of some 5,000 square miles on both banks of the Gila River in eastern Arizona. Much of it was low lying, and in summer the temperature often hovered around 110 degrees. The vegetation mainly consisted of cactus, mesquite and dejected cottonwoods along the river banks. Sandstorms were frequent, and centipedes and rattlesnakes were endemic nuisances.

As though the barren waste were not enough punishment, the Indians at San Carlos were regularly short-changed by the civilian contractors who supplied their rations — usually with the collaboration of the reservation authorities. A military observer once made a check of the scales used to weigh the Indians' weekly beef ration and found that each week the government was being charged for 1,500 ghost pounds of meat. Moreover, the cattle herd used to supply the ration was pastured on the south side of the Gila River, while the slaughter house was on the north side. On ration day, having held the stock off water the day before, the beef contractor would slowly drive the animals through the river, allowing them plenty of time to slake their thirst on the way. "The government was paying for half a barrel of Gila River water delivered with each beef," the military observer reported.

San Carlos was continually nibbled away by whites who found something they wanted around its perimeter. On the southeast, Mormon farmers moved in and squatted on fields planted by Indians who were trying to conform to the government's determination to convert them into farmers. Two copper strikes on the west side and another to the east cut thousands of acres out of reservation lands. Coal and silver discoveries to the south swallowed another chunk. A Tucson grand jury found that one agent, J. C. Tiffany, used Indians as semi-slave labor to dig coal on reservation lands for the benefit of white speculators who were his partners.

Geronimo hardly stayed long enough to get a clear picture of these myriad forms of wretchedness. Although the agent tried to win his support by appointing him

spokesman for all the Chiricahuas, he derived no satisfaction from this hollow honor, coming as it did from a white man. The novelty of free rations soon dimmed and after a few months, he fled back to Mexico with a few other Chiricahuas. He returned voluntarily in 1880, following a harrowing winter of near-starvation in the Sierra Madre but, again, he did not stay long.

His next breakout was prompted by more than simple restlessness. During the spring of 1881, an Apache mystic named Noch-ay-del-klinne gained sway over many of the San Carlos residents by preaching a simple but inflammatory doctrine — that dead chiefs would rise again and reassert Apache greatness. In August, the agent sent a detachment of 85 soldiers to arrest this disruptive spiritual leader at his camp in a remote quarter of the reservation. Perhaps because the Apaches did not understand the troopers' intentions, a battle broke out, and the medicine man was killed, along with several soldiers and Indians. The Army immediately rushed reinforcements to the scene to head off further violence. Geronimo, alarmed at the increase of troops, hearing rumors that he was to be arrested and hanged, vanished into Mexico with 74 followers.

Over the next two years, he and other Apache raiders periodically recrossed the border to attack American settlements, growing more audacious all the time. On March 21, 1883, a war party ventured within 10 miles of the populous silver-mining town of Tombstone, Arizona, and killed three men. A few days later the same warriors appeared in the vicinity of Lourdsburg, New Mexico, and waylaid a buckboard that was carrying a federal judge, H. C. McComas, and his wife and six-year-old son. The Apaches killed both of the adults and took the boy captive.

These outrages finally stirred the government to negotiate an agreement with Mexico whereby soldiers of either nation were permitted to cross the border when chasing renegades. The pleased beneficiary of this pact was General George Crook — a brilliant veteran of Indian campaigns all across the West — who had recently been assigned to the Southwest. Crook developed another important tactical advantage on his own. Firmly believing that it took an Apache to catch an Apache, he augmented his main cavalry force with 193 Indian scouts to track down the holdouts amid the desolate crags of the Sierra Madre. Crook had no difficulty in

Seated in Mexico's Cañon de los Embudos
— Canyon of Tricksters — Geronimo *(left
of center)* agrees to surrender to General
Crook *(second from right)* on March 27,
1886. The next night he reneged and fled.

persuading Indians to take on this role: in their desperation for adventure and relief from reservation rules, they leaped at the chance, especially if they belonged to a band that had no ties with the Chiricahuas.

The innovation paid off in May 1883, when a force of scouts surprised a renegade camp, killing nine Apaches and taking five prisoners — one of them the granddaughter of Cochise. It was a stunning blow to the renegades, for they had thought themselves virtually invulnerable in the fastness of the Mexican mountains. Geronimo's dismayed followers pressed him to meet with General Crook and negotiate the best possible terms for surrender.

The two men held a parley at an Army camp in Mexico on May 20, and Geronimo found Crook to be surprisingly generous. The general, aware that the Apaches were widely scattered, gave Geronimo two months to gather up his people and return to the res-

ervation. True to his word, Geronimo came in on his own, but he arrived in March 1884, having stretched two months to nine. He appeared at the border driving 350 head of cattle, which he proposed to use for trading on the reservation. His last brief stay was begun in deep indignation, for the authorities confiscated his cattle. To his mind this was rank injustice, since he felt he had obtained the stock fair and square — by raiding in the manner of his lifelong training.

Writing a report to his superiors in 1884, Crook proudly noted that "for the first time in the history of that fierce people, every member of the Apache tribe is at peace." But a year later, the war was on again.

Geronimo's next breakout was rooted in a minor act of defiance and a stupid Army blunder. Like most Apaches, he resented a reservation rule that prohibited liquor of any sort, including the weak beer the Indians had formerly brewed from corn. In May 1885, he and

87

Santiago McKinn (*foreground*), an Irish-Mexican lad captured by Geronimo, was freed during negotiations with General Crook. The boy's physical condition caused bitter controversy. Outwardly he seemed unharmed, but some in Crook's retinue insisted "his mind was almost ruined."

a dozen other leaders deliberately staged a spree with homemade beer, then openly admitted the deed—figuring that the authorities would hesitate to discipline so many prominent Indians. The ranking military officer at San Carlos, new to the job, composed a telegram to Crook, asking for instructions; however, before sending it, he showed it to his chief of scouts, a man named Al Sieber. As it happened, Sieber was badly hung over from a spree of his own; he mumbled that the problem did not amount to anything, and the inexperienced officer simply put the telegram aside.

Geronimo and the others grew increasingly apprehensive as they waited for some response from the authorities. The interminable delay seemed to bode ill, and finally, unable to bear the suspense, Geronimo decamped, taking along 42 men and 92 women and children. Before leaving, he sent his warriors to cut the telegraph wire, concealing this sabotage by making the cut in the crotch of a tree and tying the wire ends with a rawhide thong.

Collecting supplies on the way south, he attacked the ranch of a man named Phillips, killed him, his wife and an infant. He also hanged their five-year-old daughter on a meat hook. She was still alive when a posse arrived from Silver City, but died a few hours later.

Crook was furious when he learned about the unsent telegram. He later wrote, "I am firmly convinced that had I known of the occurrence, the outbreak would not have occurred." He mounted the heaviest campaign in the Apache wars up to that time, with 20 cavalry troops and more than 200 Indian scouts—3,000 men in all. Once again, his policy of using scouts paid off, although more slowly this time, for Geronimo knew they were coming and was more cautious.

Throughout the winter of 1885-1886, Crook's forces hunted the foe in the Sierra Madre. In January, they surprised one camp and captured the renegades' horses and supplies, although their quarry escaped. Finally, in March, Geronimo's followers persuaded him to meet Crook a few miles south of the border.

When the general arrived, he did not find Geronimo or his men looking particularly discouraged. "Though tired of the constant hounding of the campaign," Crook later recalled, "they were in superb physical condition, armed to the teeth, fierce as so many tigers. Knowing what pitiless brutes they are themselves, they mistrust everyone else. We found them in camp, in such a position that a thousand men could not have surrounded them with any possibility of capturing them. They were able upon the approach of any enemy to scatter and escape through dozens of ravines and cañons which would shelter them from pursuit."

Crook and Geronimo talked for two days, and Geronimo agreed once more to return to the reservation. "Do with me what you please," he said. "Once I moved about like the wind. Now I surrender to you, and that is all." Despite his submissive words, the agreement fell apart before Crook could convey the Apaches back across the border. On a dark and rainy night, Geronimo changed his mind and departed, taking with him the last coterie of desperate fugitives: 20 warriors and 18 women and children, 38 in all.

For some time, Crook had been under fire from Americans in the Southwest who felt that the Apaches could have been brought to bay more quickly — and also from his superior, General Philip Sheridan, a traditionalist who disapproved of the wholesale use of Indian scouts. When Crook reported the abortive dealings with Geronimo to Sheridan, he received a curt reply by telegraph: "Your dispatch of yesterday received. It has occasioned great disappointment. It seems strange that Geronimo and party could have escaped without the knowledge of the scouts." Disgusted with this response, Crook immediately asked to be relieved of his com-

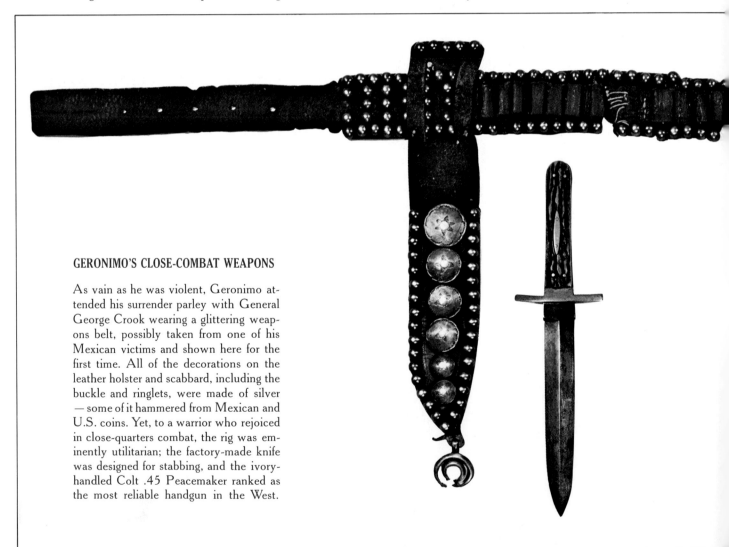

GERONIMO'S CLOSE-COMBAT WEAPONS

As vain as he was violent, Geronimo attended his surrender parley with General George Crook wearing a glittering weapons belt, possibly taken from one of his Mexican victims and shown here for the first time. All of the decorations on the leather holster and scabbard, including the buckle and ringlets, were made of silver — some of it hammered from Mexican and U.S. coins. Yet, to a warrior who rejoiced in close-quarters combat, the rig was eminently utilitarian; the factory-made knife was designed for stabbing, and the ivory-handled Colt .45 Peacemaker ranked as the most reliable handgun in the West.

mand and was subsequently transferred to the Department of the Platte.

As a replacement, Sheridan sent General Nelson Miles, with orders to "capture or destroy." Miles never, in the strict sense, managed to do either. But his work was destructive enough. One of his early decisions was to arrange for all Mimbres and Chiricahua Apaches on the reservations—including scouts who had fought with Crook—to be exiled to Florida.

For the manhunt of Geronimo, Miles mounted 5,000 troops and built 30 heliograph stations to flash Morse code messages from mountain to mountain across southeastern Arizona and into northern Sonora. (When Geronimo saw the mirror flashes, he thought they were

magic and began avoiding the mountaintops.) Miles spread his troops, trying to guard every spring and pass to prevent the Indians from moving about, but Geronimo remained more mobile than ever. In April of 1886, he and his warriors crossed the border into Arizona, killed a cattleman's wife, her 13-year-old child and a ranchhand. A few weeks later, the Apaches killed two men outside the town of Nogales, Arizona, then ambushed pursuing soldiers in a narrow canyon and took two more lives—along with horses and supplies—without suffering any casualties.

Hysteria spread through the region as the Apaches eluded the massive hunt and raided at will. Newspapers exaggerated the death toll and claimed that Geronimo

A school to "kill the Indian and save the man"

In the autumn of 1886, just weeks after Geronimo finally lost his bid to live like an Apache of old, a band of Apache children arrived at the Carlisle Indian School in Pennsylvania, where they were to be readied for integrated citizenship in the white man's world. In the words of former Indian-fighter Richard Henry Pratt *(page 45)*, founder of the institution in 1879, Carlisle's job was to "kill the Indian and save the man."

To that end, the new arrivals were quickly scrubbed, shorn, stripped of their Apache garb, issued uniforms and dresses, and assigned such tongue-tripping Anglo-Saxon names as Humphrey, Basil and Margaret. Then began a regimen of school days structured with military precision, from the rising bell at 6 a.m. to lights-out at 10 p.m. The youngsters were taught not only reading, writing and arithmetic, but such skills as carpentry and farming for the boys, and cooking and sewing for the girls. Once a student became reasonably conversant in English he was permitted to speak no other tongue. The children ate only white man's food, and in their spare time they played white man's games, including football and baseball.

Yet, while the Carlisle experience benefited some Indians—most notably an athletic Sauk-and-Fox named Jim Thorpe, who was enrolled there in 1904—it was marred with tragedy for the Apaches. Of 112 youngsters who made the long trek to Carlisle beginning in 1886, 30 had died of white man's diseases by the end of 1889, and another dozen, seriously ill, had been sent home to recuperate.

Before: Carlisle's first Apache students present a ragtag appearance upon their arrival in 1886.

After: Four months later, the same children have become a vision of well-groomed uniformity.

was leading 150 men. It was rumored that Geronimo was trying to stir an uprising of the reservation Apaches, communicating with them through signal fires. More wishful rumors said that his group had been wiped out by American or Mexican soldiers. In fact, in July, when Geronimo slipped deep into the Sierra Madre to rest, he had not suffered a single loss.

The finish was subdued—and oddly reminiscent of the end to Cochise's war. General Miles, while not giving up on his more dramatic tactics, decided to try negotiating with the enemy. His appointed emissary, Lieutenant Charles Gatewood, was, like Tom Jeffords, a man of uncommon courage who also understood the ways of the Apaches. He had been stationed on a reservation for several years and had met Geronimo on a number of occasions.

To make contact with the band, Gatewood headed across the border and began patrolling the flanks of the Sierra Madre with two scouts and an escort force of 25 men, simply listening for word of the Apaches' whereabouts. When he heard that Geronimo was sending women into the small Mexican town of Fronteras to procure mescale, he rushed to the scene. The Mexicans, he discovered, were hoping to lure the Indians into the town to massacre them. But Gatewood decided on a different approach. Paring his force down to two scouts and half a dozen soldiers so as not to alarm the enemy, he trailed an Apache woman out of Fronteras and deep into the front range of the Sierra Madre. It was late August 1886.

Watching the scouts come up a canyon ahead of Gatewood, Geronimo dispatched a warrior to conduct them into his camp. He kept one scout as a hostage and sent the other back to Gatewood to say he was ready to talk. The next day, Gatewood and his six men moved up the canyon. They were met by a warrior who said Gatewood would have to come on alone. Gatewood compromised, leaving the soldiers behind but taking his remaining scout.

Geronimo, surrounded by his warriors, met him inside the camp. Twenty feet away, he laid his rifle on the ground and came forward to shake hands. But when they sat down to talk, Geronimo deliberately sat so close that the lieutenant could feel the revolver on his hip. Geronimo asked what the U.S. government would offer if he gave himself up. Gatewood replied that he

could only accept unconditional surrender and that Geronimo would be sent to exile in Florida. At that, the renegade leader bristled. "Take us to the reservation," he demanded. "Or fight!"

Then Gatewood told Geronimo that his family already had been removed to Florida, along with the other Chiricahuas. The news was an evident shock. All at once the fighting spirit, the years of defiance, the fierce—if fitful—will for independence seemed to drain out of the old warrior. He said that he would speak with General Miles.

Using the heliograph system, the lieutenant contacted Miles and then conducted Geronimo and his last 37 followers—14 of them women and children—to a point just across the border. Geronimo very nearly fled once more; this time there was nobody to blame but Miles himself. The general—perhaps wanting to impress Geronimo, perhaps to humiliate him, perhaps trying to give him a taste of the medicine he had once administered to General Crook—made no effort to get to the parley on time. Growing nervous as he waited nine long days, Geronimo once suggested that Gatewood—whose poise and courage had thoroughly impressed him—come with him back into the mountains, presumably to take up a rewarding and adventurous life of raiding. But Miles finally arrived on September 3, and that was the end of the long road. Geronimo, offered nothing beyond an assurance that the fugitives would be reunited with their families in Florida, gave up at last.

Perhaps he was not surprised, after all these years, when he found himself the victim of one final treachery. In Florida, he was imprisoned for two years, with no glimpse of his family. Finally, in 1894 he and the remaining Chiricahuas were taken to Fort Sill, Indian Territory, where most of them died rapidly of disease and despair. Geronimo himself was turned into a human exhibit, paraded in President Theodore Roosevelt's inaugural procession in 1901 and at the St. Louis World's Fair in 1904. Stubbornly declining to become the white man's burden, he eked out a living of his own, of sorts. He made and sold bows and arrows, and peddled his autographed photographs.

The white man had overwhelmed him. Nearly everything was gone. But there was one thing nobody could wrest from him—the memory that, in the end, it had taken 5,000 whites to subdue his 38 Apaches.

The twilight years of a living legend

Geronimo, the most notorious of the Apache leaders, was about 57 years old but still a forbidding figure in 1886, when he surrendered and began a 23-year exile in Florida and Oklahoma. The portfolio of portraits here and on the following pages records his degeneration from a haughty warrior into a submissive old man who hawked pictures of himself in outlandish attire that no Chiricahua ever wore. Through it all, he nourished a forlorn hope. "I want to go back to my old home before I die," he confided to a reporter in 1908. It was not to be. The next year Geronimo died and was buried at Fort Sill, 700 miles from the crags and deserts where he had inspired such fear.

1886

1890

C. 1894

C. 1903

C. 1904

1905

His lance poised for the kill, a Comanche warrior overtakes an Osage in artist George Catlin's tribute to the master equestrians of the plains.

3 | Final champion of Comanche glory

In the late 1860s, a war chief of riveting appeal arose among the Comanches of the southern plains. He was a half-breed named Quanah; the Texans on whom he preyed would later call him Quanah Parker, after his white mother, Cynthia Ann Parker, who as a young girl had been captured by Comanches. Quanah's slashing raids and hairbreadth escapes from the U.S. cavalry rekindled war fever among the Plains Indians who were still free; and those who had already signed themselves over to a stagnant reservation existence thirsted after news of his exploits, hoping he might somehow reverse their fortunes.

His people were horsemen without peer. While many other Plains tribesmen rode to meet the enemy and then dismounted to fight, the Comanches always fought on horseback. They routinely traveled hundreds of miles to execute a lightning raid, and their prowess in battle made them prodigiously rich in captured animals: ordinary warriors often owned 250 horses, and chiefs like Quanah might have more than a thousand.

Not even Quanah and his spectacularly mobile warriors could long withstand the whites' overwhelming superiority in numbers, resources and organization. However, when the inevitable time for surrender arrived, he devoted himself to an even greater career — as a politician and financier who found ways to merge the interests of the two peoples whose blood flowed in his veins.

The two lives of Quanah Parker

In the early 1870s, it seemed to the whites that nothing but a fatal bullet could make a "good" Indian out of Quanah, the notorious half-breed Comanche chief. While the tribe's other war leaders were leading their defeated bands onto the Fort Sill reservation in Indian Territory, Quanah and his followers in the Kwahadi band kept up their murderous attacks on frontier settlements across nearly half of Texas. Cavalry Captain Robert Carter, a battle-scarred veteran of the Indian wars, described the Kwahadi horsemen as "the most inveterate raiders on the Texas border," and he blamed Quanah for "some of the foulest deeds ever recorded in the annals of Indian warfare."

Quanah fought with reckless, fanatic zeal. This much Carter learned at close hand one day in west Texas, when he and a detachment of troopers barely stood off a Kwahadi war party until help arrived from their main column two miles away. "A large and powerfully built chief led the bunch on a coal black racing pony," Carter wrote in his memoirs. "His heels nervously working in the animal's side, with six-shooter poised in air, he seemed the incarnation of savage brutal joy. His face was smeared with black war paint, which gave his features a satanic look. A large cruel mouth added to his ferocious appearance. Bells jingled as he rode at headlong speed, followed by the leading warriors, all eager to outstrip him in the race."

This demon on horseback was never truly vanquished in his many battles with the Army. Yet suddenly, in 1875, Quanah gave up his wars and his wanderings and accepted a cramped, sedentary reservation life. Moreover, the U.S. Congress later praised his public service in persuading his tribe to quit the warpath for good. Quanah was, in fact, an anomaly — a chief who was equally great in war and in the enforced peace that followed, when he emerged as an energetic and enlightened protector of his people's interests.

What caused Quanah's unlikely turnabout? Some Texans, grudging admirers of their tormentor, credited him with a statesman-like decision to save the remnants of his tribe, even though the price was his own surrender. Other Texans, aware that Quanah had been born to a white mother, figured that his white blood had somehow prompted a change of allegiance. The notion was absurd. Although Quanah seemed to lead two very different lives, he was wholly Comanche in both of them, never forswearing the heritage of a people who ranked as the greatest horse-warriors in the West.

The tribal world that shaped Quanah had begun to take shape itself sometime around the year 1700, when Comanche horsemen migrated southward from the Wyoming region. No tribe or alliance of tribes in their path could match their equestrian prowess, and by the middle of the 18th Century they had not only established themselves as reigning lords of the southern plains but had played a possibly momentous role in American history by blocking the northward expansion of the Spanish, holding the bulk of them in southern Texas.

The Comanches reached the peak of their power early in the 19th Century. They were then one of the largest Indian tribes, about 20,000 strong, occupying a range of some 240,000 square miles, mostly in Texas but also including adjacent areas of what would become Kansas, Colorado, New Mexico and Oklahoma. This enormous dominion was shared by five main Comanche bands, all completely autonomous and acknowledging no principal chief. The bands were free to carry on any war they pleased, except with fellow tribesmen. Their

Prior to tribal festivities in the 1890s, Comanche chief Quanah, his braids wrapped in beaver fur, wears traditional attire. By then a well-connected businessman, he was more likely to be seen in a suit and tie.

Hunters take their ease as women labor in a Comanche village visited by artist George Catlin in 1834. At that time, the 20,000 members of the powerful tribe controlled an enormous range centered in northwestern Texas and measuring 600 miles north to south, 400 miles east to west.

favorite targets were the outposts of New Spain—or Mexico, as the area was called after its citizens revolted against a distant monarchy in 1821. War parties sometimes thrust hundreds of miles into Mexico and returned with as many as 1,000 stolen horses.

The Spanish and Mexicans in Texas, never numbering more than a few thousand, were regarded as a feeble enemy by the Comanches. But the tribe faced a more daunting foe when Anglo-Americans began appearing in eastern Texas in the 1820s; they kept coming in such numbers that within a few years settlers were encroaching on the Indians' buffalo-hunting plains.

A long and venomous war between the newcomers and the Comanches began shortly after Texas won independence from Mexico early in 1836. In the first serious clash—an exhilarating victory for the Comanches —Quanah's mother, Cynthia Ann Parker, was taken captive. Cynthia Ann was then nine years old and living in Parker's Fort, a stockaded cluster of homesteads set up by her parents and kinfolk near the town of Groesbeck, in east-central Texas. When raiders attacked Parker's Fort, they set a pattern of savagery that both sides followed for decades thereafter. Grandfather Parker had his scalp taken and his genitals ripped off before he was killed. Grandmother Parker was pinned to the ground with a lance, stripped and allowed to live to suffer her pain and degradation.

Cynthia Ann was one of five white women and children abducted by the warriors. Like most young white captives, she adjusted readily to the Indian life and was adopted by the Comanches, who suffered from a low birth rate. In her teens, she became the wife of Peta Nocona, a rising young chief of the Noconas, one of the main bands. Early in her marriage, she gave birth to Quanah—meaning "fragrant" in Comanche. The infant looked just like a full-blooded Comanche, except that his eyes were blue-gray instead of black. As Quanah grew into a strong, tall boy, Cynthia Ann bore another son, Pecos, and a daughter, Prairie Flower.

Three children were a larger-than-average brood for a Comanche woman, and Nocona was so pleased with his productive blue-eyed spouse that, though most chiefs took several wives, he remained monogamous. Cynthia Ann was as content as her husband. In the 1850s, some white hunters met her on the plains and offered to pay ransom for her freedom. She refused, saying she

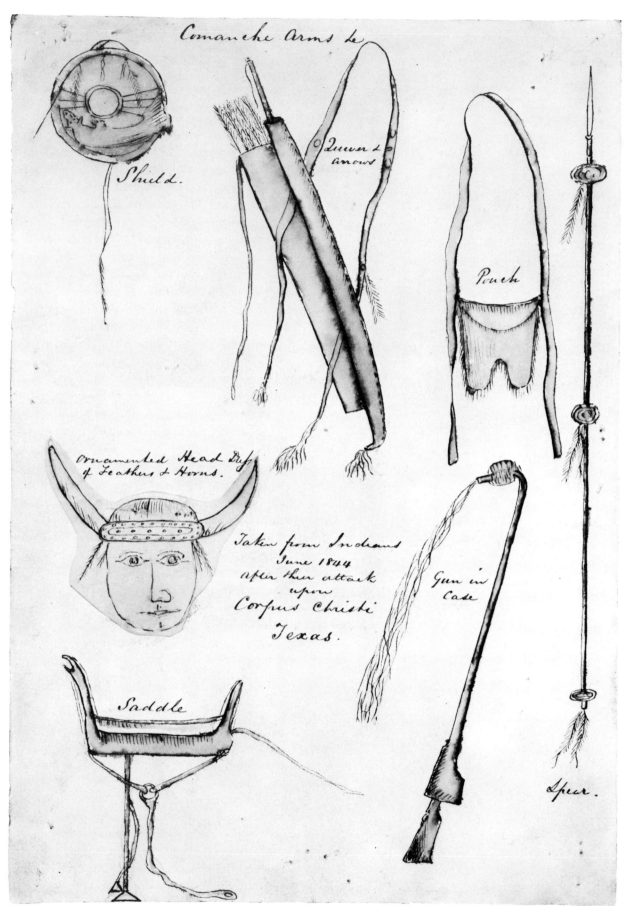

Comanche Arms &

Shield.

Quiver & arrows

Pouch

Ornamented Head Dress of Feathers & Horns.

Taken from Indians June 1844 After their attack upon Corpus Christi Texas.

Gun in Case

Saddle

Spear.

Comanche war gear, sketched by a British visitor to Texas, includes a pouch for charms that summoned divine aid in battle.

had children to care for and that she loved her husband.

Quanah, like all Comanche children, grew up on horseback. He learned to ride with his mother almost as soon as he could walk, and by the time he was five he had a pony of his own and was practicing with a small bow and blunt arrows as he rode at increasing speeds. A Comanche's boyhood was a pampered, sportive idyl, and from the time Quanah was nine or 10 he and other youths were taking midnight joy rides on the moonlit prairie, playing rough games and enviously watching the warriors parade around camp before leaving on raids. Quanah learned that Comanche men hunted to live, but lived to win honors and booty in war.

Because anyone who did not fight was not truly a man to the Comanches, many aging warriors felt that life had become purposeless, and they would bitterly quote the Comanche proverb, "A brave man dies young." More than a few elderly warriors, realizing that their skills and strength were fast slipping away, chose to commit suicide by battle. One such glorious death was witnessed—and abetted—by a troop of U.S. cavalry in 1860. The soldiers, pursuing a Comanche raiding party, saw an aged warrior dismount up ahead. He removed his moccasins, a sure sign that he did not intend to leave that spot alive. The old man fought hard and wounded three soldiers and their commanding officer before he died with more than 20 bullets in him. But while he made his brave stand, his friends were able to get away.

Quanah probably went on his first raid—and killed his first enemy—by the age of 15. The success of the mission was practically a foregone conclusion, in part because the Texas frontier was too extended to defend at all points against surprise attack, and also because Comanche raiders never neglected to plan for their retreat. If the target lay at any appreciable distance, they traveled with a change of horses in tow. The warriors would set up a temporary camp not far from the intended point of attack, and leave their spare horses there before swooping in for the kill. It took hours for any settler who escaped their scalping knives to round up a relief force, and the rescuers could not reach the ravaged settlement for hours more. By then the booty-laden warriors would have returned to their temporary camp, carefully traveling over rocky areas and through stream beds to conceal their tracks. Mounted on fresh horses, they would ride as much as 100 miles without stopping for food or rest. Even if they were tracked to their temporary camp and beyond, their pursuers stood only a slim chance of catching them.

Years before Quanah came of age, the Texans had learned that it was foolish to wait for Comanche raids and then launch vain pursuits; the best defense was to reply in kind, by surprise attack. In 1835, the Texans had established a small but tough militia, the Texas Rangers. The Rangers patrolled constantly to intercept raiding parties, and they probed deep into Comanche territory to strike vulnerable encampments.

When the Republic of Texas joined the United States in 1845, the Texans had every reason to expect the U.S. Army to take over their war with the Comanches. After the Mexican War of 1846, the Army did indeed begin building a string of forts across central Texas, but at first the posts were manned only by infantrymen, whose worth against the mobile Comanches was nil. The Texans were bitterly disappointed, but they soon got some unexpected help. In 1849, prospectors poured through Comanche territory on their way to the California gold fields, and they left a virulent cholera epidemic in their wake. Like their Kiowa allies, every Comanche band suffered heavy casualties, and the largest band, the Penatekas, lost about half of its population. In late 1854, many of the Penatekas surrendered and were consigned to a reservation on the Clear Fork of the Brazos River in north-central Texas. The other Comanche bands were able to hold out all through the 1850s, although the Texas Rangers, along with the U.S. cavalry, continued to exact a steady toll by surprise attacks. One such attack in December 1860 brought disaster upon Quanah's band.

The Noconas were confidently camped near the Pease River, with most of the men off hunting buffalo and the women drying meat for their winter food supply, when a force of 40 Texas Rangers and 21 U.S. cavalrymen—all under the command of Ranger Captain Sul Ross—suddenly struck, killing a number of Indians and taking several captives. After the battle, it was noticed that one of the women had Caucasian features and blue eyes. Even though she spoke no English, her captors suspected that she was Cynthia Ann Parker, known to be living among the Comanches. They summoned her Uncle Isaac, and he positively identified her

In the original illustrations of her narrative, Mrs. Harris grieves for her murdered husband before being dragged into the dwelling of a Comanche.

A white woman's ordeal as a Comanche captive

In raids against their traditional Spanish and Mexican enemies, Comanches frequently abducted young women for marriage—a practice they justified by the need to overcome their low birth rate. Texas settlers got their first taste of this aspect of war in the summer of 1835—almost a year before the seizure of the girl who would become Quanah's mother—when Comanche marauders ambushed a pair of emigrant families, sparing only two women. One of them later provided a vivid, if stilted, account of her ordeal in a book, *History of the Captivity and Providential Release Therefrom of Mrs. Caroline Harris.*

She and Mrs. Clarissa Plummer were taken by the Indians to a distant village where two young chiefs drew lots for them. Mrs. Harris, her body daubed with red dye, found herself the reluctant bride at "a mock ceremony uniting me to the ruthless savage whose companion I was to become." Resistance, she realized, would only have subjected her "to all the tortures that their inventive faculties could have given birth to."

Life in a Comanche tipi proved to hold more drudgery than terror. "The savage treated me as his menial servant while his own time was employed in fishing, the chase and other amusements," wrote Mrs. Harris. She also complained of the chief's inebriated homecomings: "My only safety was in flight to some neighboring swamp until he became sober."

But if she found nothing agreeable about being a chief's wife, the Comanche seemed pleased enough with the arrangement. On one occasion he led a search party that found Mrs. Harris after she had been lost in a forest for three days. "An uncommon degree of joy and satisfaction was manifested by my Indian companion," she recalled, quickly adding, "but whether it was to be imputed to genuine love, or the high value he set upon me, I never knew."

Her use of the word value was not figurative. In 1837, a white hunter, having learned of her fate, paid the Comanches a ransom of $400 and brought the two-year travail to an end.

as his niece, lost 24 years earlier. He took her and young Prairie Flower back to east Texas to live with the Parker clan.

Quanah's reaction to the recapture of his mother can only be guessed at in light of his persistent later efforts to learn of her fate. Obviously he loved Cynthia Ann, and an adolescent boy — even a fierce Comanche — was bound to be shaken by the sudden loss of a parent. Almost certainly, the loss added an urge for vengeance to his hatred for the whites who kept proclaiming themselves the masters of the Comanche range.

Quanah suffered other losses in quick succession. His father died, reportedly of an infected wound, and his brother Pecos then died of disease. With no one left to hold him in the Nocona band, Quanah joined the powerful Kwahadies, a band that lived on the edge of the Staked Plains of west Texas, a timberless tableland bordered by steep escarpments; the region's name recalled an early Spanish surveying venture.

Among the Comanches, individual warriors and whole families changed bands freely, often to follow an especially successful war chief. Quanah was probably attracted to the Kwahadies by their reputation as persistent and consummately skillful raiders. If so, he made the switch at a most opportune time, for the Comanches suddenly found themselves almost unopposed. The Civil War not only stripped the forts of U.S. soldiers, but also sent about 60,000 Texans into the Confederate Army, leaving scarcely 27,000 men behind to defend the entire state. The Comanches, together with the Kiowas and other allies, turned central Texas into a disaster area. Hundreds of settlers were massacred, and their settlements were reduced to charred ruins. When the U.S. Army finally returned after the war, an officer remarked, "This rich and beautiful section does not contain today as many white people as it did when I visited it 18 years ago."

The raiders' success was more apparent than real. The Comanche bands had not replaced the losses they had suffered in the cholera epidemic of 1849 or in the Texas Ranger attacks that followed it. So when the war-weary U.S. government called a grand peace council with the Indians of the southern plains at Medicine Lodge Creek, Kansas, in 1867, most chiefs were willing to listen — and eager for the gifts that went with the talk. However, the Kwahadies and part of the Kot-sotekas — then the two strongest hostile Comanche bands, with about one third of the tribe's population — disdained the peace talks and sent no representatives.

Over a period of two weeks in October, the peace commissioners from Washington elaborated on their plans for the Comanches, Kiowas, Arapahos and Cheyennes: the tribes were to cede their homelands, go to a reservation in Indian Territory and accept government guarantees of land, rations and protection from hostile whites or Indians.

Ten Bears, a chief of the Yamparika Comanches, protested, "We wish only to wander in the prairie until we die." But more out of weariness than hope or conviction, he and nine other Comanche chiefs signed. The government conveniently interpreted these signatures as representing the consent of all Comanches. Henceforth the Kwahadies, whose fierce raiding warranted fierce retribution, would be attacked with special fervor for trumped-up reasons: for clinging to homelands they had not signed away, and for breaking a peace they had never agreed to.

During the council, Quanah, who may have been lurking nearby, sought news of how the talks were going. As an up-and-coming young warrior who looked forward to a future rich in battle honors, he was dead set against accommodation. In one debate with Comanche leaders, Quanah declared, "My band is not going to live on the reservation. Tell the white chiefs that the Kwahadies are warriors."

It was apparently during the Medicine Lodge talks that Quanah learned of his mother's fate. Cynthia Ann had tried repeatedly to leave the Parkers and return to the Comanches, but her well-meaning relatives kept thwarting her attempts. Then in 1864 her daughter Prairie Flower died of disease. Cynthia Ann, overcome with grief, starved herself to death.

From the first, the Medicine Lodge Treaty was honored mainly in the breach by both sides. The Kwahadies, having shunned the peace talks, ignored the treaty terms and continued their marauding. Quanah took part in one raid in the vicinity of Gainesville that nearly ended in disaster. The war party was intercepted by soldiers while en route home, and the Indians' leader was killed. Quanah distinguished himself by assuming command and using sound judgment in breaking off the fight. Thereafter he led several raiding parties as a war

At an 1847 peace council in central Texas, painted by the daughter of a German emigrant, Comanche chiefs grant a right of way through their

chief and participated in others as second in command to Bull Bear, the leading Kwahadi chief.

Meanwhile, the treaty-signing Comanches and Kiowas entered their shared reservation in Indian Territory. But they were soon embittered by their government rations of pork and cornmeal, by the Indian agent's efforts to teach them how to farm, and by the intrusion of whites and eastern Indians who stole their livestock. Before the decade was out, thousands of resentful Comanches were leading a dangerous double life: languishing on the reservation through the winter, then leaving in the spring to hunt buffalo and do some raiding on their own or with the holdout bands.

Washington did not tolerate this situation for long. In 1870, a crack Army officer was given command of the 4th Cavalry and assigned to put a halt to the raid-

ing in Texas; he was a 30-year colonel named Ranald Slidell Mackenzie, whose brilliant Civil War service had prompted General Ulysses S. Grant to call him "the most promising young officer in the Army." Grim, unapproachable and mercilessly tough, Mackenzie cared nothing for Army spit-and-polish. He allowed his troopers to wear dirty uniforms and long hair, and he told them to discard their sabers, which he regarded as useless. But he molded a force that could fight in the guerrilla style of the Indians under any conditions of terrain and weather. One of Mackenzie's early moves was to set up patrols out of Forts Richardson, Griffin and Concho, keeping men in the field at all times.

In September 1871, Mackenzie assembled some 600 troops for an invasion of the Kwahadies' home ground along the little-known Staked Plains. Soon after

land in exchange for $3,000 in presents. The pact hastened their downfall by persuading would-be settlers that Comanches were manageable.

hitting the trail, Mackenzie's command made contact with war parties led by Quanah and Bull Bear. The wily chiefs did not oblige Mackenzie by fighting a pitched battle. Arrogantly they pursued their pursuers across the plains, and from time to time small groups of warriors would make lightning thrusts at the long column and then wheel and vanish before the troopers could form ranks to follow them. Shortly after midnight on October 10, Quanah led a wild charge through Mackenzie's encampment, ringing cowbells and flapping buffalo skins to panic the cavalry horses. The stampede enriched Quanah with 66 prime mounts, including Mackenzie's own prized animal.

In the morning, Mackenzie sent a small detachment of troopers to try to recover the lost horses. They came upon the Comanches about three miles from the mouth of Blanco Canyon. A group of warriors, with Quanah in the forefront, sallied forth to meet them. Quanah charged straight at the soldiers, killed one and dismounted to take his scalp while the rest of the overmatched troopers beat a hasty retreat.

The relentless Mackenzie continued to hound the Kwahadies into the Staked Plains. But on October 12, a howling blizzard put an end to the futile chase. Heading back toward home, Mackenzie spotted two Comanches observing his troops. He went after them and caught an arrow in the hip, a wound that incapacitated him for a time. It was a dismaying end to a frustrating mission, but he had learned valuable lessons about Comanche tactics and their highland refuge.

By March of 1872, Mackenzie was back in the field again, hunting Comanche raiders and keeping a sharp eye out for the New Mexican traders who were supplying them with repeating rifles in exchange for stolen Texas cattle. On one mission in September, Mackenzie's scouts found the Kotsotekas encamped on McClellan Creek at the edge of the Staked Plains, where they had set up housekeeping after spending the winter on the reservation. The colonel and his 231-man force surprised the camp, killed 23 warriors and took 124 captives—all at a cost of only two troopers killed and two wounded.

The Kotsotekas' loss of their families was a crippling blow to their shaky morale; most of the band straggled back to the reservation, this time to stay. Even the Kwahadies—now the last hostile Comanche band of any importance—were noticeably quiescent. They curtailed their raiding for fear that the Comanche captives would suffer cruel retribution.

In turn these reactions were interpreted by the U.S. government as a sign that all the Comanches were finally ready to accept peace and the reservation. To further that end, the Indian agent released the captives as a gesture of conciliation in June of 1873. The Kwahadies promptly resumed raiding. Once again, Mackenzie was called upon to protect the frontier, and for a time his vigorous patrolling kept Quanah on the run.

This standoff was broken in 1874 by the appearance of large numbers of white buffalo hunters on the plains of the Texas Panhandle, where they presented an immediate threat to the Indians' basic food supply —a threat that was more urgent than the chiefs realized. The buffalo herds were doomed by two new technological advances. Until recently, whites had hunted the buffalo largely for ruglike robes, which could be taken only in winter when the animals' hair was long; dried buffalo hide was too soft for use in commercial leather goods. But by 1870, a new tanning process had made the hide commercially workable, and it turned buffalo hunting into a year-round business. At the same time, the hunters' efficiency was greatly increased by the development of high-powered Sharps rifles that could kill a full-grown buffalo at 600 yards.

Now the buffalo plains became a vast slaughter house, with only the time-consuming work of the skinners limiting the rate of kill. A top marksman might bag more than 200 animals a day, enough to keep 15 skinners busy. So many riflemen joined the hunt that up to

Forty thousand buffalo hides, worth about $120,000 at tanneries in the East but a priceless staple of the Plains Indians' culture, wait for an eastbound train at Dodge City, Kansas, in 1874. During that decade, professional hunters slaughtered buffalo at the rate of more than a million a year.

40,000 hides a day were shipped east from Dodge City, Kansas, alone. The buffalo herds, once numbering some 30 million animals, would be reduced to a total of fewer than 1,000 beasts by 1886.

With Kansas already nearly stripped of buffalo by 1874, the hide hunters drifted south that March and set up a base near the deserted trading post of Adobe Walls on the South Canadian River. During the Medicine Lodge talks, the peace commissioners had promised to keep whites off the Indians' buffalo grounds in the Texas Panhandle, but the government now made no effort to prevent the incursion of buffalo hunters. Indeed, some key Army officers encouraged their bloody work, figuring correctly that the slaughter of the buffalo would inevitably starve the hostiles into dependence on reservation rations. General Philip Sheridan praised the buffalo hunters for "destroying the Indians' commissary. For the sake of lasting peace, let them kill, skin and sell until they have exterminated the buffalo. Then your prairies will be covered with speckled cattle and the festive cowboy."

The presence of white hunters on the Texas buffalo plains infuriated the Indians and drove them to take unprecedented action. Diehard Comanche, Kiowa, Arapaho and Cheyenne bands rallied around two inspirational leaders and formed an intertribal federation to fight the whites. One of the leaders was Quanah, fast becoming the fighting hero of every Comanche warrior. The other was a young Kwahadi medicine man, Isa-tai, whose name is variously translated as Little Wolf, Rear End of a Wolf and Coyote Droppings.

Isa-tai started the pan-tribal movement with some grandiose claims. The Great Spirit, he said, had drawn him up into heaven, conversed with him at length and sent him back to earth endowed with magical powers. Isa-tai boasted that he could belch up ammunition by the wagonload and make warriors and their horses impervious to bullets by means of a magical paint. Most important, Isa-tai prophesied that an all-out Indian attack would drive the white men away and bring back the buffalo, and he urged the Comanches to hold a sun dance to prepare for the assault.

Isa-tai had demonstrated some talent as a weather forecaster, and his meteorological reputation lent a certain credibility to his new predictions and won him a following among warriors who wanted desperately to

believe him. As for Quanah, he may well have recognized Isa-tai as an ambitious fraud and used him to serve ambitions of his own. Bull Bear, still the leading Kwahadi chief, lay dying of pneumonia, and Quanah was certain to succeed him if he organized a successful attack on Adobe Walls.

Quanah approved of Isa-tai's suggestion for a sun dance, even though the Comanches had never celebrated the rite before. The Comanches put on their amateurish ceremony late in the spring of 1874, near the junction of Elk Creek and the North Fork of the Red River. After the celebration the Comanche chiefs met in council with the leaders of other dissident bands. The council came to agreement on three main points: all bands would cooperate in unrelenting war against the whites; Adobe Walls would be the first target; and Quanah would lead the allied forces in the attack.

On June 26, Quanah's army of 700 mixed warriors stole up on Adobe Walls under cover of darkness. Twenty-eight men and one woman were lodged in the base, which consisted of three main buildings located about 100 yards apart. The whites were sound asleep in the early morning hours, and they might have been slain in their sleep—but for what appeared to be an extraordinarily fortuitous mishap. A loud crack rang out, rousing all the hunters. James Hanrahan, who operated the saloon at the little settlement, said that the noise had been caused by the splitting of the ridgepole that supported his establishment's roof. The noise may in fact have been a gunshot, surreptitiously fired by Hanrahan, who suspected that Indians were lurking nearby and wanted to keep the party vigilant. In any case the men, including a soon-to-be-famous youth named Bat Masterson, propped up the ridgepole and were enjoying Hanrahan's well-lubricated hospitality when they spied, in the gray predawn light, Quanah's warriors moving into attack positions.

The warriors charged and the hunters started firing, but Quanah had lost the battle the moment he lost the element of surprise. His warriors' training and outlook prevented them from accepting the heavy losses it took to carry the strong point in one all-out assault. Quanah ordered repeated attacks—and repeatedly withdrew as casualties mounted. The chief often charged at the head of the pack. Once he backed his horse against the door of a building and tried in vain to batter it down. In an-

other attack, his mount was shot out from under him and he had to crawl to cover behind a buffalo carcass. Moments later, Quanah was briefly stunned when a bullet, spent after its flight over a long range, ricocheted and hit him in the back. His superstitious warriors blamed the unseen blow on some strange new magic.

The hunters' magic — Sharps rifles with telescopic sights — finally ended the seige on the third day. A warrior was knocked off his horse by a sharp-shooting buffalo hunter at a distance later measured at about 1,500 yards — nearly a mile. It was the end of Isa-tai's bid for power and fame. The medicine man, rather than Quanah, was held responsible for the defeat.

The buffalo hunters had lost only three men. Total Indian casualties were hard to estimate, for the warriors had — as usual — carried off all the dead they could reach. Just 13 Indian bodies had been left behind. The hunters decapitated them all and stuck the 13 heads on sharpened poles around their base.

After Adobe Walls, the Indians scattered and vented their fury in wide-ranging attacks. All across the plains, from Texas to Colorado, white men were disemboweled and staked out to die alone in agony. White women were raped, mutilated, killed and dismembered. The vengeful orgy was so violent that Washington sent out an ultimatum informing the tribes that all Indians who did not enroll on the reservation by August 3 would be attacked as hostiles. Soon thereafter, five columns of cavalry and infantry were sent to converge on the Comanche and Kiowa holdouts. The southern column — some 600 soldiers under Colonel Mackenzie's command — was awarded the dubious honor of carrying the campaign to the Staked Plains and smashing Quanah's Kwahadies, the hard core of Indian resistance.

Just before dawn on September 28, 1874, after an all-night forced march prompted by his scouts' reports, Mackenzie had a great stroke of luck at Palo Duro, a

A Comanche painting on deerskin commemorates the abortive assault of 700 Indians on 28 buffalo hunters and merchants at the tiny Texas settlement of Adobe Walls in 1874. The buildings are surrounded by puffs of gunsmoke from the hunters' own Sharps rifles, and two prone warriors attest to the deadly effect of the long-range weapons. At the lower right, Quanah, the leader of the attacking force, lances a hunter hidden in a wagon — one of only three whites who were killed at a price of dozens of Indian lives.

Quanah's spectacular war bonnet boasted a total of 60 eagle feathers, each one decorated with bright stripes of beadwork at the base and tipped with a plume that was made from the hair of a white horse.

vast chasm unknown to the whites until then. From the rim he discerned, far below, a large encampment of Comanches, Kiowas and Cheyennes whose overconfident chiefs — not including Quanah, who was elsewhere at the time — had neglected to post enough sentinels. Mackenzie found a narrow trail that zigzagged some 900 feet down the sheer wall of the canyon. His troopers dismounted and led their horses down the trail, slipping and sliding as they went. They were nearing the bottom when the encampment awakened to the threat. Warriors began sniping at the helpless soldiers on the steep trail. But most of the Indians scrambled to escape as the troopers reached the canyon bottom. Mackenzie's men swept through the village, burning tipis and capturing more than 1,000 horses.

In the aftermath of the Palo Duro attack, Mackenzie added a new master stroke to his strategic repertoire. He knew from experience that the Comanches would keep on trying to recapture their horses. So he gave a few hundred choice ponies to his Indian scouts, and he ordered the rest to be slaughtered, thus depriving many warriors of the mounts they needed to hunt buffalo.

Little groups of Comanches and Kiowas began surrendering with the onset of cold weather. Not until April 1875 did the first Kwahadies straggle into the reservation, half starved and ill clad. But Quanah and some 400 of his people had more than enough horses to hold out still longer. In fact they were hunting buffalo that spring when a white doctor who had learned of Quanah's whereabouts from reservation informants passed him a message from Mackenzie. If Quanah would come in to the reservation, his people were promised good treatment; but if he held out longer, Mackenzie would exterminate his band. The messenger was astonished when Quanah personally guaranteed the surrender of the last diehard Comanches.

Quanah was as good as his word. Leading his contingent of Kwahadies, with a herd of 1,500 horses in tow, he entered the reservation on June 2, 1875. Colonel Mackenzie was at the Fort Sill headquarters when Quanah enrolled, and the two great enemies came face to face. It was a brief and undramatic meeting; they were both too proud to make overtures or to reveal their feelings at a moment that must have been deeply stirring to each of them. Thus the Comanche war chief began his second life — as a peaceful reservation Indian.

Quanah spent 35 of his 65 years traveling the white man's road, and from that day at Fort Sill when he embarked on the journey, he was a model of vigorous, imaginative, responsible citizenship. He did far more than disprove the widely held view that Indians could not adapt to change. Quanah initiated change whenever it promised to benefit the Comanches, and when he fought unfavorable change it was not as a rebel but as a loyal opponent of the ruling order who defended peace and the law as strenuously as he formerly practiced war. He cooperated intelligently as a free Comanche—not to be mistaken for a white man's Indian.

The early years on the reservation sorely tested Quanah's commitment to the peaceful, sedentary life, if only because he and his people never seemed to get enough food. The regular rations guaranteed by the government were often delayed or insufficient. In 1878, the whole tribe was given a pass to leave the reservation to hunt buffalo—but they found only the bleached bones of the animals gleaming everywhere in the sun. The men with Sharps rifles had done their work well.

The plains were not empty, however. Great herds of longhorns now grazed where buffalo once roamed—and this usurpation proved to be a boon of sorts. To get the cattle to Eastern markets, Texas ranchers had to drive their longhorns along trails that led through Indian Territory to Kansas railroad towns—Dodge City, Caldwell and a handful of others. Quanah, with the agent's permission, began charging the cattlemen one dollar per head for the privilege of crossing reservation lands. The fees added up to a tidy income that could be used by the tribe to buy cattle of their own.

As soon as his responsibilities allowed, Quanah won the permission of the Indian agent to satisfy his longtime curiosity about his mother's family in Texas. He set out alone, clad in Comanche buckskin, speaking little English and armed only with a letter from the agent: "This young man is the son of Cynthia Ann Parker, and he is going to visit his mother's people. Please show him the road and help him as you can."

In his pilgrimage, Quanah met with occasional hostility; at least one farmer threatened him with a shotgun when he appeared at his cabin. Curiously, though, some Texans grew friendlier when they learned his identity. Although he had ravaged their land fearfully, they considered him a son of Texas and called him Quanah Parker. The chief adopted the surname as his own.

Following a map that a stranger drew for him, Quanah located Cynthia Ann's Uncle Silas in east Texas. Old Silas and his family made Quanah welcome. He stayed on for a while and slept in his mother's bed. During this interlude, he improved his English and studied farm tasks—the milking of cows, the making of butter, the cultivation of cotton.

Then, having laid to rest the ghost of his past, Quanah returned to the reservation and to the job of bettering the Comanches' lot. He gradually made a big business out of grazing rights. Since the Comanche-Kiowa reservation had three million acres, more than enough for the Indians' own cattle, Quanah arranged to lease pasturage to wealthy Texas stockmen like Burk Burnett, Dan Waggoner and Charles Goodnight. At one point, Waggoner alone leased 650,000 acres. Such arrangements brought in as much as $200,000 annually, and usually meant $30 to $50 a year for each and every Comanche.

Quanah's dealings with the Texas stockmen steadily broadened his horizons. Since the grass leases had to be approved by the Commissioner of Indian Affairs, Quanah made several trips to Washington and used the visits to lobby in Congress for Indian interests. The chief's friendly relations with the cattle barons proved valuable in several ways. Burnett advised him on personal investments and built him a handsome ranchhouse near the town of Cache, within easy reach of the Fort Sill reservation headquarters. Far more important, the stockmen shared the Comanches' financial stake in keeping the tribe's grazing lands open and intact, and they made powerful allies in Quanah's struggle to preserve the reservation, guaranteed by treaty as "a permanent home."

As early as the late 1870s, land-hungry "boomers" in Kansas and Texas were exerting pressure on the federal government to make all or part of Indian Territory available to white settlers. In 1889, a portion of the Indians' land, soon to be organized as Oklahoma Territory, was opened to white homesteaders. But the boomers, unsatisfied, demanded the opening of the Comanche-Kiowa reservation.

Presumably any plan that accomplished their goal would provide tracts of farmland for individual Indian families and would make a cash settlement for the loss

Master of a star-spangled manor

Of all the Plains Indian chiefs whose unhappy duty it was to lead their people into the white-dominated world of a reservation, none handled the transition more skillfully than Quanah. When he surrendered with his band of Kwahadi Comanches in 1875, Quanah spoke little English and had never lived in a house, eaten at a table or ridden in a wagon. But long before his death in 1911, he had mastered the speech of his mother's people well enough to hammer out shrewd deals leasing reservation lands to Texas cattlemen; he was a major shareholder in a railroad; and he was at ease lobbying for Comanche interests in Washington's corridors of power.

His remarkable adaptation to white ways brought him honors, wealth and a 12-room show-place home for his family. Yet no amount of pelf and circumstance tempted him to foresake his Comanche heritage: when he was buried beside his white mother, it was in the full regalia of a Comanche chief.

On one of his frequent trips to Washington in the 1890s to obtain approval for land-leasing deals, Quanah is accompanied by the youngest of his eight wives, Tonacey, modishly attired in a gown made of satin.

Quanah's home near Cache, Oklahoma, was locally known as the Comanche White House. Built for him by cattle baron Burk Burnett, it bore 22 stars on the roof—symbols of authority. They were inspired by the star insignias of U.S. Army generals.

← Acknowledging his dual heritage, Quanah sits for a living-room portrait in his chief's finery, flanked by a painting of his mother and an icon of her people's "Jesus road" — a religion he respected but did not follow.

Five of Quanah's 25 children try, with mixed success, to smile for the camera in this 1892 photograph. All were encouraged to learn the white man's ways, and two of his daughters took white husbands.

Awaiting the arrival of guests at his breakfast table, Quanah assumes the place of honor beneath a large advertising poster, one of several used as decorations on his dining-room walls. Two of his wives are among those present, seated to his left.

of the rest of their land. But Quanah realized that the Comanches were strangers to the concept of private property; though about half of them were already self-sufficient farmers or herders, even these fast-adapting members of the tribe were not fully ready to shift for themselves in a world full of devious and greedy whites. On a trip to Washington in 1892, he tried to prevent Congress from authorizing negotiations with the Indians. In this effort, he received vigorous assistance from a lawyer representing Texas cattlemen who wanted to maintain the reservation as surplus pasturage. But all the lobbying was in vain.

In October 1892, a number of Kiowa and Comanche leaders were persuaded to sign an agreement that dissolved their three-million-acre reservation. The tribes would retain 551,681 acres of communal land; in addition, each individual was to receive 160 acres, along with a share of a $2 million cash payment.

Quanah and the cattlemen's lawyer again took their case to Congress, this time trying to prevent ratification of the agreement. Quanah insisted that the leaders who signed did not represent all of the Comanches and Kiowas. He also claimed that a translator had misrepresented the terms of the agreement in order to obtain signatures. Impressed by these arguments, Congress refused to approve of the transaction for almost a decade. But the reservation lands were dismembered in the end and with the break-up Quanah lost a strong force for tribal solidarity.

As busy as he was with politicking and tribal finance, Quanah found time to serve his people in other roles. In 1902, he was elected deputy sheriff of Lawton, Oklahoma—a town in the vicinity of Fort Sill—accepting this position because he rightly believed that it would help him to keep young Comanches out of trouble. Six years later, he was elected president of the local school district—which he had helped create.

But his most important function was as a judge. After acting as unofficial judicial aide to the Indian agent, he was chosen chief judge of a three-man Court of Indian Offenses, which was founded in 1886 and which met twice a month until it was discontinued along with the reservation system 15 years later. Quanah's verdicts were rather strict by Indian standards, and a few of them baffled white observers. In one particularly tough case, he found it impossible to choose between two Indian litigants who were contesting rights to a plot of land. Unable to find a satisfactory precedent in the white man's law, Quanah reverted to Comanche standards. With the aid of Indian police, who had been organized to keep order on the reservation, the chief dug into the litigants' pasts to find which man had won the greatest war honors. It turned out that one litigant had rescued an unhorsed comrade during a fight long ago. On the ground that he was more courageous than his rival, Quanah decided in his favor.

In his various public roles, Quanah often spoke for all the Comanches, sometimes with instinctive tact, but just as often with forceful bluntness. Thus in 1898, at a July 4th picnic given by Congressman Bird McGuire in Hobart, Oklahoma, Quanah criticized the whites for their careless exploitation of the once-verdant plains. "We fear your success," he told his white audience. "This was a pretty country you took away from us —but you see how dry it is now. It is only good for red ants, coyotes and cattlemen." He was outspoken in his opposition to several white programs, among them the Army's efforts in 1892 to organize several Indian cavalry battalions. Quanah urged Comanche men not to enlist, explaining to the recruiters: "My people quit fighting long ago, and we have no desire to join anyone in war again."

To do his duty effectively as a Comanche chief, Quanah necessarily made practical compromises, but he seldom compromised his Comanche heritage in his private life. Over the years he took eight wives; at one time he had five. White officials told him repeatedly that this was against the law, that he must set a good example for all Comanches. No less a personage than the Commissioner of Indian Affairs ordered Quanah to choose one wife and to tell the others to go away. Quanah put an end to the subject with a shrewd retort: "You tell them."

The Comanche religion, based on winning the aid of spirits hidden in nature, was just right for Quanah—simple, undemanding and highly personal. But his desire to hold to the religion's tenets presented him with certain problems in diplomacy. Clergymen of several sects set up missions on the reservation and vied for Indian converts—especially influential chiefs. Quanah carefully cultivated the friendship of the ministers and tactfully obliged them all by telling Indian groups, "The Jesus

Writing a letter to the Governor of Texas in 1909, Quanah sought to expedite the transfer of his mother's grave to the Comanche-Kiowa reservation. Congress had allocated $1,000 for the project in gratitude for his help in keeping the peace.

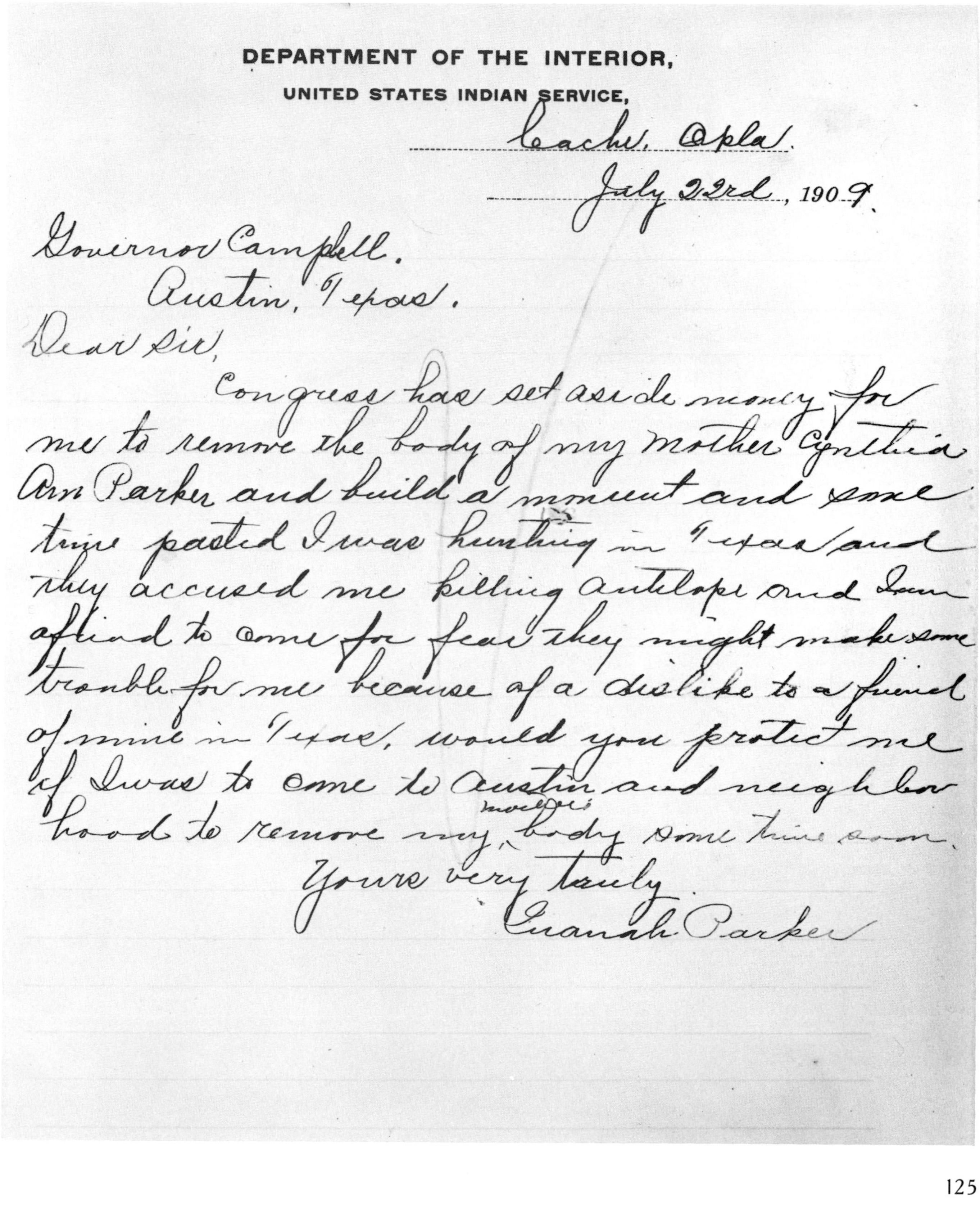

DEPARTMENT OF THE INTERIOR,

UNITED STATES INDIAN SERVICE,

Cache, Okla.

July 22rd, 1909.

Governor Campbell.
Austin, Texas.

Dear Sir,

Congress has set aside money for me to remove the body of my mother Cynthia Ann Parker and build a monument and some time pasted I was hunting in Texas and they accused me killing antelope and I am afraid to come for fear they might make some trouble for me because of a dislike to a friend of mine in Texas, would you protect me if I was to come to Austin and neighborhood to remove my mother's body some time soon.

Yours very truly,

Quanah Parker

road is good." But he joined no sect—not even the Methodist congregation of preacher White Parker, one of his 25 children.

Such was the respect that he inspired among whites that in 1886, promoters who founded a new town halfway between the Red and Pease rivers, in what had been the heartland of the free Comanches, named their creation Quanah. The chief traveled to the community and made a reverent speech of thanks. "May the Great Spirit always smile on your new town," he said to an assemblage of settlers. "May the rain always fall in due season. May the earth yield bountifully for you. May peace and contentment dwell with you and your children forever." Within four years of its birth, the town became a county seat. Quanah the man invested $40,000 of his cattle-derived affluence in a small railroad that passed through Quanah the town; the name of the line was the Quanah, Acme & Pacific Railroad.

Quanah had much to be thankful for. He was, some people said, the wealthiest Indian in America. He traveled widely and was received by the great and the famous; he rode in President Theodore Roosevelt's inaugural procession and went hunting with the President in Comanche country. His life of service on the reservation won him many honors. His people and the U.S. government both recognized him as the principal chief of the tribe, and they later agreed that after Quanah, no Comanche would bear the title of chief. What more could he ask of life?

Only the impossible—the preservation of the Comanches as a distinct people. It had been Quanah Parker's duty to preside over the peaceful liquidation of his tribe. In his lifetime, the Comanches had dwindled from perhaps 20,000 nomads, including 4,000 battle-ready warriors, to fewer than 1,200 people, settled among whites and leading a life barely recognizable as Comanche. Quanah would gladly have traded all his wealth and his honors for one intact band, roaming through the Staked Plains in search of buffalo.

But at least he could die in a manner that acknowledged the old ways. Taking to his bed with pneumonia on February 22, 1911, he called for the tribal medicine man. At the end, in keeping with Comanche tradition, the medicine man flapped his hands over Quanah like the wings of an eagle—the messenger of the Great Father, calling the chief's spirit to an Indian afterworld.

Recessing from his appointed duties as presiding judge of the reservation court in the 1890s, Quanah Parker relaxes in his office beneath a painting of Custer's Last Stand. His verdicts were unorthodox by white standards: a drunk might get four days in jail while a manslaughter offense netted 10.

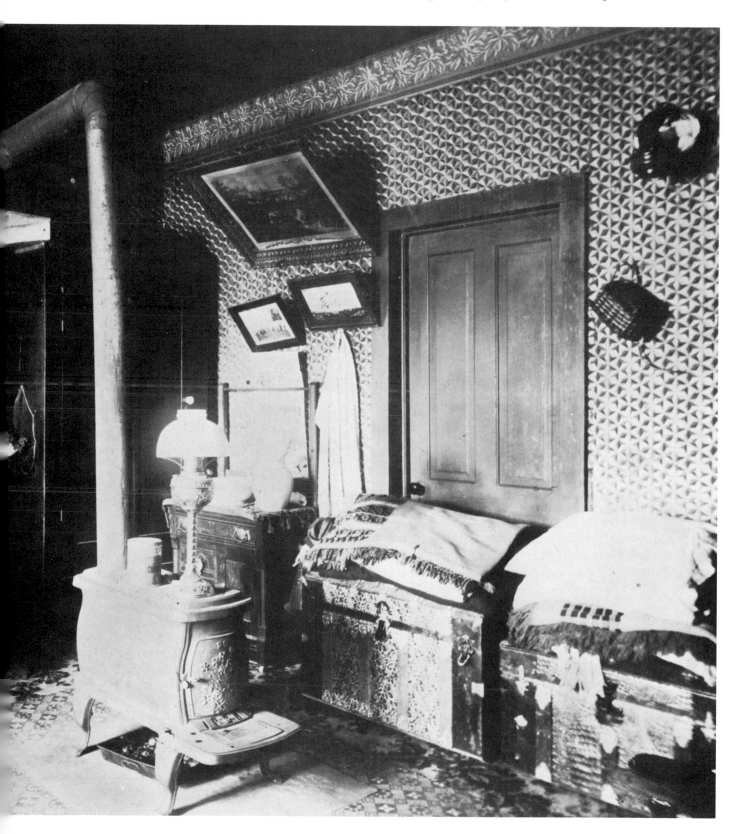

At the ritual breakfast concluding an 1892 peyote meeting, food containers are formally aligned in front of the crescent-shaped peyote altar.

The peyote ceremony: a release from misery

Worldly wise in business and politics, Quanah Parker also exercised a leadership role in less mundane matters: he was a proponent of the ceremonial use of peyote, a hallucinogenic drug that offered solace to Comanches as reservation life eroded their tribal values. Largely because of his proselytizing, the rite began to spread widely among other Plains tribes shortly before the turn of the century. Ultimately it became the focus of an Indian religion known as the Native American Church.

The peyote rite centered around the eating of the bitter-tasting "buttons," or the aboveground part, of the peyote cactus, a spineless species about the size of a radish found in northern Mexico. The buttons produced auditory hallucinations, visions in refulgent colors and a deep sense of brotherhood among those participating. Peyote was also believed to possess curative powers, and it was this supposed attribute that apparently aroused Quanah's enthusiasm. Initially opposed to its use, he became a convert after attending ceremonies in 1884 and gaining relief from a stomach ailment.

A peyote meeting was held at night in a special tipi and ordinarily was

PEYOTE BUTTON

attended only by men. They seated themselves around a small clay altar, symbolizing the mountain range where, according to legend, peyote was discovered. After the leader of the ceremony distributed the buttons, sacred songs were chanted, accompanied by a drum and rattles. By the time the rite ended with breakfast at daybreak, each man might have consumed anywhere from four to 30 buttons.

Quanah frequently presided at such meetings, wielding ritual gear like the items shown opposite (the staff and the kettledrum may actually have been his). On one occasion, attempting to explain the peyote ceremony in terms a white listener could understand, he stated: "The white man goes into his church house and talks about Jesus; the Indian goes into his tipi and talks *to* Jesus."

128

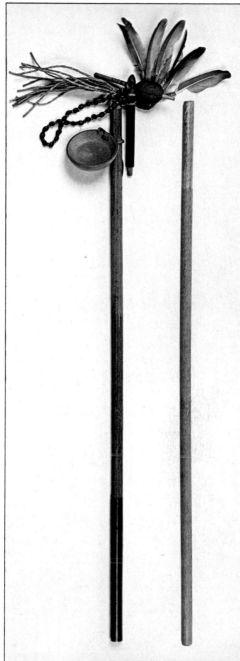

TWO-PIECE PEYOTE STAFF

FEATHER AND BEAD FAN

GOURD RATTLE

POUCH FOR PEYOTE BUTTONS

The sacred paraphernalia of the peyote cult, indispensable to the performance of its night-long rites, was provided by the leader of the group. As soon as the peyote was distributed from a distinctive buckskin-fringed pouch, the celebrants took turns singing to the throb of a kettledrum and the rattle of a pebble-filled gourd. The drum, the gourd and the long, symbol-laden staff — which might later be taken apart for convenient storage—were passed from hand to hand, along with a feathered fan that represented the birds linking God and man.

DRUM

4 | Protecting a way of life

While most tribes either bitterly resisted or reluctantly submitted to the white invasion of their ancestral wilderness, a few chose a third alternative—alliance with the whites. It was a course as logical to them as continuing to resist their ancient Indian foes.

Much like feudal Europe with its many tiny principalities, the West was a patchwork of tribes with no common language or culture. Each tribe regarded itself as autonomous, its customs superior, its members unique. Even the names they chose reflected their sense of singularity: the Cheyennes called themselves Dzi-tsi-istas, meaning "our people"; the Apaches were Tinde, or "the people"; the Kiowas were Ka-i-gwu, "principal people."

Because warfare among these proud nations was a way of life, the only hope of survival for the smaller tribes was to forge alliances with stronger forces. When the white men came, it was quickly apparent that they would make the most powerful allies of all.

No chief who chose this course was more steadfast than Washakie of the Eastern Shoshonis. A man of steely will, he would not brook any challenge to his policy of cooperation. When one of his sons was about to join a war party against the whites in revenge for broken promises, Washakie said, "My son, rather than see you take up arms against the white man, I will strike you dead at my feet." His son desisted.

The Shoshonis' friendship with the whites began with the visit of the explorers Lewis and Clark in 1805 and was fostered by more than three decades of commerce with beaver hunters who roamed their mountain homeland. Accompanying one party of trappers was Alfred Jacob Miller, a Baltimore-born artist who compiled a pictorial record of a tribe that found it possible to choose peace and yet stay proud.

In an idyllic panorama of the Shoshonis' high plateau country, a chief and two of his aides watch

from a bluff that overlooks the Sweetwater River while a party of warriors comes back from a marauding expedition against an enemy tribe.

Jubilant at the arrival of summer in her highland domain, a bare-breasted Shoshoni maid swings from a branch as a demure friend looks on.

132

Savoring a moment of solitude at the edge of camp, a warrior smokes his pipe — "the great solace of his leisure hours," said artist Miller.

Firing rifles as they gallop in a great processional circle around their camp, some 2,000 Eastern Shoshonis— according to artist Miller's estimate

— present a spectacular greeting to the fur-trapping contingent *(far right, middle ground)* that had brought the painter to the West in 1837.

ABRAHAM LINCOLN

JAMES GARFIELD

ANDREW JOHNSON

THOMAS JEFFERSON

Washakie–tough-minded ally of the white man

The event went almost unnoticed by newspapers whose editions were being otherwise filled with lurid stories about the rampages of the Sioux and Cheyennes on the northern plains. In the autumn of 1876 the U.S. government paid ceremonious homage to an Indian chief — Washakie of the Shoshonis. Unlike the Comanche war chief, Quanah, who had cooperated with the whites only after he saw that resistance was futile, Washakie had early decided that the best interests of his people lay in accommodation with the endless stream of foreigners who were invading his land and bringing a new civilization. And so from the outset he had given them his generous support — including invaluable military assistance.

It was as a reward for these services that Washakie was being honored by his allies in a remarkable celebration. The setting was Camp Brown, a military post on the tribe's 1,520,000-acre reservation in Wyoming Territory, and the natural backdrops were magnificent. This was mile-high land, just east of the Continental Divide, well watered by rivers and creeks, rich in game. To the northwest lay the Grand Tetons and Yellowstone National Park, established four years earlier. Not far to the south was the famed South Pass, where throngs of Oregon-bound pioneers, Mormons and forty-niners had breached the barrier of the Rockies. Washakie had done much to assure the safety of their passage.

Now, as bugles sounded, soldiers formed ranks on one side of the parade ground and Shoshoni warriors lined up on the other. Agent James Irwin stepped forward from a phalanx of Indian Bureau dignitaries and presented the venerable chief with a handsome saddle elaborately trimmed with silver. Then he started on a solemn speech.

This gift, Irwin said, was sent by the Great White Father in Washington, President Ulysses S. Grant, to his great friend in Wyoming, Chief Washakie of the Shoshonis. The President was aware that the chief had saved the lives of many emigrants by guiding them and providing protection against hostile Indians in the early days of the Oregon Trail. He was grateful, Irwin continued, that Washakie and his warriors had fought alongside United States soldiers against the Sioux and the Northern Cheyennes, enemies of the government, and he wished to express his particular gratitude for the aid given to General George Crook in recent operations against those enemies. Furthermore, he commended Washakie's efforts to educate the Shoshoni people. "President Grant," concluded the agent, "is one of your admirers."

Throughout the speech the chief remained with his arms folded and his face immobile. But tears welled from his eyes, and when it came time for him to speak he had no words.

Irwin prompted him: "What reply shall I send to the Great Father in Washington?"

Washakie still did not speak.

Irwin continued his urging: There must be something Washakie could say so that the President would know how pleased he was. A few words would do.

Washakie remained silent for a moment more, and finally he said: "When a favor is shown a white man, he feels it in his head and his tongue speaks. When a kindness is shown to an Indian, he feels it in his heart, and the heart has no tongue. I have spoken."

The agent expressed pleasure at this response. "That is just the reply I wish President Grant to receive,"

Chiefs who were friendly to the whites were rewarded with peace medals, minted by 21 administrations. Each issue bore the incumbent President's likeness on one side; the obverse usually conveyed a simple message of brotherhood. Lincoln's medal, however, offered a moral lesson: agriculture as a promising alternative to the quest for scalps.

Washakie of the Shoshonis wears a medal issued to mark his long friendship with the whites. This picture, taken in 1866, was sent to President Andrew Johnson to show the chief's gratitude for the award.

he told Washakie. "Something out of the ordinary."

Whatever Grant himself thought of the old chief's words — and his reactions are not on record — every authority concerned with the Western Indians knew well that this chief and these people were indeed something extraordinary. While a number of tribes had voluntarily chosen not only to walk the white man's road but also to fight shoulder to shoulder with U.S. soldiers, none had done nearly so much to facilitate white settlement of the West as the Shoshonis. Their reasons were selfish, to be sure: the need for trade goods, the wish to be protected from powerful Indian enemies, and the desire to win favor with newcomers who seemed destined to inherit the future. Yet those motives were by no means craven or demeaning. One had only to look at Washakie to see that this was so. He carried himself with the dignity and quiet strength of a man who was a stranger to fear. Even the Sioux chiefs, Red Cloud and Crazy Horse — his enemies — acknowledged him as the greatest of all Indian warriors.

The friendship between the white man and the Shoshonis began at about the time of Washakie's birth, shortly after the turn of the 19th Century. The Shoshonis were then scattered from South Dakota through the Wind River country in present-day Wyoming, parts of Montana, Utah, Idaho, Nevada and California. Linguistically and culturally related to the Utes of the Colorado Rockies, and to the Paiutes of the Great Basin, they were a fierce fighting people who early acquired the horse and contested with the Sioux, Crows, Blackfeet, Cheyennes and Arapahos for mastery of the Montana and Wyoming grasslands.

The first meeting between the Shoshonis and the white man was an auspicious one. On April 7, 1805, the explorers Meriwether Lewis and William Clark, still in the early stages of their great 7,689-mile Western reconnaissance, set out from their winter camp near what is now Bismarck, North Dakota, and followed the Missouri westward into the virgin wilderness. With them was a guide-interpreter whom they had recruited during the winter, a French-Canadian trader named Toussaint Charbonneau. He brought along his young Shoshoni wife, Sacajawea, only about 16 years of age. She had been taken captive five years earlier by a war party of Hidatsas, and Charbonneau had subsequently acquired her from her captors in a game of chance. Six weeks before the expedition got underway, Sacajawea gave birth to a boy, and for more than four months she carried the infant in a cradleboard on her back as she accompanied the explorers toward the Pacific.

When the party reached the headwaters of the Missouri, Sacajawea found herself in familiar territory, and on August 17 she caught sight of a group of her own people. As recorded in the journals of Lewis and Clark, she "began to dance and show every mark of the most extravagant joy, pointing to several Indians, sucking her fingers at the same time to indicate that they were of her own tribe." The expedition leaders proceeded cautiously into the camp, exchanged salutations with Chief Cameahwait, and sent for Sacajawea to serve as an interpreter. She came into the tent and had already begun to interpret when suddenly, the explorers related, "in the person of Cameahwait, she recognized her brother. She instantly jumped up, and ran and embraced him, throwing over him her blanket and weeping profusely."

This joyous reunion and Sacajawea's subsequent testimony to the good will of the white men completely won Cameahwait over. After the explorers distributed gifts of clothing, knives, tobacco, beads and mirrors, the chief gave them some desperately needed aid — pack horses to carry their gear and the services of Indian guides for their journey through the mountains ahead. The expedition left the encampment on August 19, having forged a friendship that would embrace virtually all whites who followed in their footsteps.

The boy who would be called Washakie was not then living among the Shoshonis. Only half-Shoshoni by birth, he spent his first four or five years with his father's people, the Flatheads, whose heartland was the Bitterroot Mountains of present-day Montana. After his father was killed in a raid by Blackfeet, his mother returned to her own tribe — a shift that seemed to afflict the boy with a lingering sense of rootlessness. In his early twenties, he transferred his allegiance to yet another tribe, the Bannocks of present-day Idaho, before finally settling permanently among the eastern branch of the Shoshonis a few years later.

At some point in his wanderings, his childhood name — Smells of Sugar — was replaced by the name Washakie, variously translated as the Rattler, Gambler's Gourd, Shoots Straight or Shoots on the Fly. In all like-

On a sight-seeing excursion in 1868, white families pause to visit a Shoshoni camp near the newly laid tracks of the Union Pacific. "It is good to have the railroad through this country," said Washakie, who had previously welcomed wagon trains, the Pony Express and the telegraph.

lihood, he earned it by some intrepid deed: he apparently owned a rattle that he used to frighten enemy horses in battle; and the record of his kills suggests that he was an excellent shot.

Shortly after Washakie joined the Eastern Shoshonis, a raiding party of Blackfeet penetrated their range and made off with many of their horses. Washakie gathered a pursuit force, followed the trail of the marauders all the way to the Missouri River in Montana—almost 600 miles to the north—and brought back not only the stolen horses but the scalps of most of the raiders as well. In another clash with the Blackfeet, he did not fare quite so well: an arrow caught him below his left eye, leaving a deep scar. The wound did not diminish in the slightest his appetite for combat, although in the mellowness of old age, Washakie professed regret for the bloody deeds he committed in his prime. "As a young man I delighted in war," he recalled. "When my tribe was at peace, I would wander off sometimes alone in search of an enemy. I am ashamed to speak of these years, for I killed a great many Indians."

At the same time he was pursuing a growing friendship with the whites. A horde of leathery adventurers had swarmed into the Rockies on the heels of Lewis and Clark, seeking the pelts of beaver, otter and marten. Their heyday began in 1825 with the devising of a regular—and raucous—system of commerce between East and West. That summer and each summer afterward, the trappers rendezvoused at an agreed-upon location in the wilderness to meet traders and pack trains journeying all the way from St. Louis. After bartering their furs for guns, ammunition, coffee, flour, tobacco and prodigious quantities of whiskey, they proceeded to compensate for the year's privations with a month of carousing.

More than 800 souls gathered at the 1825 rendezvous, and as the years went by the number doubled and quadrupled. By the time the summer conventions hit full stride in the mid-1830s, Washakie had become a man of considerable influence among his people. Recognizing the possibilities of profit in the white man's annual fur fair, he encouraged the Shoshonis to do some trapping themselves so that they could trade for guns, ammunition, tools and cloth. The Shoshonis soon found that they could gain as much from the mountain men as from the traders by supplying them with

something the traders did not stock: young women.

Father Pierre Jean De Smet, a Jesuit missionary who spent a lifetime of labor among Western Indians, attended the 1837 rendezvous, and while he disapproved of some of the behavior he saw, he was deeply impressed by the arrival of the Shoshonis: "Three hundred of their warriors came up in good order and at full gallop into the midst of our camp. They were hideously painted, armed with war clubs and covered all over with feathers, pearls, wolves' tails, teeth and claws of animals, outlandish adornments with which each one had decked himself out according to his fancy.

"Those who had wounds received in war, and those who had killed the enemies of their tribe, displayed their scars ostentatiously and waved the scalps they had taken on the ends of poles, after the manner of standards. After riding a few times around the camp, uttering at intervals shouts of joy, they dismounted, and all came to shake hands with the whites in sign of friendship." Among them, perhaps, was Washakie, whose close friends included two of the most renowned of all the mountain men, Kit Carson and Jim Bridger.

The year 1840 marked the last of the annual rendezvous. Although trappers continued to work the mountain ranges for the next few years, the days of abundance were over. The beaver stock, upon which the bulk of the fur trade was based, was close to depletion; and in any event beaver hats were no longer in style, having been replaced in the fashion world by elegant silk toppers. The Shoshonis, too, were in a period of transition. Their principal chief died in 1842 and, after a few months of turmoil, Washakie—recognized as one of the greatest warriors of his tribe—took over the chieftainship.

His ascendancy coincided with the start of a new era in the development of the West. In 1843 a caravan of 120 wagons and more than 1,000 pioneers, heading toward a new life in the lush valleys of California and the Pacific Northwest, lumbered along the 2,000-mile Oregon Trail. Four thousand came the next year, and the traffic continued to swell steadily, reaching a peak of 55,000 by mid-century.

The majority of the tribes in the region—the Sioux, Crows, Cheyennes and Arapahos—looked upon the great highway with growing alarm and hostility. They responded as they would have to the harassment of another Indian tribe: by attacking and plundering. Those pioneers who were foolish enough to attempt to travel across the plains by themselves often lost their scalps. Nor was there guaranteed safety in numbers, because the Indians sometimes picked off wagons that straggled behind the trains — although they seldom dared to take on a whole convoy.

But even though the emigrant road cut through the heartland of the Shoshonis, and even though the swarms of emigrants were running off Shoshoni game and destroying Shoshoni root-digging grounds, Washakie saw matters in a different light. Beset by the very same enemies that were attacking the whites, but farseeing enough to realize that the whites in the long run would make the strongest and therefore the most acceptable allies, he did not harass the emigrants but gave them his protection. This, in the main, consisted of holding his own restless young warriors in check. Beyond that, he ordered them to intervene when they saw pioneers within the Shoshoni territory under attack by neighboring tribes. He also instructed them to help wagons ford treacherous creeks and to round up livestock that had strayed from the wagon trains. And he warned that any Shoshoni who stole from a white man would be sent into exile.

In 1859, the Oregon Trail put out a new shoot, the 346-mile Lander Road, named for engineer Frederick Lander. It crossed the Continental Divide 20 miles north of South Pass, dropped down into the upper Green River valley, and followed the Snake River. Again, it cut directly through land occupied by the Shoshonis. Washakie was disturbed by this new intrusion but still not moved to belligerence. Instead, he used subtle diplomacy when he met Lander, who reported the meeting between himself and "the celebrated Wash-i-kee" to the Commissioner of Indian Affairs:

"He remarked that it was never the intention of the Shoshoni tribe, at least his portion of it, to fight the whites, and that he had always taught his young men that a war with the 'Great Father' would be disastrous to them. He said, before the emigrants passed through his country, buffalo, elk and antelope could be seen upon all the hills; now, when he looked for game, he saw only wagons with white tops and men riding upon their horses; that his people are very poor, and had fallen back into the valleys of the mountains to dig roots

and get meat for their little ones." Even now, noted Lander, the chief did not propose to quarrel — "notwithstanding the building of this new road would destroy many of their root grounds and drive off their game."

Lander was a man who could take a hint. Aware of the dangers of alienating a chief who had a following of some 6,000 souls, he used his good offices to obtain from the government regular gifts of guns, ammunition, food, cloth, tools and ornaments as compensation for the "destruction of their root and herding grounds by the animals of the emigration."

By now, the Oregon Trail was a pulsing artery through the West for all manner of travelers. From April 1860 through October 1861, the tireless riders of the Pony Express galloped over the route in darkness and daylight, fair weather and foul, delivering the mail from St. Joseph, Missouri, to San Francisco in an incredible 10 days. Telegraph linemen, stringing the cross-country wires that would put the Pony Express out of business, added their tracks to the broadening trail. So did stagecoaches laden with passengers, and post and wagon freighters carrying bulk goods to every outpost in the burgeoning West.

Regular users of the Oregon Trail learned to look to Washakie for succor. A daughter of the Mormon leader Brigham Young recalled the Shoshoni chief's helpfulness: "Washakie, I remember, was located near the Sweetwater mining country at the time two of my uncles were Pony Express riders, and as a child I heard them say many times, when the Indians were bad on the trails, 'If we can only make Washakie's camp we are safe.'"

Once, during a raging snow storm, several wagon freighters stumbled into the chief's camp for shelter. One man, whose feet were severely frostbitten, was unable to walk and his friends begged Washakie's advice and aid in treating him. The chief absented himself for a few minutes and came back with one of his own wives. After carefully cutting off the teamster's boots, he told him to place his feet against the bared breasts of the woman and remain for hours in that position. By the next day the teamster could walk again. History does not reveal what the woman thought of this therapy.

In sharp contrast to such gentle deeds was Washakie's steely treatment of his own people. He had to

A quick stop by a junketing President

In the summer of 1883, a milestone was passed in Indian-white relations: for the first time, a United States President visited Western Indians on their own soil. The deserving recipients of this honor were the Shoshonis, whose friendship with the government had endured for nearly 80 years and who had been invaluable military allies. In actual fact, however, it was not gratitude nor even simple good will that prompted President Chester Arthur to travel to their reservation in Wyoming. It was trout. Suffering from poor health, Arthur felt he needed a quiet sportsman's holiday at Yellowstone National Park. In planning the trip, his aides scheduled a stopover at the Shoshoni agency —Fort Washakie—simply because its location and facilities qualified it as a suitable way station.

The President, accompanied by a dozen or so cronies, a 75-man cavalry escort and 175 pack animals, arrived at the agency on the evening of August 7. The following morning, Arthur dutifully reviewed a welcoming procession of tribesmen, witnessed a spectacular mock battle between the Indians and cavalrymen, then paid a call on Chief Washakie in his lodge. In a ceremonial exchange of gifts the chief gave Arthur a pinto pony intended for his daughter Nell; the President responded by grandly designating Washakie an Army scout —hardly a title worthy of a warrior who had led regiment-sized Shoshoni forces into battle against enemies of the United States. Despite this faux pas, Washakie presumably remained a gracious host; Arthur emerged from the lodge shaking his head and describing the chief as "amazing."

Forthwith, the President's party left for Yellowstone, where its members enjoyed a plentiful harvest of trout and bagged three antelope, a bear and a bevy of small game.

The next visit by a chief of state to a Western Indian tribe would take place two decades later, when another sportsman, Theodore Roosevelt, obtained relief from the pressures of his office by going wolf-hunting with a Comanche named Quanah Parker.

Shortly after his hurried but historic visit with the Indians, President Chester Arthur *(seated, center)* relaxes with members of his entourage in the locale that inspired the trip — game-rich Yellowstone Park. On his right sits General Philip H. Sheridan, commander of the Division of the Missouri, who had planned the President's itinerary.

Shoshonis — together with Arapahos who shared their reservation — line up to meet President Arthur. The chiefs hold umbrellas to distinguish them from ordinary warriors. Washakie did not attend; observing protocol, he awaited Arthur in his lodge.

exercise firm control over them to maintain his policy of cooperation with the whites. A not-always-benevolent despot, he literally dictated to his tribe and made free use of force to exact compliance. Frederick Lander described his brand of chieftainship thusly:

"He obtained his popularity in the nation by various feats as a warrior and, it is urged by some of the mountaineers, by his extreme severity. This has, in one or two instances, extended so far as taking life. 'Push-i-can,' another war chief of the Shoshonis, bears upon his forehead the scar of a blow of the tomahawk given by Washikee in one of these altercations."

Pushican, scarred as he was, fared better than a hapless warrior named Six Feathers, who was in the habit of beating his wife cruelly and often. An Army officer whose name and interest in the matter are not on record remonstrated with Washakie for permitting such uncivilized behavior. Washakie replied that sometimes wives must be beaten to make them obey. But such unmerciful beating, the officer persisted, showed that the chief did not have his people under sufficient control. Stung by this disparagement of his authority — and also ready to accept the white man's judgment that wife-beating was wrong — Washakie promptly went to Six Feathers and ordered him to stop. Two days afterward he caught Six Feathers doing it again, whereupon he shot and killed him on the spot. He, Washakie, was judge, jury and executioner, and few of his people disobeyed him more than once.

Nor did they successfully contest his leadership, although the size of his following fluctuated with the fortunes of the tribe and the inconstancy of the white man, who promised much in gratitude to the Shoshonis but did not always deliver. Many of Washakie's young warriors resented his close association with the whites and his increasing disinclination to take the offensive against Indian enemies. Some complained openly that he had become soft, that he was too feeble to win in combat and too much of an old woman to take enemy scalps. The war blood, they told each other, had ceased to flow in his veins; and they had begun arguing about who should succeed him.

Washakie overheard their rebellious talk. It angered him, but he said nothing. One evening he rode quietly out of camp to test his skill alone. A few days later, when he reappeared as unexpectedly as he had departed, he brought with him seven fresh scalps. He had been on the warpath, he announced, and had encountered a band of hostile Indians; these were the trophies he had singlehandedly obtained. "Let him who can do a greater feat than this claim the chieftainship," he challenged, holding up the scalps for everyone to see. "Let him who would take my place count as many scalps." There were no takers, and no more questions about his courage.

Despite his atavistic response to challenge, the percipient Washakie had been convinced for a long time that the Shoshoni life style of hunting and fighting was an anachronism in the new age that had dawned with the coming of the whites. Since 1858 he had been making known to government officials his wish for a reservation for his tribe. He wanted a settled homeland for his people, and nothing but the Wind River valley would do. Even though his native environment had been considerably affected by the hundreds of thousands of travelers who had passed through it on the overland highway, the Wind River heartland of the Eastern Shoshonis was by the end of the 1860s still rich in buffalo. It would offer an ample supply of food until the Shoshonis learned to grow their own crops and graze cattle in the fertile river valley.

In the summer of 1868, the government — in the person of Colonel Christopher C. Augur — finally granted Washakie his desire: the Wind River valley would be the Shoshonis' home forever. Before committing himself, Washakie went through each sentence and paragraph of the proposed treaty with the aid of two interpreters. He made sure that it provided for everything he considered necessary on a reservation: a school, instructors, a church, a mill, a hospital, farm implements and seed, and an Army post to help protect the Shoshonis against the powerful enemies who would, no doubt, come raiding.

On July 4, Washakie finally placed his X-mark on the treaty. "I am laughing because I am happy," he said, "because my heart is good. When the white man came into my country and cut the wood and made the roads, my heart was good and I was satisfied. You have heard what I want. The Wind River country is the one for me. We may not be able to till the ground for one, two or three years. The Sioux may trouble us. But when the Sioux are taken care of, we can do well." ◉

Department of the Interior,

OFFICE OF INDIAN AFFAIRS,

Washington, D.C., *November 18*, 1873.

This is to certify that *Man-afraid of his Horse*

is a *Chief* of the *Ogallalah band of Sioux*

Indians.

This *Band* is at peace with the United States, and

Man-afraid of his horse is recognized as a *Chief*

of said *Band* by the United States, whose influence has been to

preserve peace and harmony between said *Ogallalah band of Sioux*

Indians and the United States, and as such is entitled to the

confidence of all persons whom he may meet.

This certificate to be renewed on the 1st of January and July of each year so

long as the above named shall be entitled to the benefits thereof.

In testimony whereof, I have hereunto subscribed my name and procured

to be affixed the seal of the Department, on the day and year

first above written.

Edw. P. Smith

Commissioner

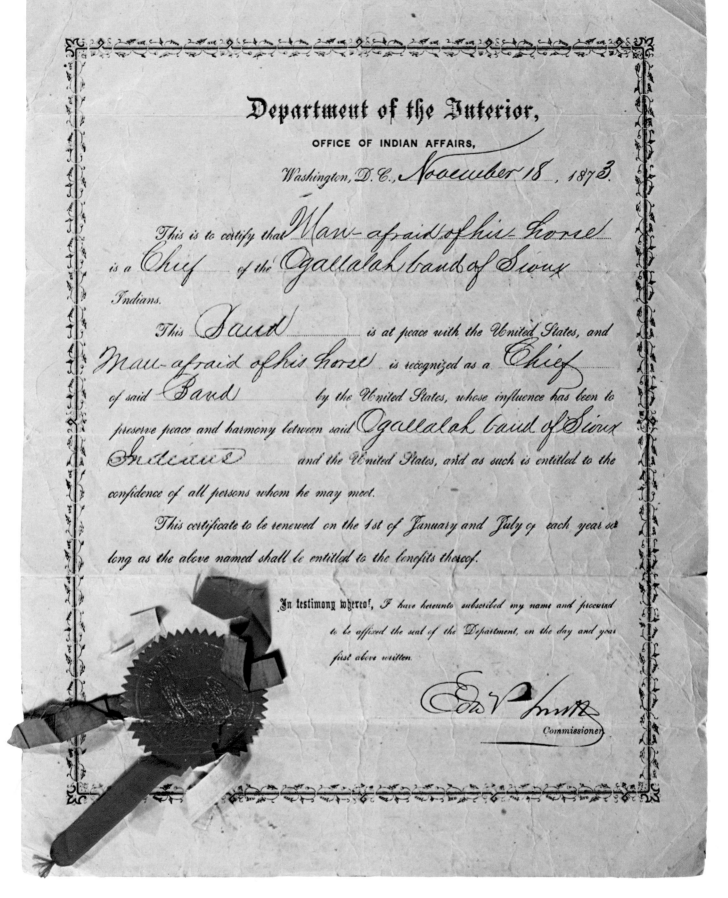

Sky Chief of the Pawnees demonstrated his regard for the whites by wearing frock coats and supplying guards for railroad-building crews.

Four chiefs who chose to ride with the tide

A number of tribal leaders in addition to Washakie chose to join the whites rather than fight them — for reasons both gross and subtle. Chief Ouray of the Utes, for instance, was motivated in good part by a fondness for the white way of life. The perfect host, he even plied his dinner guests with wine and cigars. Ouray maintained firm control over his people until he signed away a large chunk of tribal land in 1872 — and the Utes later discovered that the government had rewarded him with a stipend of $1,000 a year for life.

Chief Guadalupe of the Caddos also felt an affinity for white culture. But he supplied the Army with scouts because he viewed the war to control the land not so much as a dispute between whites and Indians as between farmers and raiders. The Caddos were farmers.

The Crows, too, provided the Army with scouts, but their motives were a combination of an old enmity and astute favor-seeking. Chief Plenty Coups (*right*) advised his warriors to join a campaign against the Sioux because "When the war is over, the soldier-chiefs will not forget that the Crows came to their aid."

Sky Chief of the Pawnees (*left*) provided the same service for very much the same reason. However, it cost him dearly in 1873, when an immense force of vengeful Sioux took a Pawnee hunting party by surprise. A troop of the 3rd Cavalry raced to the rescue of their Indian allies, but by the time they arrived, the Sioux had forced the Pawnees to pay with 150 lives — including that of Sky Chief — for presuming to send scouts into battle against them.

A prophetic dream of white conquest spurred Chief Plenty Coups to side with the Army.

Guadalupe of the Caddos not only called for his own people to accept white ways but also tried to convert other southern plains tribes.

Ute chief Ouray, an iron-willed autocrat, singlehandedly kept his militant band in line by shooting all opponents of his peaceful policies.

These last words were prophetic, for the Sioux and their allies would indeed have to be subdued before the Shoshonis could find peace in their Wind River valley. The Sioux were the most powerful Indians on the northern plains, about 20,000 strong, well equipped with firearms, and imbued with the spirit of conquest. For more than a century they had been moving steadily west from the headwaters of the Mississippi River. First they drove the Omahas and the Iowas from the coveted hunting lands in present-day South Dakota; then they swept inexorably on toward the Black Hills, where they confronted and overcame the Kiowas and the Cheyennes, compelling them to flee southward. In 1822, still on the move, they won a victory over the Crows and established their dominance over much of eastern Wyoming—within easy striking distance of the Shoshonis.

Washakie had a deeply personal reason for hating and fearing these neighbors. In 1865 a war party of 200 Sioux attacked his summer camp on the Sweetwater River, taking with them about 400 of the Shoshonis' horses. Washakie led a countercharge, driving back the enemy and recovering the horses, but in the engagement his oldest son was killed and scalped before his eyes.

Settling on the reservation brought the problems Washakie had predicted. In the spring of 1869, forty-five of Washakie's finest young warriors set off in search of a Sioux war party that had beset Shoshoni hunters in their Wind River hunting grounds. The Shoshonis caught up with the enemy but found themselves hopelessly outnumbered. In the bloody contest that followed, the Sioux swept the field and left all the Shoshonis for dead. Three of the 45, in fact, survived and reached the safety of their camp, one crawling 18 miles on his hands and knees in the snow to get there. A wave of similar incidents followed, and in September 1869, Washakie complained to the authorities at nearby Fort Bridger that "my reservation has been invaded many times by my enemy, the Sioux."

With these events to spur him on, Washakie drilled his warriors for long hours each day in mock battle tactics and cavalry maneuvers learned from his Army friends. He knew that his Shoshonis could not hope to handle the Sioux without the aid of a superior force; but some day, he was resolved, he would have his reck-

Resplendent in his war bonnet, Washakie looms over his
tribal council in this studio photograph taken during the
1870s. During his six decades as chief, the council was
merely a rubber stamp; Washakie told one emissary from
Washington, "Whatever I do, the others will agree to."

oning with the enemy, and he would be ready for it.

That day was still nearly seven years in the future. And when it came at last, it came because the white man had decreed it.

In the spring of 1876, Brigadier General George Crook of the Department of the Platte, regarded by no less an authority than William Tecumseh Sherman as "the greatest Indian-fighter the Army ever had," was selected to spearhead a campaign to subdue the bellicose Indians of the northern plains — the Sioux and their allies the Cheyennes. Crook had no intention of essaying such a mission with white soldiers alone. His extensive field experience had convinced him that a white army needed Indians to stalk Indians.

No white man had the Indian's intimate knowledge of his own terrain or his skill in tracking both animals and men. From the dust in the sky an Indian scout could tell whether what lay ahead was a herd of buffalo or a thousand warriors. From a faint trail of hoofprints, an occasional moccasin track, a patch of crushed grass and a scattering of pony droppings he could interpret the nature and size of the party, how long ago it had passed that way, where it had come from and where it was going. Broken branches, blazed trees and stones overturned without clear cause — all these might be read as Indian messages. A bird song or the cry of an animal could be identified as the forewarning of attack. And scouts organized into groups could also fight. Skilled in the quick skirmish, the darting attack, the capturing or stampeding of enemy horses, Indian scouts served as the military's guerrilla arm.

Thus, when General Crook received his orders to march north from Fort Fetterman in southeastern Wyoming as part of a three-pronged attack against the rebellious Sioux, he instantly thought to seek the services of the Shoshonis. And he was confident of a favorable response. Washakie had been waiting since 1865, when he had first offered the government his assistance in military action against the Sioux, for just such an opportunity to settle accounts with the most hated of his old antagonists. To Crook's emissaries he readily promised his wholehearted cooperation.

Meanwhile, Colonel John Gibbon had marched east from Fort Ellis in southern Montana. Early in April he met with the chiefs of the Crows at their agency on the Yellowstone River, with the object of recruiting scouts.

"I have come down here to make war on the Sioux," Colonel Gibbon told them in a cannily pitched enlistment speech. "The Sioux are your enemy and ours. For a long while they have been killing white men and killing Crows. I am going down to punish them. If the Crows want to make war upon the Sioux, now is their time. If they want to prevent them from sending war parties into their country to murder their men, now is the time. If they want to get revenge for Crows that have fallen, now is their time."

This prospect was so agreeable to the young Crow warriors that 30 of them went with Gibbon as scouts when he returned to his own camp, and another contingent promised to join General Crook two months later. As a result of their decision, the Crows found themselves fighting side by side with Washakie and his well-drilled warriors at the Battle of the Rosebud.

In the first week of June, Crook set up a camp and supply depot on Goose Creek, a tributary of the Tongue River, near the Wyoming-Montana border. Here he received a bold message from the Sioux war chief, Crazy Horse. Every soldier who crossed north of the Tongue River, declared Crazy Horse, would die.

Crook, now knowing approximately where to find the elusive Sioux, meant to cross as soon as his Indian scouts arrived. On June 14 he was joined by 176 Crows under their chiefs, Medicine Crow, Old Crow and Good Heart, and later in the day by 86 Shoshonis led by Washakie and two of his sons. Lieutenant John Bourke of Crook's staff was dazzled:

"A long line of glittering lances and brightly polished weapons of fire announced the anxiously expected advent of our other allies, the Shoshonis, who galloped rapidly up to headquarters and came left front into line in splendid style. No trained warriors of civilized armies ever executed the movement more prettily. Exclamations of wonder and praise greeted the barbaric array of these fierce warriors, warmly welcomed by their former enemies but at present strong friends, the Crows." Crook rode out to review them in their regalia of feathers, brass buttons and beads, "and when the order came for them to file off by the right, they moved with the precision of clockwork and the pride of veterans."

General Crook's total force now numbered 1,302 men: 201 infantry, 839 cavalry and 262 Indian fighter-

scouts. That evening, he held council with his officers and the Indian chiefs. Washakie and his Crow counterparts asked to be allowed to use their own methods when going after the Sioux, and the general agreed to give them a free hand. The meeting was adjourned early because it was thought that the Shoshonis, having ridden 60 miles that day, would need to rest. On the contrary, what they needed was to prepare for battle in their own manner, which meant a night of war dancing. Wrote Bourke:

"A long series of monotonous howls, shrieks, groans, and nasal yells, emphasized by a perfectly ear-piercing succession of thumps upon drums, attracted nearly all the soldiers and many of the officers not on duty to the allied camp. Crouched around little fires not affording as much light as an ordinary tallow candle, the swarthy figures of the naked and half-naked Indians were visible, moving and chanting in unison with some leader. No words were distinguishable; the ceremony partook of the nature of an abominable incantation, and as far as I could judge had a semi-religious character."

Early in the morning of June 16, Crook and his Indian allies broke camp, crossed the Tongue River and turned northwest into hostile Sioux country. Indian scouts riding ahead of the main army galloped back in the afternoon with their reports: they had discovered the trail of a vast force of Sioux, and they had seen a herd of buffalo fleeing after being disturbed by a party of Sioux hunters.

The command camped that night on the headwaters of Rosebud Creek. Before dawn the next morning, they rose and marched downstream. At about 8 a.m., Crook called a halt in a huge natural amphitheater encircled with hills and bisected by a stream. There he ordered his men to unsaddle and let the horses graze until the rear of the column caught up. Some of his units pulled up on one side of the stream, some on the other.

To the north rose a line of low bluffs backed by a series of ridges leading up to higher ground. From the valley, nothing could be seen of what lay beyond the heights. Washakie and the Crow chiefs were uneasy. Somewhere up ahead was the enemy; and Crook's men were resting in the valley — out in the open, divided and unprepared. General Crook was convinced that the Sioux were encamped in a great village, the exact whereabouts of which had yet to be determined, and that his best course was to find it and destroy it. His Indian allies, however, regarded Crazy Horse as too shrewd and skillful a leader to present a stationary target. Surely he would have plans of his own. Therefore Washakie and the Crow chiefs had their warriors take up positions on the ridges north of the valley amphitheater, and they sent scouts beyond the hills to see if they could find fresh traces of the enemy.

Within half an hour the scouts, one seriously wounded, rode back at a headlong gallop. "Sioux! Sioux!" they shouted. "Many Sioux!" Shots rang out as the vanguard of the advancing Sioux clashed with Army pickets. A horde of charging enemy riders, riding low along the sides of their horses, appeared on the ridges to the north and out of the hills to the west.

Only one segment of Crook's army was ready to do battle — the advance company of Shoshonis and Crows. Undaunted by the size of the attacking force, they boldly countercharged. Fifteen hundred Sioux took part in the first assault, while Crazy Horse kept the remainder of his warriors — perhaps 2,500 — concealed in the hills to draw the pursuit of Army detachments or, as seemed most likely in the first moments of battle, to deliver the final blow to the disorganized troops in the valley. But the Sioux attack did not unfold exactly according to plan. The Shoshonis and Crows, only 500 yards in advance of the main command, blunted the thrust for as long as Crook needed to shape up his troops. With the onslaught held in check, Crook sent units of his command forward to support his Indian allies and deployed other units to favorable points in the valley.

Washakie, meanwhile, was in his element. Lieutenant Bourke wrote later: "The chief of the Shoshones appeared to great advantage, mounted on a fiery pony, he himself naked to the waist and wearing one of the gorgeous headdresses of eagle feathers sweeping far along the ground behind his pony's tail." The old chief was everywhere: riding alongside General Crook and discussing tactics with him through an interpreter, up at the front exhorting his warriors to greater efforts, consulting with his fellow chiefs, and even helping to defend a wounded officer.

The latter was Captain Guy Henry, a company commander whose unit was occupying the end of a ridge which was under fierce attack. A bullet pierced Henry's left cheek and came out under his right eye, cov-

General George Crook was considered the Army's top Indian-fighter, but he failed to keep his forces on the alert before the Battle of the Rosebud, despite Washakie's warning that a mass of Sioux was nearby.

ering his face with blood. Henry tumbled from his horse, unconscious. As he lay prostrate on the field his men gave ground, and the enemy galloped exultantly toward him expecting to exact the ultimate trophy—his scalp. But Washakie, along with a Shoshoni warrior named Little Bob and several other scouts, took positions around the fallen man and kept the hostiles at bay until some troopers arrived and carried the captain to safety and to his eventual recovery.

The first wave of Sioux, stopped in their tracks by the Shoshoni-Crow forces, fell back, regrouped and charged again, this time in greater numbers. Again the scouts countercharged to halt the advancing foe. Some dismounted and began firing from the ground. Others rode recklessly into the midst of the enemy. Men and horses died violently in the dust and gunsmoke, and the fragile wild roses that carpeted the hills and hollows were trampled into a mulch of dirt and blood. The

Sioux darted and feinted, giving ground; the Shoshonis and Crows drove forward relentlessly until they found themselves venturing too far from the supporting troops and were forced to retreat, but again they had stopped the hostile threat.

General Crook—perhaps unaware of the Sioux's numerical superiority—still did not appreciate the full measure of his danger. Shortly after noon he ordered Captain Anson Mills to disengage his cavalry companies, head north up Rosebud canyon, and attack the Indian camp that the general was convinced lay some miles ahead. In theory the hostiles would be diverted into taking out after Mills, who would then be supported by the rest of Crook's men.

Contrary to Crook's reasoning, the Sioux did not change the location of the battlefield but instead attacked the weak point created by the removal of the unit. Crook immediately realized the error of dividing his forces and dispatched couriers ordering Captain Mills to come back. Mills, a cool and quick-thinking officer, wheeled his cavalrymen out of the canyon and made a great half-circle along the high prairies to return to the battlefield. This time good fortune was with the Army: Mills came in behind a major contingent of Sioux warriors that was advancing toward Crook's men and took them completely by surprise. Finding themselves in a rapidly developing pincers movement, the Sioux broke into a gallop around Crook's line and made a clean getaway. Again, the white men had been caught unprepared by the Indians, and their flurry of pursuit dwindled away.

Only the alertness and fighting mettle of the Shoshonis and Crows had saved Crook from disaster in the face of the Sioux's sudden, skillfully executed mass attack. As it was, the general was left in undisputed possession of the battlefield, and thus could claim a victory of sorts. Yet the battle was a strategic defeat for him, because it left his forces unexpectedly bloodied and in disarray, unable to pursue the hostiles and prevent them from striking in force elsewhere. For the 25,000 rounds of ammunition used by his troops, 13 Sioux lay dead on the field. Twenty-eight of his own allied army had been killed and 56 severely wounded. The casualties gave him no recourse but to return to his base camp on Goose Creek to the south. Crazy Horse and his warriors were alive and free to fight another day—or in an-

Outnumbered more than three to one, General Crook's forces try to fight their way through waves of Sioux at the Battle of the Rosebud. Though taken by surprise, the troopers managed a stalemate—but only because their Shoshoni and Crow allies bore the brunt of succeeding Sioux charges.

other eight days, to be exact, when they would meet and massacre a force of cavalrymen under Lieutenant Colonel George Custer, some 30 miles to the north, on the Little Bighorn River.

Washakie's contribution at the Battle of the Rosebud did not go unrecognized. It was shortly after his service to General Crook that he was presented with the gift saddle from President Ulysses S. Grant in the stirring ceremony at Camp Brown and was moved to unaccustomed tears.

He continued to lead Shoshoni scouts on the warpath for the United States until the defeat of the Cheyenne chief, Dull Knife, in the Big Horn Mountains late in November 1876. After that, he fought no more but remained on the Army payroll as a scout for as long as he lived. In 1878 he was again paid tribute; Camp Brown was renamed Fort Washakie—a compliment that pleased him perhaps more than any other.

As he passed his 80th birthday, then his 90th, his mind and his zest for knowledge continued to be as lively as ever. He spent part of nearly every day with the farmer-teacher assigned to the Shoshoni agency, peppering him with questions about the economics of farming and the correct utilization of water in irrigation. At regular intervals he rode off to the farthest reaches of the valley to inspect the farmlands of his people, and he frequently visited the school to inquire into the progress of the pupils.

Finally, blindness and the weight of his years confined the old chief to his log cabin beside the Little Wind River. On the night of February 20, 1900, Washakie called his family to his bedside. Straining to catch his fading voice, they heard him say: "You now have that for which we so long and bravely fought. Keep it forever in peace and honor. Go now and rest. I shall speak to you no more."

Two days later he was buried with full military honors at Fort Washakie. In the mile-and-a-half-long cortege that followed the flag-draped casket to the grave site were his own Indian police, employees of the agency, officers and soldiers of the fort, and all the grieving men and women of his tribe. When the coffin was lowered into the grave a squad from Troop E of the 1st U.S. Cavalry fired three volleys in farewell salute; and the poignant notes of "Taps" echoed through the hills that embraced Washakie's beloved Wind River home.

A delegation of Sioux moderates, visiting Washington for talks with President Rutherford B. Hayes in 1877, pauses in an art gallery during a gov-

ernment-conducted tour of the capital. Such tours were standard practice, planned to impress Indians with the white man's power and culture.

5 | Pacifist on the warpath

In the autumn of 1877, a missionary-reared Nez Percé chief called Joseph emerged as the tragic hero of a national morality play. The drama had begun 22 years earlier, when the tribe ceded a small portion of its ancestral range in the Pacific Northwest at the treaty council sketched here. This concession only whetted the whites' land-hunger. By the time Joseph became a chief, the government claimed about 90 per cent of the original tribal domain and was trying to evict his band and four others from the disputed land.

A pacifist, Joseph opposed both the white officials and the Nez Percé hotheads who called for war—until the Army attacked his people to put them on a reservation. At that, the chief took up arms. In a battle for freedom covering almost a quarter of the continent, his people won many a clash and earned universal admiration for their courage in the face of severe hardships. But they failed to win acceptance for the basic principle that Joseph voiced: "All men were made by the same Great Spirit. They are all brothers. The earth is the mother of all people, and all people should have equal rights upon it."

An unfinished watercolor by a government artist shows the colorful arrival of the Nez Percés at an 1855 peace talk near Walla Walla.

Chief Joseph: the epic journey of the "Indian Napoleon"

Throughout the summer of 1877, Americans from coast to coast read, with increasing awe and pity, the newspaper coverage of one of history's greatest epics of group courage and endurance. Five bands of Nez Percé Indians, totaling about 700 men, women and children, had fled from their homeland in the Pacific Northwest and were trying to find a refuge from the U.S. Army—perhaps among friendly tribes on the plains, perhaps in Canada. Anywhere would do. During their zigzagging 1,700-mile flight, the Nez Percés were constantly pursued and attacked by vastly superior government forces, whom they repeatedly defeated, fought off or somehow outwitted.

As the desperate trek continued, many newspaper readers came to agree with the estimate of *Harper's Weekly* that the refugees had "a great deal of right on their side," and found themselves rooting for the underdog Indians and for the heroic figure identified as their leader. He was a tall, powerful young man named Joseph, and he appeared to be a military genius—an "Indian Napoleon," as the press described him.

Actually, Joseph was not the leading chief of the Nez Percés or even a war chief. He was a civil chief, and while he helped to plan the Nez Percés' brilliant strategy as a member of the council of leaders, he modestly minimized his military skills, saying: "The Great Spirit puts it in the heart and head of a man to know how to defend himself." Joseph's authority was subtler and more durable than a war chief's power. It rested on his rocklike dignity and calm, and his unswerving devotion to duty and to principle. His people—or at least that faction of the tribe caught up in an unwanted war

—tacitly recognized him as their guardian in their time of greatest need.

The plight of the fugitive Indians was fraught with bitter ironies. In spite of the massive chase mounted by the U.S. Army, the Nez Percés had never presented any threat to the white man. The entire tribe consisted of only 3,600 people, divided into many small, autonomous bands. In former days they had been widely scattered throughout the rugged uplands where Oregon met the future states of Idaho and Washington. They did fight occasionally with the Plains tribes to the east, and their young men usually gave a good account of themselves. But the Nez Percés had always been friendly in their dealings with white men, and asked nothing more of them than peace.

The Nez Percés—so-called by French-Canadian trappers for their pierced noses, through which they wore ornaments of shell—had made their first contact with whites in 1805, when the explorers Lewis and Clark stopped by on their way west. The visitors found them an advanced and enterprising tribe, already masters of the arts of selective horse breeding. The men gelded unpromising colts and sold off scrub mares to neighboring tribes, and by breeding only the best animals they built up the finest horse herds possessed by any Indians. But the American explorers admired the Nez Percés for more than their skills as stockmen. Meriwether Lewis ranked them "among the most amiable men we have seen. Their character is placid and gentle, rarely moved into passion."

Decades later, toward the end of the fur-trapping era, white missionaries found them to be most receptive to Christian tenets. In 1836, the Reverend Henry Spalding founded a Protestant mission on Lapwai Creek in Nez Percé country. One of his early converts was Joseph's father, Old Joseph, the leading chief of one of the richest Nez Percé bands. His eldest son, born in April

---

Still youthful and vigorous nearly 30 years after the 1877 war, a forgiving Joseph declared at the end of his life, "I have no grievance against any of the white people."

1840 and given the tribal name Thunder Rolling in the Mountain, was baptized by Spalding and given the name Joseph. He and his little brother Ollikut ("Frog"), born about two years later, spent much of their childhood around the Lapwai mission.

Under Spalding's stern tutelage, the Nez Percés became good farmers and cattle-raisers. But by the late 1840s, the increasing influx of white settlers, and the attendant rise in friction between peoples of different cultures, prompted Old Joseph to move his band southward to their ancestral domain in and around the Wallowa Valley. Joseph's Wallowa band and its four nearest neighbors were thenceforth known as the Lower Nez Percés because they inhabited the southern part of the tribal homeland.

In 1855, the U.S. government decided to settle the various tribes of the Northwest on reservations and thus clearly determine what land was available for development by whites. The Indians, including the Nez Percés, were summoned to a grand council in Walla Walla, Washington Territory. The Nez Percés' loose tribal organization, which gave a chief authority only over his own band, caused some problems in negotiations; government commissioners tried to simplify matters by designating one man as principal chief—an Upper Nez Percé leader whose persuasive oratory had won him the name Lawyer. In the end, however, this ploy proved unnecessary. Fifty-six Nez Percé chiefs, among them Old Joseph, signed the treaty, and it was a reasonably fair one. Although the tribe lost a small portion of its traditional range, the 10,000-square-mile reservation that remained was considered by the Indians to be room enough. In addition, they were promised $200,000 worth of goods in compensation for the territory they gave up.

These mutually satisfactory arrangements were disrupted in the autumn of 1860 by the start of a gold rush in Nez Percé country. Although prospecting was expressly forbidden under the treaty, neither the government nor the Indians tried very hard to stop the ragtag invaders. The Nez Percés gladly sold the prospectors horses and cattle, and patiently waited for them to go away. As the gold petered out, more and more miners did depart, some of them stealing Nez Percé horses in order to travel in style. But many whites remained behind as farmers and ranchers, and dissension

between them and the Indians increased dangerously.

Much of the trouble was over fences. Both whites and Indians would tear down each other's fences to use for firewood or to let their livestock through to other pasturage, whether or not the beasts trampled crops en route. But the Nez Percés' basic complaint was against the prejudice and inequities that characterized the administration of the Indian Bureau, the territorial officials and the white man's courts. Indians received stiff punishment for minor misdemeanors, while a white man could kill an Indian in plain view of other Indians but escape prosecution for the lack of white witnesses. The Nez Percés concluded that they could never receive justice from their white friends.

In an effort to ensure protection for the Nez Percés—and also to acquire more land for the whites in the process—federal authorities called another council in 1863. They presented the chiefs with a new treaty, which proposed to reduce their tribal holdings from 10,000 square miles to just a little more than 1,000. This prospect permanently split the tribe into two factions. The Upper Nez Percé chiefs, led by Lawyer, willingly signed the treaty. The agreement called for no sacrifice on their part, since their accustomed range lay within the reduced reservation, along Lapwai Creek. But the Lower Nez Percé chiefs, led by Old Joseph, were being asked to give up their homeland in the south and move north onto a reservation which, they maintained, was too small for the whole tribe. They refused to sign and departed in anger.

Back in his beloved Wallowa Valley, Old Joseph tore up his Bible—the "Book of Heaven" as he had always called it. This was no mere peevish gesture. The chief and other Christianized members of the Lower Nez Perce bands were so disillusioned by the white man and all he stood for that they quickly reverted to their ancestral nature worship, and they soon became susceptible to the preachments of one Smohalla, a medicine man whose so-called "Dreamer" cult had begun to spread through the Pacific Northwest. Smohalla's principal doctrine was that the Indians' lands were an inalienable gift from the Great Spirit, and it lent religious sanction to the Nez Percés' determination to keep their ancestral domains.

In the troubled years that followed, Old Joseph steadily failed in health, but his policy of passive resistance

was stubbornly maintained by his two very different sons. The younger, Ollikut—a huge man and enormously popular—advanced rapidly toward the status of war chief, winning many honors in his skirmishes with the Plains tribes, especially the Nez Percés' traditional enemy, the Blackfeet. Meanwhile Young Joseph —shorter than Ollikut, but nonetheless standing six feet two inches tall and weighing 200 pounds—took over more and more of his father's duties as civil chief.

Young Joseph's hardest chore was the futile routine of conferring with white officials and disputing their contention that the 1863 treaty obligated all Nez Percés, even the nonsigning bands, to move onto the reservation at Lapwai Creek. In the face of cajolery, orders and eventually threats, Young Joseph remained polite and friendly, but fearless and adamant. Though he earnestly desired peace with the white man and vigorously opposed Lower Nez Percé chiefs who spoke of war,

his intransigence convinced the authorities that he was the backbone of the resistance movement.

In 1871, Young Joseph inherited the full weight of chieftainship. As he later described his farewell to his dying father, the blind old man sent for him, took his hand and said, "My son, my body is returning to my mother earth, and my spirit is going very soon to see the Great Spirit. When I am gone, think of your country. You are the chief of these people. They look to you to guide them. Always remember that your father never sold his country. You must stop your ears whenever you are asked to sign a treaty selling your home."

Joseph buried his father in his beautiful Wallowa Valley, commenting: "I love that land more than all the rest of the world."

Who really owned that land? Major Henry Clay Wood, assistant adjutant of the Army's Department of the Columbia, made a thorough legal study of the ques-

167

Leaders of opposing Nez Percé factions were sketched at Walla Walla in 1855 by soldier-artist Gustavus Sohon. Lawyer *(left)* urged cooperation with the whites for "peace, plows and schools," while Old Joseph refused to cede ancestral lands.

Lawyer
Hal-hal-hoostsot
Head Chief of the Nez percé Tribe
25 May 1855

Joseph Taun-i-tak-hes.
Chief of the Nez percé Indians
29 May 1855

tion and reported to the department commander, General O. O. Howard: "The nontreaty Nez Percé cannot in law be regarded as bound by the treaty of 1863; and in so far as it attempts to deprive them of a right to occupancy of any land its provisions are null and void."

But the legal rights of the nontreaty bands were of small concern to several key officials. Governor Lafayette Grover of Oregon wanted the Lower Nez Percés to vacate his state to make way for civilization. Indian agent John Monteith wanted them near him on the Lapwai reservation so that he could control them better. Early in 1877, the Commissioner of Indian Affairs asked General of the Army William Tecumseh Sherman to order U.S. troops to put the nontreaty bands on the reservation.

That May, General Howard called all of the Lower Nez Percé chiefs to Lapwai, instructed them to select land for their bands, and gave them exactly 30 days to

move their people, possessions and herds to their new homes. "If you are not here in that time," Howard warned Joseph, "I shall consider that you want to fight, and will send my soldiers to drive you on."

Chief Too-hool-hool-zote, another of the recalcitrant leaders, shouted at Howard, "I am *not* going on the reservation!" But Joseph persuaded the chiefs to avoid bloodshed as long as possible. Though the 30-day deadline was short, they rode south to comply with it as best they could.

Joseph's band, consisting of a few hundred people, hastily rounded up their nearest horse and cattle herds; the rest they would have to leave behind to be usurped by white settlers. Then they dismantled their village and bade farewell to the Wallowa Valley. On their way north, they had to ford the Snake and Salmon rivers, both of them swollen with melted snow. But they arrived just outside the Lapwai reservation with more than a week to spare, and there they camped with the four other nontreaty bands.

All of the chiefs and leading warriors met to discuss their predicament. Though members of the rebellious Dreamer cult taunted Joseph with charges of cowardice, he patiently insisted that war with the whites would be foolhardy. After the council, Joseph and Ollikut led a small party south to butcher some cattle they had abandoned in their rush to make the deadline.

While Joseph was gone, the encampment seethed with talk of war, which soon triggered violence in the band of the 70-year-old Chief White Bird. On June 13, a young hothead named Wallaitits set out with two companions to avenge the death of his father, who had been killed in a brawl with a white man three years back. The bloodthirsty trio failed to find the culprit, but they killed four whites—all of whom had committed some brutality against Indians in the past. Their triumph, such as it was, encouraged 21 young warriors to stage another foray. On this mission, they killed at least 14 whites, some of them were women and children. Throughout the region, farmers and ranchers fled in fright to the small towns.

The Nez Percés were frightened too. When Joseph returned to camp from his meat-packing trip, he discovered that many families, fearful of punishment if they now set foot on the reservation, were striking their tipis and preparing to flee. Though no member of Joseph's own band had been involved in the atrocities, he guessed correctly that individual guilt or innocence would not matter to the whites and that General Howard would want to thrash all five nontreaty bands. The peace-loving chief resigned himself to fighting if any Nez Percés were attacked.

During the next few days, Joseph urged all of the chiefs to adopt rules for humane conduct in case of war: stop the young men from killing women or children; let there be no scalping of the dead or slaying of wounded soldiers; if there was to be savagery in the conflict, let it be done by whites, not Nez Percés. The chiefs agreed to do their best to keep their headstrong young warriors under control.

Amid all the talk of death, one of Joseph's wives brought forth new life; a daughter, his second, was born just in time to detain Joseph as the bands scattered. One of the bands, led by the noted chief Red Echo, de-

cided to risk white wrath and go onto the reservation. Some of Joseph's people left with Chief Looking Glass (so called because he wore a small mirror around his neck) and camped with his band on Clear Creek. Chiefs White Bird and Too-hool-hool-zote, with their small bands, went to camp on White Bird Creek, and there Joseph joined them with the rest of his band as soon as his wife and infant daughter could travel.

Meanwhile, the white authorities began marshaling formidable forces to crush the rebels. General Howard sent messages by courier and telegraph to seven Army posts in his Columbia department, ordering all available soldiers to Lapwai. Outside his department, assorted troops were shipped from San Francisco, artillery units from Alaska, and an infantry regiment all the way from Atlanta, Georgia. Eventually some 2,000 U.S. soldiers, plus countless local volunteers, Indian auxiliaries and supply workers, would be brought to bear on the breakaway bands, which could not field even a tenth as many fighting men. On the eve of war, it seemed that the Nez Percés stood no chance.

That was the opinion of General Howard. He wired his superiors, "Think we shall make short work of it," and he quickly assigned missions to the troops already on hand at Lapwai. As a cavalry column departed on June 15 under the command of Captain David Perry, Howard saluted and called banteringly to Perry, "You must not get whipped."

Perry replied, "There is no danger of that, sir." Then the jaunty young officer rode off to what was one of the worst defeats the United States Army ever suffered at the hands of Western Indians.

Captain Perry's orders were simply to protect the refugee settlers who had flocked into Grangeville, a small town about 50 miles southeast of Lapwai headquarters. But Perry learned at Grangeville that Joseph, White Bird and Too-hool-hool-zote were encamped 15 miles away at White Bird Creek, and he could not resist such a golden opportunity. So Perry augmented his 103 cavalrymen with 11 civilian volunteers and confidently galloped off to punish the disobedient bands. At midnight on June 16, his men settled down behind a long ridge that overlooked the Indian camp. Perry was planning to take the Nez Percés by surprise at dawn, but the troopers soon learned that their presence

Members of the "Dreamer" cult that took hold among the Nez Percés by 1860 surround the prophet Smohalla *(center, white shirt)*, who preached that the Indian dead would arise and drive the white man from their land. Joseph shared Smohalla's reverence for land, but not his antiwhite bias.

had already been detected by Indian boys who were out herding the horses.

At first light on June 17, Perry deployed his men in three groups and sent them over the ridge, down the long rugged slope toward the creekside camp. Meanwhile the Nez Percé chiefs, forewarned by their scouts of Perry's approach, had decided to make one more attempt to avert war. Six Indians, carrying a white flag, rode upslope to arrange a parley with the leader of the troops. If the truce effort failed, the chiefs had only 60 or 70 warriors at their disposal, but they may well have roughed out their battle plan beforehand.

Lieutenant Edward Theller, in command of the skirmish line at Perry's center, was leading an advanced patrol when he saw the truce team approaching. Moments later, one of Theller's men fired twice, doing no damage but flagrantly violating the flag of truce. The last chance for peace had disappeared.

A Nez Percé rifle cracked, and Perry's bugler fell dead. Gunfire then became general, and soon the cavalry's second bugler was killed, leaving Perry unable to send quick commands to his men along the strung-out battle line. The Nez Percés were clearly the better marksmen. They knocked troopers out of the saddle with arrows, shotguns and old rifles, while the soldiers, equipped with the latest arms, sprayed bullets harmlessly at elusive targets.

Joseph seems to have divided his time between fighting on the slope and directing operations in the camp below, where the noncombatants were packing up for a prearranged move. The camp was in no danger, because the warriors were advancing steadily, carrying the battle to the cavalry. In fact, the Indians were brilliantly disproving the military axiom that a small force cannot outflank a larger one.

On Captain Perry's left, the dismounted volunteers struggled to hold a rocky knoll. But the position became untenable as warriors swung past it; the volunteers, afraid of being cut off, scrambled back to their horses. The Indians occupied the knoll and from there began an enfilading fire on Theller's exposed skirmish line in the center.

As Perry's left flank gave way, Joseph's brother Ollikut led a charge against Perry's right. It crumpled. With both flanks collapsing, Perry frantically ordered his center to retreat. His men's horses reared and

plunged, panicked by the din. At the height of the confusion, the warriors stampeded a herd of their horses through Perry's center. Clinging unseen to the sides of the loose horses were the few Nez Percés who had repeating rifles. Once past the center they began firing on the troops from the rear.

Captain Perry no longer aspired to win a battle; he was now trying to save some part of his command, and even that prospect seemed dubious. Lieutenant Theller and 19 of his men retreated by an ill-chosen route, and a party of warriors trapped them against a rock ledge in a ravine. All 20 of the cavalrymen fought gallantly, and all were killed.

Somehow Perry managed to disengage his survivors and retreat from the battlefield. At this juncture, the captain had reason to think he had made good his escape, for most Indian tribes lacked the military sophistication to drive home a victory; their warriors would simply cease fighting to scavenge the battlefield for booty and scalps. But the extraordinary Nez Percés barely paused to take rifles — and nothing else — from the dead. Swiftly they formed a large pursuit force and forced the fleeing enemy to fight a rear-guard action for the rest of the morning. The warriors did not break off the chase until Perry's survivors reached the town of Mount Idaho, 18 miles from the battlefield.

The casualty figures told a nearly incredible story. Captain Perry had lost about one third of his command — 34 men dead and four wounded. Not a single Nez Percé had been killed and only two were wounded.

For almost a week, the shock of the battle paralyzed the area. White settlers, expecting widespread hostilities, huddled together in the towns. The Nez Percés, though elated by their victory, were uncertain about what to do next; they did some pillaging and waited for the Army's reaction. As for General Howard, the debacle had taught him never again to underestimate the Nez Percés and he cautiously marked time until reinforcements arrived.

On June 22, the general mustered a force of nearly 400 soldiers, plus about 100 supply workers and Indian scouts, and he led them southeastward to seek out and crush the breakaway bands. Howard moved slowly to the deserted battlefield at White Bird Creek. After burying the dead, his troops tracked the bands to the Salmon River. There they were startled to see a war

THE Nez Perces CAMPAIGN IDAHO

"NEZ PERCES"

ON PICKET.

IN PURSUIT OF THE INDIANS

U.S CAVALRY CHARGING ON THE RED SKINS.

Keller

One-armed General O. O. Howard, who had promised a quick victory, doggedly pursued the Nez Percés from Idaho to Montana.

174

Colonel John Gibbon, a veteran of campaigns against the Sioux, took a Nez Percé camp by surprise, and sustained a leg wound—and 40 percent casualties overall.

Colonel Samuel Sturgis, an Indian-hater since his son's death at the hands of Sioux, chased the Nez Percés through the Absaroka Mountains but failed to corner them.

Colonel Nelson Miles finally halted the Nez Percés just 40 miles short of refuge in Canada. Later, he championed Joseph's long struggle to return to his homeland.

party waiting for them on the far shore, just beyond rifle range. This insolent display had been planned by the chiefs to lure Howard's main force out of position and into a wild goose chase. The general obliged.

On July 1, Howard's troops crossed the swollen Salmon River unopposed and followed the bands into the dangerous mountains to the south. Although the Nez Percés were encumbered by their families and herds, they completed a circuitous 25-mile move in just 36 hours and, on July 2, recrossed the Salmon several miles upstream from their first crossing. Howard followed them to their second crossing point, but his ponderous column, unable to ford the stormy river there, had to retrace its whole agonizing route through the mountains. Not until July 7 did Howard recross the Salmon at the same spot where he had started his futile chase six days before. Meanwhile the Nez Percé bands had swung east, staging raids on Howard's thinly defended rear areas. In one attack, war chiefs Five Wounds and Rainbow wiped out an 11-man patrol.

On July 6, the Indians pitched camp on the South Fork of the Clearwater River. There they were joined by Chief Looking Glass's band and also by the band of Red Echo, who had been inspired to sacrifice the security of the reservation when he had heard of the victory at White Bird Creek. The five nontreaty bands were now all assembled together and at peak strength, with 150 men of fighting age, plus about 550 older men, women and children.

The Indians relaxed now, enjoying their successes, certain that General Howard was several days' journey behind them. They repaired their equipment, grazed their 2,000 to 3,000 horses and cattle, raided for supplies and skirmished on a small scale to keep the local defenders pinned down. The chiefs met to air their views on the situation, but since each band had the right to do as it pleased, the council made no special effort to agree on a course of action.

The days of respite were ended abruptly just after noon on July 11, when the Nez Percé encampment on the valley floor was startled by a cannon shot from the bluffs to the northeast. That shot, and the Gatling gun fire that followed it, announced the appearance of General Howard, who had finally extricated himself from the

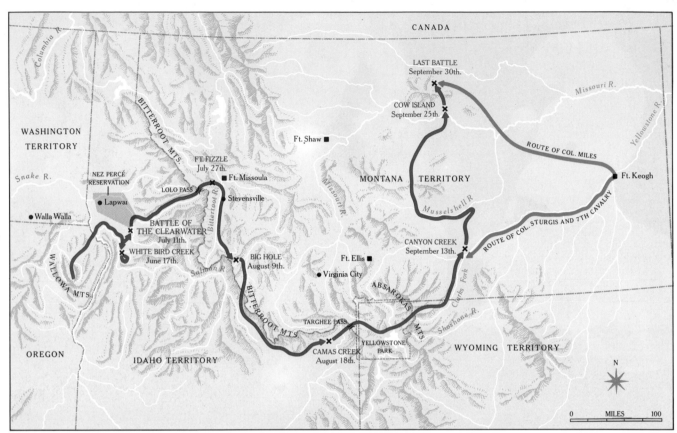

THE NEZ PERCÉ RETREAT began in June 1877 and lasted for 108 days. Chief Joseph, upon returning from a hunt in the Wallowa Mountains *(left),* found his camp near Lapwai in turmoil after hotheads had attacked whites. Expecting retaliation, he sought escape. As the Nez Percés headed east to look for help from other Indians they fought a series of successful battles against superior U.S. Army forces. After a setback at Canyon Creek, however, they turned northward hoping to reach safety in Canada. They finally surrendered, exhausted, on October 5 — 40 miles from the border, and about 1,700 miles from their starting point.

mountains and hurried north with a beefed-up command of nearly 600 men. Howard prepared for a classic battle of the sort he had participated in at Gettysburg.

Though the Nez Percés had been caught with their guard down, they quickly recovered. Brave old Too-hool-hool-zote saw the troops skirting a long ravine to enter the valley down its distant eastern slope, and instantly he raced eastward with 24 prime warriors. They took strong positions across the steep slope and halted the descending soldiers with deadly volleys.

The chief and his little skirmish line held firm until the threat of a flanking movement forced them downhill to the valley floor. There they held again, and were joined by warriors under Ollikut, Five Wounds and Rainbow. Another contingent attacked Howard's supply train in the woods to the north, and still other Indians drove the herds to safety out of the open western end of the valley.

All of this purposeful Nez Percé activity only served to convince General Howard that he was fighting against a force of as many as 300 first-class warriors. And so, having learned at a great cost to respect this enemy, he overcautiously went on the defensive. Along the eastern end of the valley, Howard deployed his troops in a huge circle, stationing himself and his staff in the center. The general stubbornly held this defense line for 30 hours.

The Nez Percés countered with an un-Indianlike tactic and pulled off an improbable feat. At intervals all around the soldiers' defense perimeter, the warriors dug rifle pits and built rock piles to protect themselves. An army of 600 troopers had been surrounded by about

100 Nez Percés with no formal military training.

Nez Percé horsemen joined their dug-in comrades, and the fighting went on through the blazing hot afternoon. Chief Joseph was seen from time to time, fighting as an ordinary warrior. The soldiers, cut off from water, fought thirst as well as the Nez Percé sharpshooters. Sergeant Michael McCarthy wrote staccato impressions of the hectic scene: "The enemy everywhere fronting us or galloping by us firing from horseback. Musketry all around our position like firecrackers on fourth of July. Howitzers booming, Gatling guns, Indians yelling, soldiers cheering, and the mules of our immense pack train braying loud enough to drown all other sounds. The sun on burnt necks, and the thermometer somewhere around 100, and no water."

Late in the day, the Indians began losing interest in the battle. They had little to gain by continuing the siege and much to lose by an assault on the Army position. In small groups, about half the warriors left their trenches and returned to camp. Firing continued into the night, but it was light and desultory.

On the morning of July 12, Howard finally realized that he was opposed by only a token force. So the general turned aggressive again and ordered his command to advance on a broad front. The Nez Percé warriors gave ground steadily, but made sure that the women and children had time to make their getaway toward the town of Kamiah to the north. When the soldiers reached the Indian campsite, they captured some tipis, food supplies, utensils and clothing. Tom Sutherland, a newspaper reporter tagging along with Howard, sent back an account of these finds, and added: "For my part I found a much worn pair of small moccasins and an absurd little rag doll under a tree."

Though Howard lost 13 men dead, about three times the Nez Percé casualties, he greatly exaggerated the enemy losses and proudly claimed a major victory. But one of his officers reported the battle more objectively: "The Indians were not defeated. Their loss must have been insignificant and their retreat to Kamiah was masterly, deliberate and unmolested, leaving us with a victory barren of results."

To the Nez Percés, reassembling in the Kamiah area, the Battle of the Clearwater was an instructive draw and a somber turning point. The outnumbered warriors had proved themselves capable of coping with the Army's battle tactics, but their leaders concluded that the bands would fight better if they were integrated under the joint command of the council of chiefs. This meant that each band would have to give up its autonomy and abide by the council's decisions.

The issue was settled in a momentous council meeting, called on July 15 to discuss options for the next move. Joseph declared himself in favor of returning south to fight for their home domains. "I do not want to die in a strange land," he said. But the other chiefs wanted to journey east across the Bitterroot Mountains to the Great Plains, where they might form a military alliance with some old tribal friends, the Crows. Joseph deferred to the principle of united action. Looking Glass, who had often traveled over the 150-mile-long Lolo Trail that led toward the plains, was unanimously voted headman for the journey. With that decision, the five bands became a single group of expatriate refugees.

The Nez Percés — warriors, wounded, families and herds — started up the Lolo Trail on July 16. It was a cruelly arduous route, rising to altitudes of 7,000 feet. The way was blocked by tangled underbrush, jagged boulders and trees uprooted by powerful winds. General Howard, who resumed his pursuit after spending two weeks regrouping his forces, reported that the Indians had "jammed their ponies through, up the rocks, over, and under, and around the logs, and among the fallen trees . . . leaving blood to mark their path; and abandoned animals, with broken legs, or 'played out,' or stretched dead by the wayside." The soldiers noted scarred trees along the route; apparently the fugitives had been hungry enough to eat the inner bark.

In just 11 days, the Nez Percés reached Montana and the end of their mountain trek. Emerging from Lolo Canyon on July 27, they entered the cliff-sided narrows of Bitterroot Valley and found their way blocked by a sturdy timber barricade. Captain Charles Rawn, sent 12 miles from Fort Missoula on orders telegraphed ahead by General Howard, was manning the road block with 35 soldiers, nearly 200 volunteers and a party of Flathead Indians. Looking Glass, Joseph and White Bird went forward to ask Rawn for permission to pass, assuring him that they would not molest the people of Montana. Rawn would not agree; but the volunteers, believing that the Nez Percés would honor this pledge and unwilling to provoke attacks on their vulnerable settlements, deserted the captain in droves.

The next morning, while Rawn braced for a frontal assault, the Nez Percés bypassed his barricade with a startling maneuver. As one observer described it: "About 10 o'clock we heard singing, apparently above our heads. Upon looking up, we discovered the Indians passing along the side of the cliff, where we thought a goat could not pass, much less an entire tribe of Indians with all their impedimenta. The entire band dropped into the valley beyond us and then proceeded up the Bitterroot." Captain Rawn's barricade was promptly dubbed Fort Fizzle by the volunteers who took part in the aborted skirmish.

The Nez Percés, eager to calm the jittery settlers, were on their best behavior as they rode up the Bitterroot Valley. Reaching the town of Stevensville, they went into the stores to buy provisions, and though the merchants charged exorbitant prices, they paid without a murmur, spending the profits they had earned as stockmen. Several warriors, entering a ranchhouse that had been deserted as the bands approached, took 200 pounds of flour and 30 pounds of coffee; but on orders from the chiefs they left behind ample payment: seven of their horses. They even used the rancher's branding iron on the animals to make the transaction official.

From Stevensville, the Nez Percés moved south along the Bitterroot Valley, traveling at the leisurely pace of 15 miles a day. Neither they nor the settlers bothered each other. It seemed to be true, as several chiefs held, that they had left their war back in Idaho. Looking Glass, knowing that General Howard was many days behind them, drew the dangerous conclusion that they were perfectly safe, and he even refrained from sending out scouts in the belief that it would break his peace pledge to the Montanans.

The Nez Percés had crossed the Continental Divide and dropped down into the Big Hole Valley before they

Joseph's brother Ollikut, a genial giant, led the warriors of their band. In one counterstroke during the retreat, he succeeded in stealing 200 of General Howard's mules.

got their first intimation of trouble ahead. They were resting, grazing their herds and hunting antelope when, on the pleasant evening of August 8, a medicine man named Pile of Clouds uttered a warning: "Death is on our trail." And death caught up with them the very next morning in the form of a new enemy.

Colonel John Gibbon, from Fort Shaw on the Sun River, had joined the chase five days' march ahead of General Howard. This tough, resourceful campaigner, transporting his 163 soldiers and 35 volunteers 35 miles a day in hired wagons where the terrain permitted, gained nearly 20 miles a day on the Nez Percés without tiring his men. On August 7, Colonel Gibbon's advance patrol spotted the Indians in Big Hole Valley, and the following night his main force moved into attack position just 150 yards from the fugitives' camp.

At dawn on August 9, Gibbon's men charged on foot and caught the Nez Percés fast asleep. The soldiers splashed across a waist-deep stream and ran through the camp, firing and clubbing at the Indians as they emerged from their tipis. Unarmed warriors were shot down as they dashed for cover in thickets around the camp. Men too old or dazed to flee were shot where they stood. Women were shot down; one of Joseph's wives was seriously wounded. Joseph himself was seen racing by, carrying his infant daughter to safety —and none too soon. The skulls of other babies were crushed by soldiers' boots or rifle butts.

In and around the western half of the camp, Gibbon's men did their bloody work efficiently, but some of the warriors—and some women too—were dying hard. When one warrior was shot by a captain, his wife snatched up his rifle, shot the soldier in the head and kept on firing until she was riddled with bullets.

For interminable minutes, the Nez Percé resistance was disorganized and desperate. But the soldiers' attack line had not been long enough to envelop the eastern end of the camp, and it was there that Joseph, White

Chief Looking Glass headed the Nez Percés' eastward trek through the Bitterroot Mountains, using trails he had taken on buffalo hunts.

Bird and Looking Glass began rallying their people, mounting a counterattack. "Now is our time to fight!" they shouted. "You can kill left and right. Now fight!"

They fought. A ragged line of warriors advanced against the troops, who were caught in a deadly crossfire from Nez Percé snipers along the river. Now the soldiers were falling, and it was Colonel Gibbon who broke off the battle. At eight a.m., he ordered his troops to withdraw to a wooded hill.

With the troops safely established on the hill, the scattered noncombatants came back to camp to bury their dead and to pack up and flee once more. Gibbon himself later wrote: "Few of us will soon forget the wail of mingled grief, rage and horror which came from the camp 400 or 500 yards below us when the Indians returned to it and recognized their slaughtered warriors, women and children."

The battered bands departed, moving slowly to minimize the pain of their wounded. To forestall pursuit, Ollikut and a party of sharpshooters kept the troops pinned down for nearly 24 hours before they raced away on their ponies. Fortunately for Gibbon's men, General Howard had put on an uncommon burst of speed and arrived two days after the battle with much-needed food and medical supplies. The colonel, himself suffering from a leg wound, said to the general, "Who could have believed that those Indians would have rallied after such a surprise and made such a fight?"

By the Army's count, Gibbon had lost 29 dead, and the Indians had left 89 dead on the battlefield. By the Nez Percés' reckoning, all but 12 of their dead were women, children and old men; but the 12 fighting men they had lost included three irreplaceable war leaders, Red Echo, Five Wounds and Rainbow. The people blamed their tragic losses on Looking Glass: his slow rate of march, his decision to rest in Big Hole Valley. In their bitterness, they resolved to treat all whites as potential enemies, and their grief was laced with fury when their scouts reported that General Howard had allowed his Indian scouts to scalp the Nez Percé dead back on the battlefield.

Howard resumed his pursuit on August 13 and began gaining ground. He was only a day's march behind the Nez Percés when they stopped on Camas Prairie for the night of August 18. To relieve the pressure, Ollikut raced back through the darkness with 28 warriors,

raided Howard's camp at Camas Creek and drove off about 200 pack mules. The Nez Percés gained three days on Howard while his troops scoured the local settlements to replace their lost mules.

On August 22, the bands crossed Targhee Pass, eluding an Army detachment sent to intercept them, and zigzagged eastward through Wyoming's Yellowstone region. In their search for supplies, warriors took what they wanted from prospectors and held some tourists captive for a while. The young men also broke Joseph's cardinal rule for humane warfare and killed several white noncombatants.

While the Nez Percés were struggling through the rugged mountains east of Yellowstone Park, Looking Glass galloped ahead to confer with the Crows in Montana. Looking Glass asked the Crow chiefs for their armed support, or at least for permission to live among them briefly. But the Crows had scouted for the U.S. Army and feared its power. Looking Glass hurried back to his people with nothing better than a half-hearted pledge of neutrality from one of the two Crow factions.

The weary Nez Percés were stunned by the bad news. They had now traveled well over 1,000 miles, and the refusal of the Crows to help them meant that their last hope lay in reaching Canada, hundreds of miles more to the north. The council of chiefs agreed that they must make the journey. They would try to get help from their old enemies, the Sioux, led by Sitting Bull, who had fled across the Canadian border earlier that year.

Somehow the Nez Percés pulled themselves together and struck out anew. They tapped their last reserves of strength and drew ever more heavily on the courage of Joseph, who alone among the chiefs had not lost prestige through errors in judgment. Joseph was their rock, their guardian, their only permanent reference point in a world of hectic movement.

Army units from four separate commands were now converging on the fugitives, and the council of chiefs had to plan an escape carefully. They could not move due north because the Absaroka Mountains were too hard to climb on horseback; they first had to travel east, along either the Shoshone River or Clarks Fork of the Yellowstone River, and then veer north. The chiefs chose the Clarks Fork route, even though scouts reported the way blocked by soldiers. Using an old trick, the Nez Percés allowed the soldiers—a 7th Cavalry unit under Colonel Samuel Sturgis—to see them starting toward the Shoshone River, then doubled back under cover and cut behind the colonel's decoyed force.

The bands pushed on to the headwaters of the Clark Fork and followed the river toward the Yellowstone. Sturgis, hopping mad at being outfoxed, picked up their trail and closed ground. The Nez Percés turned north up Canyon Creek, a dry stream bed with banks 10 to 20 feet high. When Sturgis and his 350 soldiers reached the creek, Nez Percé sharpshooters held them off while their families hurried on ahead. The warriors fought a slow retreat for seven miles, then left their path blocked with boulders.

After General Howard learned that the Nez Percés had escaped again, he was not merely angry, he was nearly desperate. His repeated failure to corner the fugitives had earned him censure from his superiors. Now he played what was virtually his last card. He wrote a message to Colonel Nelson A. Miles at Fort Keogh on the Tongue River, advising him to move all his available troops into the Nez Percés' line of march northward. Miles, something of a glory-seeker, but capable and energetic, was just the right man for a last ditch effort. On September 18, the day after he received Howard's note, the colonel departed with seven companies of infantry and a troop of cavalry.

Meanwhile, the Nez Percés had broken out of the mountains and gorges, onto rolling terrain that was easier to travel. But many of the people were wounded or sick, and they slowed the others. Because they were a burden, some of the old and the ailing began dropping out, wandering off to die alone.

On September 17, the bands forded the Musselshell River and pushed on north. They crossed the Missouri River eight days later, pausing on Cow Island to fight for and seize some food from an Army depot there. Then they plodded north again. Cold winds were blowing now, reminding them that autumn had come.

At the end of September, the bands made camp on Snake Creek near the Bear Paw Mountains. They had now traveled more than 1,600 miles, to within 40 miles of the Canadian border, but it seemed that they were too weary to travel farther. The council of chiefs decided to stay there long enough to kill some buffalo, providing nourishing food and warm robes for the com-

ing winter. It appeared to be a sound decision, for General Howard was several days behind them. However, the chiefs did not know that Colonel Miles' troops were bearing down on them.

At 6 a.m. on September 30, Miles' Cheyenne scouts spotted the Bear Paw encampment, and his hard-riding command approached it concealed by a mountain spur. Two hours later, Miles closed in with nearly 600 men. A wintry chill had begun to set in. When Miles ordered his troops to charge, a cavalry captain said, "My God, have I got to go out and be killed in such cold weather?" It proved to be a prophetic remark.

The Nez Percés were packing up to move on when they saw Miles's cavalry top the surrounding bluffs and begin its charge. The warriors, whom Miles soon would call "the best marksmen of any Indians I have ever encountered," held their fire until the bluecoats reached a range of 100 yards, then they opened up. Many a cavalryman was knocked from his saddle. In the first charge, one battalion had 53 casualties out of 115 men; the warriors carefully picked off all but one of the officers —including the captain who had complained about the weather. This withering fire was too much for the attackers to withstand. They stopped their charge and dived for cover in the gullies that crisscrossed the flats. Miles then threw a ring of troops around the whole camp, and the siege began.

Joseph and his 12-year-old daughter Sarah were out across the creek, catching horses to use that day, when a cavalry unit swept around them to capture the herds. Joseph ran into the open, shouting to some nearby warriors, "Horses! Horses! Save the horses!" Several Nez Percés jumped on ponies and fled north toward the Canadian border. Joseph put his daughter on horseback and sent her galloping after them. Then he raced through a line of soldiers, back to the camp to help direct the defense. His wife was waiting at their tipi door. She said, "Here is your gun. Fight!"

At 1 p.m., Miles ordered a second charge, and Joseph met it head on. When an infantry unit reached the tipis, Joseph's warriors killed three soldiers quickly and fought the rest through draws and gullies until nightfall. But by the end of the day, Joseph knew the worst about the Indians' casualties.

Among their dead was Too-hool-hool-zote, the brave and cunning old chief. The crushing blow for Jo-

Chief Joseph and General John Gibbon, bitter enemies during the Nez Percés' flight, make their peace 11 years later. Gibbon blamed the plight of the Western tribes on the incompetence of reservation officials.

seph was the loss of his beloved brother Ollikut, the good-natured giant.

On October 1, a two-day storm blew in, bringing cold rain, followed by swirling snow. An Indian woman later recalled, "Children cried with hunger and cold. Old people suffering in silence. Misery everywhere." Chief Joseph was tormented to see his people suffer so much. But he and Looking Glass had sent six of their trusted warriors to the Sioux in Canada, and Joseph still held out a wan hope that they would succeed in persuading Sitting Bull to come to their rescue. He did not know that all six Nez Percés had been killed by hostile Assiniboin Indians.

Colonel Miles, too, thought that Sitting Bull might intervene. To avoid a bigger battle, he began to nego-

tiate with Joseph for the prompt surrender of his people. Joseph refused to agree to unconditional surrender, demanding assurances that the remaining Nez Percés would be returned to Idaho.

The bloody stalemate and the watchful waiting ended on October 4, when General Howard reached the battlefield with the vanguard of his army. The Nez Percé leaders met to decide finally whether or not to give up. As they talked, Chief Looking Glass heard the sound of horses' hoofs approaching and, thinking that it was the warriors returning with word from Sitting Bull, he went outside to make sure. He was killed instantly by a bullet in the forehead.

Looking Glass was the last casualty in the terrible war. Joseph and White Bird were the only chiefs left to decide the fate of the Nez Percés. In a council of warriors, Joseph, for the sake of his dying people, chose surrender. White Bird promised to yield after supervising the roundup of his own band. But on the next day, October 5, Joseph stood alone in avowing that the Nez Percés would resist no longer. White Bird, instead of fulfilling his promise, had slipped through the guard lines and made his escape to Canada with 14 warriors and a number of women.

In his camp, before a translator and recording officer, Joseph spoke words that would soon touch the hearts of Americans everywhere: "It is cold and we have no blankets. The little children are freezing to death. My people, some of them, have run away to the hills and have no blankets, no food; no one knows where they are — perhaps freezing to death. I want time to look for my children and see how many of them I can find. Maybe I shall find them among the dead. Hear me, my chiefs. I am tired; my heart is sick and sad. From where the sun now stands, I will fight no more forever."

Then Joseph stepped out into the blood-spattered snow and extended his rifle to General Howard. The general gave Colonel Miles the honor of accepting the surrender. When the soldiers took a count of their prisoners of war, they found that the 700 Nez Percés who had fled on June 15 had been whittled down to 431, only 79 of them men.

The war was over, but not the sorrow and suffering of the Nez Percé survivors. Half-starved, their clothes in tatters, they were taken first to Fort Lincoln, Dakota Territory. En route, as they passed through Bismarck, a band saluted Joseph by playing "The Star-Spangled Banner," and the townspeople turned out to cheer their bravery and give them food. Colonel Miles had planned to return the captives to the Lapwai reservation, but General Sherman, his superior, was insistent that they be treated with severity and "must never be allowed to return to Oregon."

Late in the fall, the Nez Percés were put aboard a train under heavy guard and transported to Fort Leavenworth, Kansas. During the winter, as the government deliberated on what to do with them, more than 20 Nez Percés succumbed to malaria. Joseph later said: "We buried them in this strange land. The Great Spirit who rules above seemed to be looking some other way,

and did not see what was being done to my people."

In May, the Nez Percés were moved to the Quapaw tribe's reservation in Kansas. They stayed only a month before being relocated on another Kansas reservation, where 47 more Nez Percés died by October. In the hope of improving his people's lot Joseph traveled to Washington, talked with lawmakers and gave interviews to the press. He spoke without rancor, dwelling on the great principles that have always concerned moral men: "We only ask an even chance to live as other men live. . . . We ask that the same law shall work alike on all men. . . . Let me be a free man — free to travel, free to stop, free to work, free to trade where I choose, free to choose my own teachers, free to follow the religion of my fathers, free to think and talk and act for myself."

In June 1879, the captives were moved to Indian Territory. Among the Nez Percés who sickened and died there was Joseph's little daughter, who had been born on the eve of their flight from Idaho. By 1883, the plight of the Nez Percés had become a national issue; and the next year Congress, bowing to the sympathetic public and press, authorized the Secretary of the Interior to dispose of Joseph's people as he saw fit. He saw fit to be lenient.

On May 22, 1885, the surviving Nez Percés — 268 of the 700 who had fled — boarded a train for the Pacific Northwest. But even now their woes were not over. Only 118 of them were permitted to rejoin their tribe on the Lapwai reservation in Idaho. The other 150 were sent to the Colville reservation in Washington Territory. One of the exiles was Chief Joseph, whom certain officials considered too dangerous to trust with his own people.

In 1901, Joseph told an interviewer: "My home is in the Wallowa Valley, and I want to go back there to live. My father and mother are buried there. If the government would only give me a small piece of land for my people in the Wallowa Valley, with a teacher, that is all I would ask." The United States government did not oblige him, although he made the trip to Washington to ask this favor of President Theodore Roosevelt. The end came soon afterward. On September 21, 1904, while he sat by the fire in his tipi, he suddenly pitched forward on his face. The reservation doctor commented, "Joseph died of a broken heart."

A circle of tipis, at Nespelem in Washington's Colville reservation, was the last home of Joseph and 149 exiled Nez Percés. The chief, repeatedly denied permission to return to his native Idaho, said, "I have asked some of the great white chiefs where they get their authority to say to the Indian that he shall stay in one place. They cannot tell me."

In the lava beds, Captain Jack's last stand

General Edward Canby

Kientpoos, or Captain Jack

Not all Indian wars were waged in the Western heartland. In fact, the most one-sided Indian struggle was the bizarre Modoc War of 1873, fought in northern California by a hotheaded splinter group of an otherwise friendly tribe. For six months some 50 Modoc riflemen led by their wily leader Kientpoos—nicknamed Captain Jack by the local settlers—holed up in a maze of ancient lava beds and, outnumbered by as much as 20 to 1, fought the U.S. soldiers to a standstill. Among the Army's 181 casualties was Brigadier General Edward R. S. Canby—a victim of Captain Jack and the only general ever to be killed fighting Indians.

An infantry company, part of the huge military force General Canby assembled against the Modocs, forms up before an attack in 1873.

The fearsome lava beds, shown here with a solitary figure to provide scale, presented the Modocs with a virtually impregnable refuge.

The Modoc War was triggered on November 29, 1872, when U.S. cavalrymen rode into the tribe's villages on the California-Oregon border with orders to remove the Modocs to a nearby government reservation—"peaceably if you can, forcibly if you must."

Twice before, Captain Jack had obediently led his people to a reservation, only to leave because of friction with the Klamaths, another tribe confined there. This time he refused to budge. Confused shooting broke out, and Captain Jack's Modocs fled 10 miles southward to take refuge in the 1,500-year-old lava beds on the shore of Tule Lake. In this fantastic jumble

of ridges, pits, caves and chasms, about 12 miles long and 10 miles wide, Captain Jack and his band of 165 men, women and children made their stand.

The Army mustered a strike force of three cavalry troops and two infantry companies to dislodge the Indians. But the first assault, on January 17, was crippled by a combination of dense ground fog and an unreasoning fear of Modoc snipers that sent the soldiers scrambling for cover. An embarrassed General Canby, the highest-ranking officer in the Northwest, took command and boosted his force to 700.

Soon afterward a peace commission that eventually included General

Canby was established to negotiate the Modoc surrender. For weeks the talks dragged on in the no-man's-land between the lines. Captain Jack and his lieutenants held fast to their demand for a small reservation on their old lands. The spectacle of a tiny band of Indians defying the government drew nationwide admiration and sympathy.

But not for long, for Captain Jack made a fearsome blunder. Shamed by the taunting of several of his braves— led by the power-hungry medicine man Curly Headed Doctor—Captain Jack rashly agreed to a treacherous scheme. Naïvely thinking a leaderless army is as helpless as a leaderless war party, the

A battery of howitzers that were fired in support of the Army's spring offensive merely forced the Modocs deeper into their cave shelters.

Modocs planned to assassinate the peace commissioners. At a parley on Good Friday, April 11, Captain Jack drew a hidden revolver and shot the unarmed Canby in the head.

Canby's death outraged the nation; General William T. Sherman ordered Canby's successor to crush the Modocs, adding, "You will be fully justified in their utter extermination."

On April 15, a 1,000-man army, including artillery and 72 Indian scouts, began a three-day attack. But for all its fury, the offensive was blunted by the terrain and took only one Modoc life, and that by accident. The tragic conclusion still lay ahead.

An Army scout, identified by the crossed cannons on his hat, takes aim at the Modocs.

Wary of Modoc sharpshooters who caused most of the Army's casualties, soldiers of a guard detail peer anxiously toward their elusive foe.

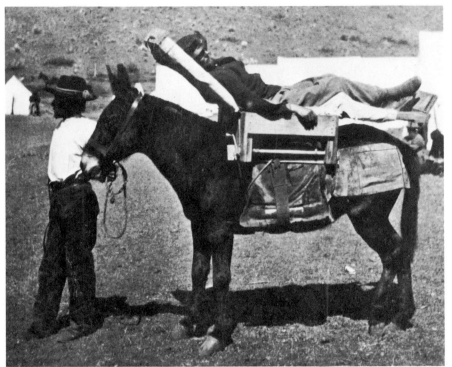

A mule-borne stretcher carries one of the Army's wounded to the rear for treatment.

In the weeks after the Army's futile assault, the besieged Modocs were finally forced from their refuge and cut off from their water supply. Casualties and defections took their toll. His spirit broken, Captain Jack surrendered on June 1, 1873. Without benefit of counsel, he was tried for Canby's murder and hanged with three of his men. Two others were spared, but not until the morning they were to swing with Captain Jack. Even after death the hero-villain of this strange war had one last indignity to undergo. In accordance with government policy, Captain Jack was decapitated and his head shipped east for scientific analysis.

The rock-roofed entrance of this cave opened into a shelter that was roomy enough to house Captain Jack and his family for three months.

In irons, Captain Jack *(right)* and another leader of the Modoc renegades await trial by an Army court shortly after their surrender.

6 | The threatened world of Sitting Bull

When Sitting Bull was inaugurated as a Sioux chief in the 1860s, he composed a song for the event. "The chiefs of old are gone," he sang, addressing himself to the role he was inheriting. "Myself, I take courage."

An outstanding warrior, a revered spiritual leader, a wily politician, Sit-ting Bull parried every attempt to reduce the Sioux lands for as long as he could. When a white emissary urged him to go to a reservation and accept government rations, he answered bluntly, "We can feed ourselves."

Sitting Bull's great stature as a tribal leader stemmed in no small part from his gift for simple, almost poetic, eloquence. His words often reflected the inspiration that he drew from the ancestral Sioux world that he so passionately loved. Indeed, he once remarked that in the morning, when he walked barefoot upon its soil, he could "hear the very heart of the holy earth."

The Big Horn Mountains in Montana present a majestic backdrop for Sitting Bull's camp, which was painted in 1873 by Henry Cross.

From the Little Bighorn to Wounded Knee

Early in June, 1876, Sitting Bull of the Sioux made ready to supplicate the deity Wakan Tanka, the Great Mysterious. He scrubbed all paint from his face, bound the stem of his ceremonial pipe with sprigs of fresh-picked sage and, taking three witnesses with him, climbed a lonely butte and prayed toward the sun: "Wakan Tanka, save me and give me all my wild game animals. Bring them near me, so that my people may have plenty to eat."

These things he had asked many times, but now he wanted a more immediate favor. The Sioux were facing a showdown with the U.S. Army, and he wished for divine aid in battle—and perhaps even a portent of how the fighting would go. In hopes of winning his god's blessings, he made a vow to sponsor a sun dance, the most solemn of religious ceremonies. He further promised to offer up, during its performance, "a scarlet blanket"—a copious flow of his own blood.

All that could be done to ensure success in war had already been done. From this bluff along Rosebud Creek about 60 miles south of its confluence with the Yellowstone River, Sitting Bull overlooked an awesome assemblage of Sioux—perhaps 15,000 souls, among them some 4,000 fighting men. Most of the bands here belonged to the Teton Sioux tribal division that, for nearly a century, had dominated a range extending from the western portion of present-day North and South Dakota deep into Montana, Wyoming and Nebraska.

The great camp had no acknowledged supreme leader, but one man claimed the deference of every warrior present: Sitting Bull, chief of the Hunkpapa band, who could count more than 60 coups. True, there were

chiefs whose credentials as warriors were as great or greater. For instance, Crazy Horse of the Oglala band was considered a fighting man without peer. But Sitting Bull was something more, something extraordinary. He was said to be a familiar of the spirit world, which spoke to him in dreams or through animals. A member of his own band said, with stark simplicity, that Sitting Bull was "big medicine."

He needed all his gifts now, and all the guidance that his offering of blood might win, for the whites intended to crush the Sioux once and for all. Surveying almost three miles of tipis stretched out before him, Sitting Bull prayed: "Let good men on earth have more power, let them be of good heart, so that all Sioux people may get along well and be happy."

Sitting Bull was born in 1831 at Grand River, in what is now South Dakota, the only son of a Hunkpapa warrior called Returns-Again. At first, Returns-Again named his son "Slow" because, as an infant, he was deliberate in his ways, careful rather than abrupt in seizing food or objects. He kept the name only into the first years of adolescence.

Returns-Again was a mystic, as his son would be. On occasion he could communicate with animals. It was a gift of particular significance when it involved the revered buffalos, considered by the Sioux to be spiritual beings as well as the principal source of food, clothing and most things useful to man. One night, while on a hunt, Returns-Again and three warriors were squatting over a campfire when they heard strange sounds—a muttering vaguely like speech. As the noise came nearer they saw that it emanated from a lone buffalo bull which had approached their fire. After brief puzzlement, Returns-Again understood that the bull was repeating, in a snuffling sort of litany, four names: Sitting Bull, Jumping Bull, Bull Standing with Cow and Lone Bull. As

After the conquest of Custer, Sitting Bull was the most famed of chiefs—"the hero of his race," said an officer who knew him in the 1880s, when this portrait was made.

195

the only man present who grasped the message of the beast-god, he concluded that he was being offered a choice of new names to take for himself or give to others; he promptly adopted the first, Sitting Bull.

In time, his young son grew up in the warrior tradition of the Sioux, feasting on the battle tales of older men. When Slow was 14, his father gave the boy a coup stick, the slender wand with which he could gain prestige by touching or striking an enemy in battle.

The chance to use it came when a 20-man war party set out on a raid to capture horses from a traditional enemy, the Crows. The boy painted his gray pony red and himself yellow, and sneaked away in the raiders' wake. When the enemy was sighted, Slow dashed ahead of the older warriors. A Crow dismounted to aim an arrow at the charging boy, but Slow struck him with his coup stick and galloped unscathed out of range. This was all he had wanted: first physical contact with the enemy; he left the actual killing to his elders.

Back in camp, his father, filled with pride, formally divested himself of his own new name and bestowed it on the boy: "My son has struck the enemy," he cried. "He is brave! From this time forward his name will be Ta-tan-ka I-yo-ta-ke"—Sitting Bull.

Young Sitting Bull was not handsome, but women liked him, finding him courteous and gentle. He would marry nine times. Paradoxically, one of the first human beings he killed was a woman; but he took her life as an act of mercy. She was a Crow, a captive taken in a raid. Ordinarily she might have been adopted into the band, but the women of the camp came to the conclusion that she was a whore. Puritanical about sexual matters, they lashed her to a pine tree, heaped brush around her and set it afire. But before the flames reached her, Sitting Bull, then only 17, fitted an arrow to his bowstring and killed her.

As an adolescent, he became aware of special ties to the spirit world. While taking a rest during a hunting foray in the Grand River bottoms, he dreamed that a grizzly bear was poised over him and that a bird nearby was urging him to play dead. Opening his eyes and discovering that the bear and bird were real, he followed the dream's advice and froze. The grizzly, after snuffling at him, wandered away. Later, at a lake in the Black Hills, he heard a call from a spot high on a rocky crag. He climbed the butte and found an eagle perched there.

He interpreted the experience as a prophecy that he would one day rise to lead all his people.

He received his first serious battle wound in single combat with a Crow during a horse-stealing raid. He and the other Sioux warriors drove a large number of horses from the enemy camp under cover of night, but the infuriated Crows caught up with them in the morning. When battle was joined, Sitting Bull went after a Crow who wore a red shirt with ermine trimming—the garb of a chief. Both men dismounted, guns and buffalo-hide shields in hand. The Crow shot first; his bullet ripped through Sitting Bull's shield and plowed a furrow through the sole of his left foot. Then Sitting Bull fired. The Crow fell and Sitting Bull finished him off with a knife—but for the rest of his life he walked with a limp.

In a society that esteemed warfare as life's central activity, Sitting Bull advanced with the bravest fighting men. By 25 he had been made a leader of the Strong Hearts, an elite military society. The position entitled him to wear a long red sash around his shoulders. During a battle, he was required to choose a point in the midst of the melee, stake himself there by pinning one end of the sash to the ground, and never retreat unless another Strong Heart released him. The office was a worthy role for a man of Sitting Bull's temperament. His peers observed that he was like the buffalo: headstrong, fearless, opinionated, incapable of surrender—in short, bull-headed. In a winter blizzard the buffalo never turned tail as domestic cattle do; instead they faced the gale and plowed ahead.

Sitting Bull was designated the chief of the Hunkpapas in the 1860s, just when the greatest issue facing his people—the encroachment of the whites—was coming to a head. During the middle of the decade, some of the finest Sioux buffalo grounds were being disrupted by a heavy traffic of miners along the new Bozeman Trail, which led from the Fort Laramie area on the Oregon Trail northwestward to Virginia City and other gold camps in Montana Territory. Chief Red Cloud of the Oglalas, whose people resided in the path of these intruders, attacked the traffic along the trail so ferociously and persistently that, by 1868, the government was ready to make peace at a high price.

Washington offered the Sioux, along with some northern members of the Cheyenne and Arapaho tribes, a spacious reservation encompassing the entire western

An autobiographical sketch made by Sitting Bull and copied by his uncle recalls the day he won his first war honors at age 14 by riding down and counting coup on a Crow. The image of a bull is his signature.

half of present-day South Dakota. Moreover, the proposal—to be known as the Treaty of Laramie—declared that the Powder River Country, immediately to the west of the reservation and reaching as far as the Big Horn Mountains, "shall be considered to be unceded Indian Territory" and that "no white person or persons shall be permitted to settle upon or occupy any portion of the same." In other words, this region was to be reserved for the exclusive use of the Indians, who were explicitly guaranteed that it would be a sanctuary where they could hunt for as long as the buffalo roamed there.

In May 1868 the Jesuit missionary Father Pierre Jean De Smet, who for decades had worked among Western Indians, visited Sitting Bull's camp near the mouth of the Powder River and tried to persuade him to accept the agreement. Sitting Bull was unimpressed by its terms; he focused on the fact that the treaty,

while generous-sounding, would considerably diminish the vast ancestral range of the Sioux.

In an impassioned speech he told the priest: "I wish all to know that I do not propose to sell any part of my country, nor will I have the whites cutting our timber along the rivers, especially the oaks. I am particularly fond of the little groves of oak trees. I love to look at them, and feel a reverence for them, because they endure in the wintry storms and summer's heat, and—not unlike ourselves—seem to thrive and flourish by them."

He refused to sign, although many other Sioux chiefs, including Red Cloud, accepted the terms and retired to the reservation—so large that it was serviced by five separate agencies.

Over the next few years, both the reservation Sioux and those who, like Sitting Bull, chose to remain in the unceded area, discovered that the Treaty of Laramie

197

A WARRIOR'S PRIVATE MAGIC

A Sioux warrior's most precious possession was his personal, dream-inspired "medicine bundle"—an array of religious talismans and herbs that was brought out on the eve of battle and used in intricate ceremonies designed to ward off harm. Sitting Bull reportedly prepared himself for combat with the articles below. They include *(clockwise from left)* a wooden bowl, with a stone pestle surrounded by a woven ring of herbs; a turtle-shell cup cradling a bowl which, in turn, holds birch bark and a wild radish; a rattle; a pouch of sacred paint; an eagle-bone whistle; and the skin of a mink stuffed with 10 different herbal remedies.

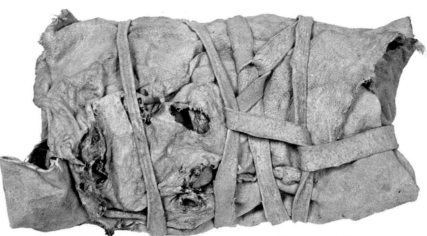

A deerskin cover protected the war-magic used by Sitting Bull.

was by no means the last word in the disposition of the old Sioux range. Predictably, the unceded territory suffered the first incursion. In 1872, surveyors for the Northern Pacific Railroad, seeking the most economical route from Duluth, Minnesota, to the Pacific, decided that the tracks should follow the south bank of the Yellowstone River, in unceded Indian lands. Officials in Washington expressed no objections; on the contrary, the Army supplied troops to protect the surveyors as they located the tracks where they desired.

That summer, the Sioux mounted several brisk attacks against the survey teams and their Army guardians. In one engagement, Sitting Bull conceived a superbly courageous and insulting gesture that quickly became famous among Sioux everywhere. At the height of the fire fight, he strode into the open between the two forces, seated himself on the ground, filled his pipe, set it alight with flint and steel, and sat there smoking while the bullets ripped past him. He did not budge until the pipe was finished and the bowl scraped clean.

Such sporadic combat would inevitably have ripened into full-scale war had the railroad survey been followed up by actual construction. Disaster was temporarily averted, however, when the U.S. economy sank into depression in 1873 and the Northern Pacific found itself without the funds to build trackage.

But the next year, the federal government itself set its sights on a precious chunk of the Sioux reservation. The Army decided that, to guard Northern Pacific workers when the construction got underway, a new fort should be erected in the Black Hills—a well-watered and heavily timbered region of granite crags on the western edge of the reservation. A reconnaissance team under Lieutenant Colonel George Armstrong Custer was sent out to locate a suitable site. Custer, a reckless glorymonger, found a way to win himself national headlines while on the mission. When geologists with the party detected traces of gold in the hills, Custer sent glowing reports to the East which led the press to hail his discovery as the new golconda. By the middle of 1875, nearly a thousand prospectors were illegally camped in the Black Hills, which the Sioux regarded as a sacred dwelling place of spirits.

The government, disinclined to evict the miners, sent commissioners to the reservation to ask a price for the region. Red Cloud, who had been criticized by his people for acquiescing to the whites earlier, said that $600,000,000 would be fair; this stupendous figure, plucked out of the air, was more than twice as great as all federal expenditures for the year. The commissioners swallowed hard and countered with an offer of $6,000,000. Compromise proved impossible.

The government promptly moved to impress its might upon the Sioux. If the Black Hills could not be purchased at the moment, then at least the unceded lands could be summarily taken away. In November 1875, the Commissioner of Indian Affairs, following the instructions of President Grant—known to the Indians as the "Great Father"—ordered that all Sioux report inside the reservation. If the order was disobeyed, the commissioner added that "they shall be deemed hostile and treated accordingly by the military force."

Sitting Bull and most other off-reservation chiefs ignored the ultimatum; and in March 1876, General George Crook took to the field with 10 companies of cavalry and two of infantry to make good the Indian commissioner's threat. His forces attacked an Indian encampment of about 100 tipis under a high bluff on the Tongue River; they set fire to the tipis but, hampered by a late-winter blizzard, failed to win a clear victory. Ironically, their victims were Cheyennes who, hearing of soldiers abroad, had been hastening across the Sioux range to find safety on the reservation. In the past, this Cheyenne band had been friendly to whites, but after the unprovoked assault, they became implacable enemies.

Sitting Bull took in some Cheyenne refugees. Calling a council, he said, "We must stand together or they will kill us separately. These soldiers have come shooting; they want war. All right, we'll give it to them." He sent couriers to every Sioux, Cheyenne and Arapaho camp, both on reservation and off, summoning them to a rendezvous on Rosebud Creek. Hundreds of men, weary of reservation life, sensing the Black Hills too would be lost if nothing were done, heeded the call. Now, in June, they were joined in a single great Indian army—and the soldiers were coming to meet them.

Three hordes of bluecoats were converging on the Indian camp. Nearest to them was General George Crook —known to the Indians as "Three Stars"—advancing with 1,047 soldiers from Fort Fetterman in the south and 262 Shoshoni and Crow scouts acquired while en

The spirited dance of the chiefs, registering the great esteem in which the Sioux hold their guest, is staged in front of the leader's tipi.

The vivid language of the Indian dance

In 1876, when Sitting Bull concluded that a final showdown with the United States Army was in the offing, he immediately sought spiritual guidance through the elaborate ritual of the sun dance. The Sioux resorted to a dance at virtually every critical moment for the tribe — and on many everyday occasions as well. Artist George Catlin, who visited the Sioux in 1832, was so impressed by their huge repertoire of dervish-like ceremonies that he said he was tempted to rename them "the dancing Indians."

Some of the dances that the artist captured on canvas during his sojourn among the Sioux were acts of supplication: thus, in the bear dance *(lower right),* hunters sought the forgiveness of a bear spirit, whose animal form they wished to slay. Other dances were strictly social; for instance, one understandably popular festival was staged to bring together young men and women under properly chaperoned circumstances. Another social event that gave Catlin particular pleasure was the dance of the chiefs *(above),* which saluted honored visitors — in this case, none other than the painter himself.

But the ceremony that most impressed Catlin was the scalp dance *(upper right),* a grisly pageant in which warriors celebrated victory over an enemy. The Indians, wrote the artist, "brandished their weapons, and barked and yelped in the most frightful manner, all jumping on both feet at a time, with a simultaneous stamp, and blow, and thrust of their weapons — as if they were actually cutting and carving each other to pieces."

A fortnight after Sitting Bull sought divine guidance in the sun dance, the Sioux staged just such a victory rite in the Big Horn Mountains, flaunting the scalps of cavalrymen who had been led by the vainglorious George Custer.

In a frenzied performance of the scalp dance, triumphant warriors wave freshly taken war trophies and re-enact their deeds of daring in battle.

Before a bear hunt, dancers, led by a medicine man covered with a bear skin, imitate the motions and sounds of their intended quarry.

This sacred buffalo skull, owned by Sitting Bull and obtained (and labeled) by a woman missionary after he died, was part of the sun dance ritual. He may have used it when he received his portent of Custer's defeat.

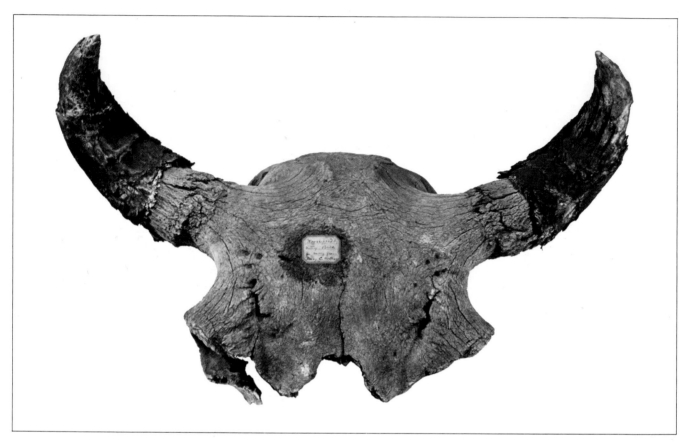

route. From the west, following the Yellowstone River, approached Colonel John Gibbon with some 450 men out of Fort Ellis in Montana Territory. And from the east, out of Fort Abraham Lincoln on the Missouri in Dakota Territory, came 925 men under the command of General Alfred Terry. Terry's force included the 7th Cavalry under the impetuous Lieutenant Colonel Custer, who had brought on much of this trouble by his ballyhoo of gold in the Black Hills.

And so the time had arrived for Chief Sitting Bull to sacrifice the scarlet blanket on his people's behalf and to arrange for the sun dance. First, men noted for their bravery were sent out to select a symbolic Enemy: a suitably forked cottonwood tree which they ceremonially struck with their coup sticks. Then a group of chaste women went to the spot and helped to fell the tree. Once down, its branches were trimmed away as high as the fork. Finally, the Enemy was carried back to camp by the men; they had to bear the burden on poles, since contact with the symbol was forbidden to everyone except the priests who presided over the ritual and those who had previously danced the sun dance.

Preparation of the Enemy entailed painting the tree red on the west side, blue on the north, green on the east and yellow on the south, then erecting it in a hole. At the top were bound a red robe, offerings of cherrywood sticks and tobacco, and two pieces of dried buffalo hide, one cut in the shape of a buffalo and the other in the shape of a man.

At daybreak on the day of Sitting Bull's sacrifice, the priests who supervised the ceremony repaired to the summit of a nearby hill and prayed for blue skies on that day; Sitting Bull would be called upon to stare at the sun, periodically shifting his gaze to the bottom rim of the sun to avoid blinding himself.

Sitting Bull could not have underestimated the ordeal ahead. He was 45 years old that summer of 1876, and he had been through this bloodletting ceremony before, as scars on his chest and back attested. However, since the idea of sacrifice held a very intense and personal meaning to a devout Sioux, he must have felt something bordering on grim ecstasy. Moreover,

Sitting Bull was given this crucifix in 1868 by Father De Smet, a Jesuit missionary who urged the Sioux to cede land to the whites in the interest of peace. The chief replied, "I will not have my people robbed."

there was the very real, mundane need to retain the respect and prestige he had already earned; only by constant demonstrations of unflinching courage could a leader lay valid claim to greatness.

His hands and feet had been painted red by the priests, and across his shoulders were blue stripes in token of the sky. Now there was the matter of the scarlet blanket he had promised Wakan Tanka, and he was about to offer it up.

He strode to the sacred tree and sat on the ground, legs outstretched, leaning against the trunk. He began to pray, a wailing, singsong petition. His chosen assistant was Jumping Bull, an adoptive brother. Years before, during a raid on an enemy encampment, the Sioux had killed all the members of a family except Jumping Bull, then an 11-year-old boy, who had excited Sitting Bull's admiration by fighting fearlessly in the face of death. Sparing the boy, he had raised him up as a Hunkpapa warrior and given him one of the names derived from his father's vision. Today, he called upon Jumping Bull to serve in his immolation.

With a needle-pointed awl in one hand and a sharp knife in the other, Jumping Bull knelt beside his brother. He began to draw blood at Sitting Bull's right wrist, piercing the skin with the awl and lifting a matchhead-sized bit of tissue, which he sliced off with the knife. The blood came immediately. Jumping Bull moved up the arm with quick precision: pierce, lift, cut — 50 cuts from wrist to shoulder. The vigilant witnesses could attest that Sitting Bull's expression did not change and that there was no alteration in the monotonous wailing of his prayer. Jumping Bull turned to the left arm and duplicated the scarification. Soon the blood covered both arms, dripping from the motionless fingers. This was Wakan Tanka's scarlet blanket. The blood gradually congealed, but the chief's agony was only beginning.

There remained the performance of the sun-gazing dance. Sitting Bull rose from his place against the sacred

trunk, stood facing the sun and began bobbing up and down on his toes in a rhythmic dance that lasted all day. He prayed as he danced and, from time to time, looked straight at the sun as it ascended toward the zenith, coursed down toward the west and disappeared in the ground haze above the crests of the Big Horn Mountains.

He continued dancing, with no food or water to replenish his energies, through the hours of darkness and into the next morning, driving himself to a state of utter exhaustion that would bring on the rite's climax. That moment arrived around noon, when Sitting Bull staggered a few steps and sank to the ground. He had fainted — or, in the Sioux interpretation, actually died a passing death. Then consciousness began to creep back. Out of the mists around him he heard a disembodied voice and saw human forms taking shape and moving against the blackness of his delirium. They were soldiers of the white man's army, entering the great Sioux encampment. But surely they were not coming as conquerors; these were men in defeat, their heads bent and campaign hats falling.

When he became conscious again, Sitting Bull knew there was to be a victory and so informed the Sioux. But he was nonetheless troubled, because the vision had also carried a warning. "These soldiers are gifts of Wakan Tanka," he told his people. "Kill them, but do not take their guns or horses. If you set your hearts upon the goods of the white man, it will prove a curse to this nation."

After the ceremony's completion, the great camp was moved. While boys rounded up the stock, the women took down the tipis, folded the heavy hide covers, and packed household goods and children on horse-drawn travois — simple sledges that were made of poles. Before night had fallen the campground was empty and the massed bands were traveling westward together, up and over a hilly saddle and on toward the Little Big-

Chiefs and white delegates meet at Fort Laramie in 1868 to hammer out a treaty pledging the Sioux a 41,000-square-mile reservation in Dakota Territory — plus clothing, rations and one cow per family. Cynical about such promises and uninterested in farming, Sitting Bull refused to attend.

Seeking safety in Canada after defeating Custer, Sitting Bull and his followers spent four years at the camp located on this contemporary map — only to return, homesick, to the United States and reservation life.

horn River, which the Indians called the Greasy Grass.

They were not fleeing, even though General Crook was almost upon them. The Sioux had not foregathered only to run away, and they were confident in their numbers and their pride. This time they would strike first and in force. The warriors painted their faces and bodies for war, and took up their coup sticks, weapons and shields of buffalo hide. About half of the warriors had guns. A few carried modern repeating rifles, but most possessed only old muzzle-loaders. The rest were armed with bows and arrows, lances and war clubs.

Led by Crazy Horse, the warriors left the camp and rode back across the saddle toward Rosebud Creek and southward. It was then — early in the morning of June 17 — that they took Crook by surprise in the Battle of the Rosebud (*pages 156-157*). In a brilliant display of generalship, unprecedented in Crook's experience of Indian-style warfare, Crazy Horse launched wave after wave of mass attacks that cut deep into the white army's disorganized defenses. When a twist of fate and the skill of Crook's Indian scouts deflected the Sioux onslaught, Crazy Horse made an orderly withdrawal from the battlefield. After the engagement, Crook claimed a victory, but it could not have been a very satisfactory one. Crazy Horse's assault had stopped his advance in its tracks, forcing him to halt, regroup, and wait for supplies and reinforcements. He fought no more that month.

Sitting Bull did not participate in the combat at Rosebud Creek. He may have been there — accounts differ — but on that day, only the third after the sun dance, his racked body was in no condition for battle. In any event, no matter how the Battle of the Rosebud was viewed, it certainly could not be regarded as the fulfillment of his prophecy. The 28 white men who were killed there, and the 50 or so wounded, had in no way been brought to disgrace.

Crook was stopped, but Gibbon and Terry were still coming. Custer was under orders to circle about and swing up on the Indians from the south, pinching them against Gibbon's force, but he threw strategy to the winds when he came across the broad trail left by the moving Sioux encampment. Uninterested in sharing the glory of a victory with the other commanders, Custer raced after the Indians, following the trail that led toward the Little Bighorn River. When he found them on June 25, he committed a disastrous error of judg-

ment. Against a numerically superior enemy, he split his force, sending Major Marcus Reno and about a fourth of the men to create a diversion, while he took five companies of cavalrymen to strike the Sioux camp from another angle.

Custer was reckless; the Sioux were overconfident. Despite several sightings of the approaching enemy, they failed to realize the immediacy of their danger. Not the first military force to relax after an illusory victory, they might have been caught unprepared but for two Hunkpapa boys out looking for stray horses. These youths crossed the cavalry's trail and found a pack shucked by a mule during the night's march. They broke it open and were breakfasting on the hard bread it contained when an Army patrol, looking for the lost pack, stumbled on them. One boy was killed; the other got back to the encampment to raise the alarm.

Even so the Indians were not fully ready when Major Reno's diversionary attack came across the river, striking the southern Hunkpapa sector of the great camp. The boy's warning caught Sitting Bull in the council lodge; he hurried to his own tipi and took up his weapons, a .45 revolver and an 1873 model Winchester carbine.

One Bull, his 23-year-old nephew, joined him, and they galloped from the camp to meet the soldiers. Sitting Bull sat on his war horse and watched as Reno's men began to fall. Within minutes, the major was trying to withdraw. "There were plenty of warriors to meet them," Sitting Bull said afterward. Indeed, Reno, against perhaps 1,000 warriors, never had a chance. When the disorganized force plunged back across the river after about 45 minutes of fighting, almost half of Reno's 150 men were killed, wounded or missing.

Thus the fulfillment of the prophecy began to unfold. There were indeed plenty of warriors, and there was no need of Sitting Bull's maimed arms that day. Nor was his advice needed in matters of tactics; Crazy Horse and other war chiefs would make his vision come true. So, when One Bull quirted his horse into the stream to follow Reno's retreating men, Sitting Bull called him back. It was time, he told his nephew, to make provision against the likelihood of more bluecoats returning to attack the women and children.

They rode north, downstream through the encampment, until they came upon a scene of wild confusion.

SITTING BULL'S NEW HOME.

Map Showing the Site of the Recent Powwow and the Indian Country Lying on Both Sides of the Border.

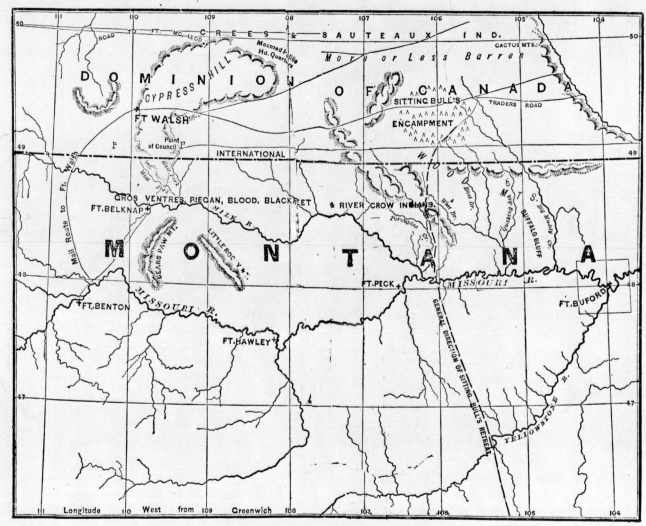

Boys were rounding up horses from the pack herd; barking dogs and excited children were everywhere underfoot; and hundreds of women milled about, uncertain whether to stay or flee. Confusion became pandemonium when a line of soldiers on gray cavalry mounts —Custer's troopers—appeared along the crest of the low hills across the river.

Firing broke out there as Sioux began to appear on both flanks of the cavalry. Instead of charging, the troopers dismounted. Sitting Bull looked on from a distance as a great mass of Sioux, exultant after cutting up Reno's force, gathered to overwhelm Custer. The deadly drama was hidden in a great cloud of dust, but the chief had seen the outcome before, in his vision.

Nobody has ever been able to determine with certainty how Custer himself was killed, except that his body was found with a bullet wound in the head and one in the chest. Another of Sitting Bull's nephews, 26-year-old White Bull, a formidable fighting man, believed he was the slayer. "A tall soldier with yellow hair and moustache saw me. . . .When I rushed him, he threw his rifle at me without shooting. I lashed him across the face with my quirt, striking the coup. He hit me with his fists on the jaw and shoulders, then grabbed

my braids with both hands and tried to bite my nose off. He drew his pistol. I wrenched it out of his hand and struck him with it three or four times on the head, knocked him over, shot him in the head and fired at his heart." Custer's death was only one satisfaction of many. In the space of an hour, the Sioux had virtually destroyed the core of the 7th Cavalry. Custer's contingent of 215 men was completely wiped out. Indian losses were not recorded; but whatever the total, the victory was worth it.

It is not known whether Sitting Bull offered up any particular thanksgiving to Wakan Tanka for the day's outcome; he may have felt that he had already fulfilled his part of the bargain with his offering of the scarlet blanket. Nevertheless, he had reason for new concern before the day was out. He had told the Sioux that Custer's troopers were gifts from their god to be slain, but

he had warned against looting. The warning went unheeded. By nightfall the camp was laden with booty — cavalry saddles, uniforms, pistols, carbines and about 10,000 rounds of cartridges.

The battle had ended, and neither Sitting Bull nor his people would ever witness another day like it. It was a triumph, but it was also the beginning of the preordained end.

In September Sitting Bull witnessed proof that the looting of Custer's men would bring grief to the Sioux. The great assembly had split up in order to hunt buffalo more efficiently. General Crook's men attacked 37 lodges of Oglala, Brule and Miniconjou Sioux at Slim Buttes, only 30 miles from the Hunkpapa encampment on Grand River northeast of the Black Hills. By the time Sitting Bull arrived at the campsite with a relief force, it was too late. The village had been destroyed.

At Fort Yates in the 1880s, Sitting Bull (*standing at center*) harangues U.S. representatives, rebuffing one of the government's periodic attempts to persuade the Sioux to sell off reservation lands. He was so adept at obstructing negotiations that authorities sometimes would not let him speak.

There were many corpses—young men, old men and women, children, babies—and the soldiers had also scalped some of the Indian dead. At Slim Buttes, the Army recovered much Custer property, including the 7th Cavalry's once-proud guidon.

In the aftermath of the defeat, some Indians gave up, but Sitting Bull did not and could not; surrender was not his way. About a month later, Lieutenant Colonel E. S. Otis, who was escorting supply wagons along the Yellowstone, received a written communication that was evidently sent by the Hunkpapa chief. "I want to know what you are doing on this road," it said. "You scare all the buffalo away. I want to hunt in this place. I want you to turn back from here. If you don't, I will fight you again."

Otis' superior officer, the veteran Indian-fighter Colonel Nelson Miles, decided to meet with the chief for a talk, hoping that he could persuade Sitting Bull to go peaceably to the reservation agency. The parley, arranged through an intermediary, began in a civil enough manner but soon degenerated into mutual angry suspicion. "No Indian that ever lived loved the white man," Sitting Bull declared, "and no white man that ever lived loved the Indian."

The meeting broke up and there was an exchange of shots. The soldiers, who had been the first to fire, drove the Sioux from the parley site and engaged them in a running battle that lasted for two days. The Indians counterattacked vigorously, setting fire to the grass and on one occasion forcing their pursuers into a traplike hollow. But Colonel Miles had artillery, which he employed with skill to keep Sitting Bull's forces from pressing too closely, and the 42-mile chase ended in a Sioux rout. In their flight the Indians abandoned camp

209

The society matron and the Sioux chief

During his long fight to salvage something of the Sioux's ancestral lands, Sitting Bull was grateful for help from virtually any quarter—even from a New York society woman. In the spring of 1889, Mrs. Catherine Weldon, a smartly outfitted widow in her middle years, arrived at the reservation on the pretext of painting the chief's portrait. Moving in with him and his two surviving wives, she had ample opportunity to achieve the real purpose of her mission: she persuaded the famous chief to make a tour campaigning against the government's efforts to open Indian reservations to white settlement—a cause that deeply concerned her as an activist in an Eastern humanitarian group, the National Indian Defense Association.

Alarmed, the Sioux's Indian agent, James McLaughlin, scuttled the plan by refusing to give the chief a pass to leave the reservation. To drive the disruptive matron away, McLaughlin circulated rumors that she was in love with Sitting Bull and had tried to arouse his warlike impulses by reading him biographies of Napoleon and Alexander the Great.

During her stay in his home, Mrs. Weldon did arouse other impulses in the chief by cooking his meals and doing housework. Sitting Bull, interpreting these actions by Sioux standards, proposed marriage. Shocked and irate, Mrs. Weldon left the reservation soon afterward, leaving the finished portrait behind. When Indian police tried to arrest Sitting Bull a few months later and ended up killing him, one of the policemen slashed the portrait—as if to kill him twice.

Mrs. Weldon's portrait of Sitting Bull shows the damage inflicted at the time of his death.

equipment, tons of meat and broken-down ponies.

After the battle, on October 27, a discouraged group of Miniconjou and Sans Arc chiefs approached Miles and attempted to surrender with 2,000 of their people. Miles, however, was not able to feed so large a number. Instead, he accepted five chiefs as hostages against the guarantee that the Sioux bands would turn themselves in at the Cheyenne River Agency. On November 30, about 40 lodges of Indians — the immediate following of the five chiefs — gave themselves up. The rest of them joined Crazy Horse.

The Sioux at the agency signed documents relinquishing all claims to the Black Hills and the Powder River country — about a third of the lands that had been guaranteed to them. They had little choice: Congress had ordered the suspension of rations and other subsistence until the Indians bowed to the white demands.

Even Crazy Horse, the brilliant Oglala leader, decided that the war was hopeless. He surrendered, although he did so with characteristic panache. He and perhaps 1,500 followers rode into the reservation the following spring decked out in war paint and feathers, carrying their shields and weapons in plain view and singing their war songs. It was a hollow gesture. Later that year, the authorities, hearing rumors that Crazy Horse was planning to make trouble again, ordered him to be locked up in the Fort Robinson guardhouse. When soldiers tried to seize him, the war chief resisted. He was stabbed in the abdomen with a bayonet and died a few hours later.

Meanwhile, Sitting Bull had turned northward toward his last refuge. In May 1877, he took his people into Canada, the land ruled by the "Great Mother" — Queen Victoria.

The sojourn north of the border lasted four years. It was a time of peace, but not of contentment. The Great Mother, acting through the North-West Mounted Police, was correct if not overly hospitable. There was no harassment by troops, but Sitting Bull's repeated requests for assignment of a vast Sioux reserve were as repeatedly refused. Moreover, at Washington's urging, the Mounted Police forbade raiding south of the border on pain of expulsion.

In October 1877, General Alfred Terry headed a peace commission to offer a full pardon if Sitting Bull would bring his people back home to a U.S. reservation. Sitting Bull replied angrily, "This country is my country now, and I intend to stay here and raise people up to fill it. We did not give our country to you; you stole it. You come here to tell lies; when you go home, take them with you."

But the band he had brought through the line of stone cairns that marked the border kept melting away until, by 1881, he had only 185 followers left. Most were his relatives, most were old, all longed for their old home, and all were hungry, since the hunting was poor in Canada. After an appeal to the Canadian government for rations was refused, Sitting Bull finally gave up, for the sake of his people. "I am thrown away," he said in despair to an officer of the Mounted Police. Then he led the last sad remnant of his band toward Fort Buford, 70 miles south of the border near the Dakota-Montana line.

Lieutenant William Bowen, who witnessed the arrival, felt pity, seeing in the 50-year-old chief "the ravages of worry and hunger he had gone through. He was getting old. Giving in to the hated whites and the final surrender of his cherished independence was a hard blow to his pride. He was much broken."

Broken in power, perhaps, but not in his proud heart. He conceded nothing. "The land I have under my feet is mine again," he told Major David Brotherton. "I never sold it; I never gave it to anybody." Quietly he handed his rifle to his eight-year-old son, Crowfoot, and indicated that it should be handed to the major.

Sitting Bull had nine years of life left to him. They were strange years, often desolate, now and then lighted by sparks of defiance, burdened with a constant weight of mortification. But some quality of the chief's spirit seemed to lift him above humiliation, leaving the essence of the man untarnished.

For two years Sitting Bull was held as a prisoner of war at Fort Randall, on the southern edge of the reservation. Then, in 1883, he was moved to the Standing Rock Agency, located on the Missouri River, 320 miles to the northwest. The whites, having nothing to fear from him, now that he had formally relinquished his weapons, lionized him. In September 1884, under the sponsorship of a showman named Alvaren Allen, Sitting Bull began a tour of 15 American cities, lured into this bizarre enterprise by an unkept promise of a

Losing ground in the white man's West

The final surrender of Sitting Bull and his 185 ragged followers in the summer of 1881 marked the finish of the Plains Indians as a nomadic, hunter-warrior people. But their acceptance of a sedentary life within reservation boundaries did not put an end to white pressure for lands assigned to the Sioux by treaty.

At that time, Western tribes still held title to almost a quarter million square miles of reservation tracts, as shown on the 1881 government map at right. But sodbusters and cattlemen were constantly pushing for laws that would open Indian-held lands for new settlement. In 1886 they threw their support behind the proposal of Senator Henry Dawes of Massachusetts, a misguided humanitarian who felt that the best way to civilize the owners was to have the government give each Indian family 160 acres for farming—plus a share in the profits gleaned from the sale to whites of all the rest.

After the Dawes Act sailed through Congress in 1887, the uncomprehending Indians were persuaded to sign away huge chunks of land for as little as 50 cents an acre—although Sitting Bull's hard bargaining helped to boost his people's reimbursement to $1.25 per acre. By 1889 the act had cost Western tribes about 61,000 square miles of reservation land— 16,000 of which had been carved out of the ancestral hunting grounds of the Sioux. Witnessing this dismemberment, one old Sioux remarked to a minister that the white men had "made us many promises but only kept one; they promised to take our land and they took it."

A map drawn for the Bureau of Indian Affairs in 1881 shows reservations held by the Western tribes (tan) and notes their populations. The sections tinted pink were being bought by treaty for white settlement.

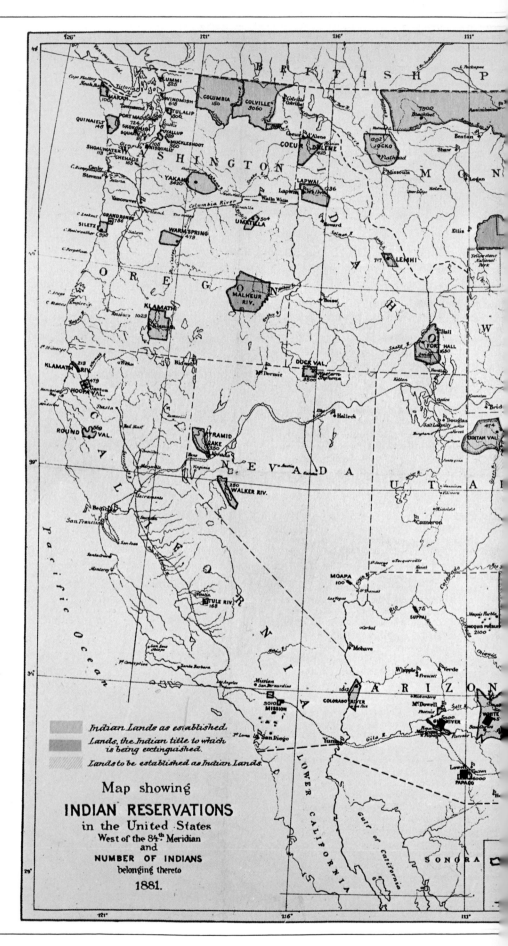

Indian Lands as established.

Lands, the Indian title to which is being extinguished.

Lands to be established as Indian Lands.

Map showing
INDIAN RESERVATIONS
in the United States
West of the 84th Meridian
and
NUMBER OF INDIANS
belonging thereto
1881.

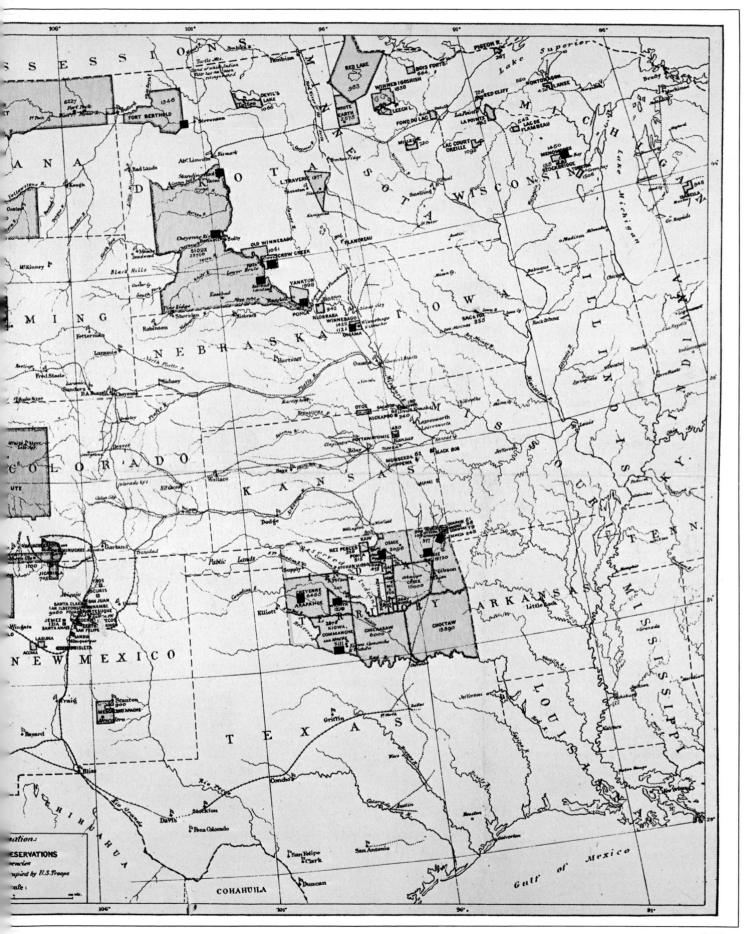

talk with the President about his people's difficulties.

Allen billed him as "the Slayer of General Custer," and had his friendly greetings to the crowds interpreted as a hair-raising account of the Battle of Little Bighorn. On this tour he was dazzled by the skills of another traveling performer, Annie Oakley, who could shoot a cigarette from the mouth of her husband or hit a dime held between his fingers. Watching her, Sitting Bull repeatedly exclaimed, *"Watanya cicilia."* His words, translated correctly for once, meant "Little Sure Shot," and the nickname stuck to her ever afterward.

In 1885, Buffalo Bill Cody took Sitting Bull on the road with his Wild West show, and on this trip he actually did meet with the President, although there is no record that he was able to discuss Sioux problems. However, he became fast friends with Cody, who paid him $50 a week and treated him respectfully. Upon the chief's retirement from show business that year, Cody presented him with a fine gray horse and a white sombrero. When a relative wore the hat one day, Sitting Bull became furious, saying, "I value it very highly, for the hand that placed it upon my head had a friendly feeling for me."

In 1887, Buffalo Bill invited Sitting Bull to travel to London with the Wild West show and attend Queen Victoria's Golden Jubilee. But not even for the chance to meet the Great Mother would the old chief go. "It is bad for our cause for me to parade around," he said. "I am needed here. There is more talk of taking our lands." Indeed there was. The government wanted to sweep away another 10 million acres of the great Sioux preserve in western Dakota, offering 50 cents an acre—an extraordinarily low price even for those times.

Sitting Bull fought back. He persuaded other reservation chiefs that the price was completely inadequate; the government, after all, proposed to sell it subsequently to homesteaders at the rate of $1.25 an acre. By the time commissioners arrived at the Standing Rock Agency in July 1888, Sitting Bull had the fight won. He had so effectively convinced the leaders there not to have anything to do with the transaction that, when they were asked to sign one of two papers indicating acceptance or refusal, most of them refused to sign either one and simply walked away.

In October of that year, Sitting Bull traveled to Washington with a delegation of 60 Sioux leaders and,

215

holding them together against temptation, pressed the Secretary of the Interior, William Vilas, until the government's offer was raised to $1 an acre. This still did not satisfy the Indians. In 1889, Congress increased the offer again, to $1.25 per acre; and the deal was further sweetened by the government's promise to give the head of each Indian family 320 acres of land—the title to be held in trust by the government for 25 years so that speculators could not swindle them out of it. Sitting Bull—who apparently was prepared to turn down any offer, no matter how high—could no longer hold the Sioux ranks in line. This time the government received the necessary signatures. Later, someone asked him to comment on the Indians' sentiments about the transaction. "Indians!" he snorted. "There are no Indians left but me!"

From that point, it was all downhill. An economy-minded Congress ordered the Sioux beef ration cut by half. They were no longer to be feared as enemies, only resented as expensive consumers of charity. In 1889 and 1890, undernourished Indian children died in epidemics of measles, influenza and whooping cough. At the same time, the Indians suffered disastrous crop failures; these were predicted by Sitting Bull, whose old powers of divination had apparently not entirely deserted him. But his communicants, the birds of the air, seemed to bring him nothing but bitter tidings. Where once an eagle had forecast that he would lead his people, now a meadowlark told him, "The Sioux will kill you." Sitting Bull accepted the new burden, possibly the heaviest; he did not question his gods.

In 1889, rumors of a miraculous Indian redemption came from farther west. In Nevada, while the sun was "dead" during an eclipse, a young Paiute mystic by the name of Wovoka had fallen into a trance. When he awoke, he told others that he had been taken up into the spirit world.

Wovoka claimed he had received a revelation of great things to come—probably in the spring of 1891. The dead would rise. Indians already alive would live forever. The buffalo would return in their millions. The white oppressors would disappear.

Commandments of the new faith, as Wovoka unfolded them, called for scrupulously innocent behavior: no fighting, no war, nothing that savored of war, no stealing, no lying, no cruelty. "A better religion than they ever had before," commented a white observer.

In addition to obeying these precepts, adherents were supposed to perform a dance that Wovoka claimed he had learned on his visit to the spirit world. By dancing regularly, he said, Indians might briefly "die" and gain a glimpse of the paradise-to-come. The ritual dance was the essence of simplicity: the worshippers—each of them painted with a sacred red pigment—shuffled counterclockwise in a circle, moving slowly at first but then picking up tempo while singing songs acclaiming the resurrection. Many participants succeeded in their quest for a trance and awoke to tell marvelous tales of meeting with dead kinsmen and seeing the hosts of the past marching into the present.

To a people in despair, defeated, subjected to humiliation, disease and grinding hardship, Wovoka's religion was almost irresistibly attractive. Apostles and delegates carried news of the revelations to most of the tribes in the West. It began to spread like fire in the dry grasses of autumn.

The faith came to be called "the ghost dance religion," a name attached by curious whites because the core of belief hinged on resurrection and reunion with the dead. When the religion first came to the Sioux reservation—brought by a Sioux mystic named Kicking Bear, who had traveled all the way to Nevada to meet Wovoka—Sitting Bull was apparently more tolerant than convinced. He danced at first, but experienced no revelation. "It is impossible for a dead man to return and live again," he told Kicking Bear. Although Sitting Bull remained unconvinced, he refused to interfere with those who performed the dance, since he respected faith in all of its guises.

Like other peoples who had picked up the new religion, the Sioux added a unique touch of their own—a small alteration, but one that appeared to taint the basic innocence of the rite. They began dancing in loose shirts, adorned with feathers or other trimmings and decorated with curious cabalistic designs. White men inquired after the meaning and function of these garments, which they called ghost shirts. They were advised that the shirts were sacred and impervious armor—proof against an attacker's bullets.

The reply stirred unease in whites, then outright alarm. What need for armor, unless a mass uprising was

217

Sacred armor for a mystical cult

Within months of the founding of the ghost dance religion by a Paiute mystic named Wovoka in 1889, most Plains tribes had seized upon its promise of an imminent, all-Indian millennium and were regularly performing the dance —said to bring on a trance in which this glorious future might be glimpsed.

The movement had no more ardent followers than the Sioux; indeed, they probably introduced its sacred costume, the "ghost shirt," which was worn by both men and women.

The ghost shirts seen here come from various tribes, but their basic design is the same. Made of buckskin, muslin or cotton sewn with sinew, each garment is decorated with symbols revealed to its owner in visions. To the Sioux, however, the ghost shirt had a special—and ultimately disastrous—significance: they believed that it had the magical power to render the wearer invulnerable to the white man's bullets.

SIOUX

KIOWA

ARAPAHO

SIOUX

218

PAWNEE

SIOUX

SIOUX

ARAPAHO

SIOUX

SIOUX

In the mistaken belief that Sitting Bull was behind the ghost dance movement, authorities asked his old friend Buffalo Bill Cody — shown with the chief in 1885 — to coax him to an Army post. But the plan was scrapped and Sitting Bull arrested instead.

being plotted? Agent James McLaughlin reported, "It would seem impossible that any person, no matter how ignorant, could be brought to believe such absurd nonsense, but the infection has been so pernicious that many of our very best Indians appear dazed and undecided when talking of it."

McLaughlin also reported that Sitting Bull, whom he deeply disliked, was the "high priest" of the ghost dance movement. Believing his own imaginings, he journeyed from the Standing Rock Agency to Sitting Bull's camp on the Grand River to try to talk the chief into prohibiting the dance. Evidently more amused than alarmed, Sitting Bull offered a mocking bargain. "You and I will go together to the tribes from which this dance came, and when we reach the last one, where it started, if they cannot produce the Messiah, and if we do not find the dead coming this way, then I will return and tell the Sioux it is all a lie. If we find the Messiah, then you are to let the dance go on."

McLaughlin demurred, taking this for double-talk. He later wrote that "the new religion was managed from the beginning, as far as the Standing Rock Sioux were concerned, by Sitting Bull, who . . . having lost his former influence over the Sioux, planned to import and use it to reestablish himself in the leadership of the people, whom he might then lead in safety in any desperate enterprise which he might direct."

Time ran out quickly in the autumn of 1890. From Washington came orders alerting the Army to take up positions to contain and put down any outbreak. The sudden and highly visible presence of troops in turn alarmed the Indians. Distrustful bands, fearing massacre by the whites, left the vicinity of their agencies and headed for the Badlands, a bleak, heavily eroded region of gullies and crags that lay to the east of the Black Hills. The Army, as apprehensive in its way as the Sioux were in theirs, labeled the fugitives hostile and mobilized to round them up. Although Sitting Bull remained at Grand River, both the Army and the Indian agent clung to a notion that, if the Indians were excited, he was the cause.

McLaughlin wanted to have Sitting Bull arrested. For a while, decision on the matter was held up by a dispute over whether the arrest should be carried out by military or civil authority. General Nelson Miles, who was contemptuous of all Indian agents, decided he would circumvent McLaughlin by a novel scheme: thinking that Sitting Bull's old friend Buffalo Bill Cody had the best chance of peacefully separating him from his people, he gave the showman the job of luring the chief to the nearest military post with promises of gifts. However, McLaughlin, resenting this infringement on his authority, persuaded Washington to cancel the plan. As it turned out, it might have been better all around if Cody had been allowed to proceed.

On December 14, 1890, having received word that Sitting Bull was determined to visit the Pine Ridge Agency south of Standing Rock, McLaughlin decided to make the arrest immediately. Aware that Sitting Bull's loyal followers would be outraged at the act, he decided that the arrest could best be accomplished by Indian policemen. He assigned the job to Lieutenant Henry Bull Head, a Sioux.

On that cold and starless winter night, a party of about 40 Sioux police — called Metal Breasts by other tribesmen because of their badges — converged on Sitting Bull's Grand River camp. At dawn they surrounded the chief's cabin. Bull Head burst through the door and dragged Sitting Bull from his bed. A kerosene lamp was lighted. Bull Head told Sitting Bull he was under arrest. Shave Head, a sergeant, said, "If you fight, you will be killed here."

At first, Sitting Bull said, "All right. Let me put on my clothes and I will go with you." But then, as the police manhandled him, trying to hold him and dress him at the same time, he began to protest. One of his wives berated the Metal Breasts, crying, "What are all you jealous people doing here?" By now, a curious throng had gathered outside.

When he was thrust out into the cold, tightly gripped by the Sioux policemen, Sitting Bull suddenly made up his mind. "I am not going," he shouted. Perhaps he remembered the meadowlark who had pronounced his fate. "The Sioux will kill you," the bird had said. "I'm not going," the chief insisted. Perhaps feeling himself betrayed by his own people, he wanted only to finish with it all at last.

Sitting Bull's followers, upon hearing his last defiant shout, acted. One of them fired a rifle at Lieutenant Bull Head. As the police chief fell, badly wounded, he managed to put a bullet into Sitting Bull. Sergeant Red Tomahawk, who had been pushing the captive, now

drew his gun and fired a shot into Sitting Bull's brain. General gunfire broke out, taking the lives of six policemen and eight of Sitting Bull's followers, including his 17-year-old son Crowfoot.

And so it was nearly over. The wagon that came to carry away the bodies of the policemen also carried that of Sitting Bull. It was placed in a homemade coffin filled with quicklime and interred in a corner of the military cemetery at Fort Yates.

Nearly over, but not quite. The last tragic act of Sitting Bull's heritage and destiny still had to be played out and another of his prophecies had to be fulfilled.

The killing of the chief exacerbated the turmoil that was already sweeping the reservation lands. Bands of Sioux fled here and there, all badly frightened, many of them still holding onto the hope of deliverance through the ghost dance miracle. Some of Sitting Bull's followers, uncertain of the Army's intentions, hurried toward the camp of Big Foot, a Miniconjou Sioux chief who lived 100 miles to the south. They met up with Big Foot while he and his people were on their way to agency headquarters near Fort Bennett on the Missouri River to procure rations.

Meanwhile, the reservation authorities had decided that Chief Big Foot was a potential troublemaker and should be taken into custody. Colonel E. V. Sumner of the 8th Cavalry was ordered to make the arrest. When he intercepted the band, Big Foot gave assurances to the officer that their intentions were peaceful and lawful. Then why, Sumner demanded, had they taken in and sheltered hostiles from Sitting Bull's camp? Big Foot replied that he had found 38 men and women who were hungry, footsore and nearly naked in midwinter. Anybody with a heart would have done the same thing, he told the colonel.

Sumner nevertheless ordered Big Foot's followers, numbering more than 300, to accompany him westward to Camp Cheyenne, where they would be kept under his watchful eye. They obeyed his orders without protest until they had traveled back to the vicinity of their own village. The Indians then announced that

Bull Head wore this badge when he led the force that arrested Sitting Bull in 1890.

they would not go any farther. Big Foot advised the colonel that they intended to return home and that they had done nothing to justify their removal. But during the night, alarmed by some reports of additional troops that were coming from the east, Big Foot's people fled toward refuge in the Badlands.

Orders came from General Miles to pursue and apprehend the fugitives. Another cavalry unit caught up with them on December 28. Carrying a white flag, Big Foot approached Major S. M. Whitside to parley. Whitside demanded an immediate surrender, and Big Foot, whose band was in no condition to fight, gave in. The troops hurried the bedraggled band southwest to Wounded Knee Creek and took up surrounding positions as the Indians set up camp.

By morning, four more cavalry troops had arrived under command of Colonel James Forsyth, bringing the escort to 470. Big Foot was now ailing with pneumonia, and Colonel Forsyth provided a camp stove to keep the sick man warm.

In the morning, Forsyth prepared to disarm his captives. To secure the field, his troops were disposed on all four sides of the Indian camp, and four rapid-fire Hotchkiss guns were set into place on a low hill overlooking the camp from the north. About 8 o'clock the Indian men came out of their tipis and sat in a semicircle in front of the troops. Colonel Forsyth issued orders that they should return to the lodges, 20 at a time, and bring out their guns. The first contingent obediently entered the tipis but, after some time, reappeared with only two weapons.

Forsyth, concluding that the Indians would not surrender the guns willingly, decided to take them by force. Troops around the warriors were moved up within 10 yards; others were detailed to go into the tipis and make a search. The soldiers went at their work with hard-handed zeal, scattering bedclothing, pawing through other property. Women inside the lodges protested with shrill cries.

Outside, resentful uneasiness quickly edged into hair-trigger tension. Then a medicine man called Yellow

DEC. 15. 1890. IND. POLICE Nº LITTLE EAGLE, AFRAIDOF SOLDIERS, HAWK MAN, BROKEN ARM, Wᴰ BULL HEAD, BRAVE HEAD, ALEX, MIDDLE. HOSTILES Nº SITTING BULL, CROW FOOT S.B.SON, BRAVE THUNDER & SON, CATCH-THE-BEAR, BLACK BEAR, ASSINABOINE & SPOTTED HORN BULL.

CAPTURE & DEATH OF SITTING I

YRIGHTED 1890 BY KURZ & ALLISON, ART PUBLISHERS, 76 & 78 WABASH AVE, CHICAGO, U.S.A.

In a fanciful 1891 lithograph, Sitting Bull, mounted on a white horse, meets a valiant end in pitched battle against soldiers. Actually, he was dragged from his bed by Indian police and shot when he resisted them.

Bird began blowing on an eagle-bone whistle and exhorting them to resist. When the soldiers began to search the warriors themselves, the situation exploded. A young Indian pulled a gun out from under his robe and fired wildly. Instantly, the soldiers retaliated with a point-blank volley which cut down nearly half the warriors. The rest of them drew concealed weapons and charged the soldiers.

Then the Hotchkiss guns on the hill opened up — on the women and children who had come pouring out of the tipis. Soon many of the tipis were burning, ripped by the explosive shells. A stumbling mass of women and children and a few warriors bolted into a ravine that led away from the encampment. The soldiers followed them, firing as they went. The Hotchkiss guns were then re-emplaced to sweep the ravine and cut down anything that moved.

Big Foot died as he tried to rise from his sickbed. Others managed to run as far as two miles from the camp before dying of their wounds. Twenty-five white men were killed and 39 wounded. Since the besieged Indians had few guns and since the troops were firing from four sides at once, it seemed likely that they caused many of their own casualties. The Indian dead numbered about 180. For three days they were left to lie where they fell while a winter blizzard swept over them.

A burial party was sent to the scene on New Year's Day, 1891. One by one the bodies, frozen in the grotesque agonies of death, were dragged from under the snow and heaved into a single pit. Four babies were discovered still alive, wrapped in their dead mothers' shawls. Most of the other children were dead. "It was a thing to melt the heart of a man, if it was of stone," said one member of the burial party, "to see those little children, with their bodies shot to pieces, thrown naked into the pit."

While collecting souvenirs, some of the men stripped the bodies. Beneath the outer layer of garments, several of the dead warriors wore the ghost shirts that were to have been impervious to bullets. Had he not already been two weeks in his grave, Sitting Bull would have seen here the final fulfillment of his vision during the sun dance on Rosebud Creek. To loot Custer's dead, he had prophesied, "would prove a curse to this nation." Custer's old regiment, the 7th Cavalry, had supplied the troops for the final holocaust at Wounded Knee.

225

Last convulsion of the Indian wars

In the turbulent days after Sitting Bull was killed, U.S. soldiers sped across the Sioux reservation to round up chiefs who might lead a full-scale uprising. On the morning of December 29, 1890, two cavalry squadrons and a company of artillerymen tried to disarm a band led by Chief Big Foot at a camp beside Wounded Knee Creek. During the confrontation, a medicine man began to perform the ghost dance, as though to suggest that the religion's prophecy of the collapse of white civilization might begin to come true here. Suddenly an Indian fired his gun, hitting no one but drawing a cataclysmic response from the soldiers' weapons. By the time a ceasefire was called about half of Big Foot's 350 followers, together with the chief himself, lay dead.

A woman who was badly hurt in the battle voiced the despair of all the survivors when she gave doctors permission to take off her ghost shirt: "Yes, take it off. They told me a bullet would not go through. Now I don't want it any more."

Within months the religion, along with its impossible promises, had faded away. But perhaps the real finale of the Indians' tragedy was enacted on New Year's Day, 1891, when white soldiers and civilians rode back to Big Foot's devastated camp and pried the victims out from under a shroud of ice and snow for an unceremonious burial.

Troopers of the 7th Cavalry survey the corpse-strewn field at Wounded Knee, blanketed by the first blizzard of the season.

Civilians hired to bury the Indians for two dollars a body pile the dead into a wagon, as cavalrymen keep watch for possible avengers.

Burial workers pause while filling a mass grave dug on the hill from which cannon raked the Sioux camp.

231

Chief Big Foot lies slumped where he fell in the first moments of the battle, with a trooper's bullet in his head.

TEXT CREDITS

For full reference on specific page credits see bibliography.

Chapter 1: Particularly useful source for information and quotes in this chapter: Mildred P. Mayhall, *The Kiowas,* University of Oklahoma Press, 1962; 6 — Lewis and Clark quote, Coues, Vol. II, p. 556; 27 — White Bear quote, Vanderwerth, p. 176; 30 — Physician quote, Mooney, "Calendar History of the Kiowa Indians," p. 177, Stanley quote, Belous and Weinstein, p. 59, reporter quote, Mooney, p. 207; 34 — White Bear quote, Mooney, p. 208; 37 — White Bear's trial speech, Capps, p. 183; 39 — Sherman quote, Andrist, p. 177; 41 — Sky Walker quote, Nye, *Carbine and Lance,* p. 233. Chapter 2: Particularly useful sources for information and quotes: Alexander B. Adams, *Geronimo,* G. P. Putnam's Sons, 1971; Britton Davis, *The Truth About Geronimo,* R. R. Donnelley & Sons Company, 1951; Morris E. Opler, *An Apache Life-Way,* Cooper Square Publishers, Inc., 1965; Dan L. Thrapp, *The Conquest of Apacheria,* University of Oklahoma Press, 1967; 66 — Carrasco quotes, Lockwood, pp. 35,36; 67 — Bourke on Cochise, Thrapp, p. 146, Bourke on Goklayeh, Bourke, p. 102, Goklayeh addressing Chiricahuas, Barrett, p. 90; 72 — Quote on Bascom Affair, *Arizona Star,* June 28, 1877; 78 — Jeffords quotes, Lockwood, p. 111; 81 — Cochise on pact, Lockwood, p. 121; Cochise dying, Lockwood, p. 129. Chapter 3: Particularly useful sources for information and quotes: T. R. Fehrenbach, *Comanches: The Destruction of a People,* Alfred A. Knopf, 1974; Rupert Norval Richardson, *The Comanche Barrier to South Plains Settlement,* The Arthur H. Clark Company, 1933; Zoe A. Tilghman, *Quanah: The Eagle of the Commanches,* Harlow Publishing Corp., 1938; Ernest Wallace and E. Adamson Hoebel, *The Comanches: Lords of the South Plains,* University of Oklahoma Press, 1964; G. Derek West, "The Battle of Adobe Walls," *Panhandle-Plains Historical Review,* Vol. 36, 1936; 103 — Carter quotes on Quanah and

Kwahadies, Carter, pp. 153,217,176; 109 — Officer describing central Texas, Rister, p. 104; 124 — Quanah quote, Jackson, p. 126; 126 — Quanah speech of thanks, Jackson, p. 127. Chapter 4: Particularly useful sources for information and quotes: Virginia Cole Trenholm and Maurine Carley, *The Shoshonis, Sentinels of the Rockies,* University of Oklahoma Press, 1964; Grace Raymond Hebard, *Washakie,* The Arthur H. Clark Company, 1930; 139 — Journal quote, DeVoto, p. 202; 154 — Col. Gibbon quote, Stewart, p. 106, Lt. Bourke quote, Bourke, p. 303; 156 — Bourke quotes, Bourke, p. 304,316. Chapter 5: Particularly useful sources for information and quotes: Merrill D. Beal, *"I Will Fight No More Forever": Chief Joseph and the Nez Percé War,* University of Washington Press, 1963; Francis Haines, *The Nez Percés,* University of Oklahoma Press, 1955; Helen Addison Howard, *Saga of Chief Joseph,* The Caxton Printers, Ltd., 1965; Alvin M. Josephy Jr., *The Nez Percé Indians and the Opening of the Northwest,* Yale University Press, 1971; 177 — Sgt. McCarthy quote, Brown, p. 190, Tom Sutherland quote, Brown, p. 195; 183 — Joseph on death of his people, *North American Review,* Vol. 128 (April, 1879), p. 430, Joseph on his home, Howard, p. 364. Chapter 6: Particularly useful sources for information and quotes: Robert M. Utley, *The Last Days of the Sioux Nation,* Yale University Press, 1963; Robert M. Utley, *Frontier Regulars: The United States Army and the Indian,* Macmillan Publishing Co., Inc., 1973; Stanley Vestal, *Sitting Bull: Champion of the Sioux,* University of Oklahoma Press, 1972; 197 — Quote from Treaty of Laramie, Vestal, *New Sources,* pp. 224-225; 220 — McLaughlin quote on absurd nonsense, Mooney, *The Ghost-Dance Religion,* p. 29, McLaughlin quote on new religion, Russell, pp. 356-357; 225 — Burial party quote on seeing dead children, Mooney, pp. 131-132.

PICTURE CREDITS

The sources for the illustrations are shown below. Credits from left to right are separated by semicolons, from top to bottom by dashes.

Cover — Paulus Leeser, courtesy Rare Book Division, The New York Public Library, Astor, Lenox and Tilden Foundations. 2 — Courtesy Rare Book Division, The New York Public Library, Astor, Lenox and Tilden Foundations. 7,8 — Courtesy of Smithsonian Institution. 9 — Henry Beville, courtesy of Smithsonian Institution. 10,11 — Courtesy of Smithsonian Institution. 12,13 — Henry Beville, courtesy of Smithsonian Institution. 14 — Courtesy of Smithsonian Institution, National Anthropological Archives. 16 — Map by Rafael D. Palacios. 18,19 — Charles Phillips, detail of watercolor, courtesy of Smithsonian Institution. 20 — Paulus Leeser, courtesy McElhaney Collection, U.S. Army Field Artillery and Fort Sill Museum. 21 — Courtesy of Smithsonian Institution, NAA. 22 — Courtesy of Smithsonian Institution. 24 — Courtesy of Lowie Museum of Anthropology, University of California, Berkeley. 28,29 — Charles Phillips, detail of watercolor, courtesy of Smithsonian Institution. 31 — Courtesy of Smithsonian Institution, NAA. 32,33 — Courtesy U.S. Army Field Artillery and Fort Sill Museum. 34 — Courtesy History Division, Natural History Museum of Los Angeles County. 35 — Courtesy of the Texas State Archives. 36 — Courtesy Rare Book Division, The New York Public Library, Astor, Lenox and Tilden Foundations. 38 — Courtesy of Smithsonian Institution, NAA. 40 — Courtesy National Archives. 42,43 — Courtesy Western Americana Collection, Yale University Library. 44 through 53 — Paulus Leeser, courtesy Private Collection. 54,55 — Courtesy Library of Congress. 56,

57 — Courtesy of Smithsonian Institution, NAA. 58 through 61 — Courtesy Library of Congress. 62 — Courtesy Prints Division, The New York Public Library, Astor, Lenox and Tilden Foundations. 64 — Lance, Frank Lerner, courtesy of The American Museum of Natural History — Sling, courtesy Museum of the American Indian, Heye Foundation — Bow and Case, Paulus Leeser, courtesy U.S. Army Field Artillery and Fort Sill Museum. 65 — War club, Paulus Leeser, from private collection of Morris E. Opler — Quiver and arrows, Paulus Leeser, courtesy U.S. Army Field Artillery and Fort Sill Museum. 68 — Courtesy Western History Department, Denver Public Library. 69 — Courtesy Museum of New Mexico. 70,71 — Paulus Leeser, courtesy Oklahoma Historical Society. 74, 75 — Courtesy of Smithsonian Institution, NAA, except bottom left, courtesy National Archives. 76,77 — Courtesy of Smithsonian Institution, NAA, except bottom right, courtesy Museum of New Mexico. 78,79 — From the collection of Jacques Noel Jacobsen Jr., Staten Island, N.Y. 80 — Victorio and Nana copied from the collections of the Arizona Historical Society, Alchesay courtesy Western History Department, Denver Public Library, others courtesy of Smithsonian Institution, NAA. 82 through 85 — Courtesy National Archives. 87,88,89 — Courtesy Library of Congress. 90,91 — Paulus Leeser, courtesy U.S. Army Field Artillery and Fort Sill Museum. 92 — Courtesy Western History Department, Denver Public Library, 94 — Courtesy Bettmann Archive. 95 — Courtesy National Archives. 96 — Courtesy of Smithsonian Institution, NAA. 97 — Cour-

tesy Kansas State Historical Society, Topeka. 98— Courtesy The Thomas Gilcrease Institute of American History and Art, Tulsa, Oklahoma. 99— Courtesy of Smithsonian Institution, NAA. 100,101— Courtesy of Smithsonian Institution. 102— Courtesy of Smithsonian Institution, NAA. 104,105— Courtesy of Smithsonian Institution. 106 — Courtesy Edward E. Ayer Collection, The Newberry Library. 108 — Courtesy Rare Book Division, The New York Public Library, Astor, Lenox and Tilden Foundations. 110,111— Painting by Louise Meusebach Marschall, copied by Paulus Leeser, courtesy Pioneer Museum, Gillespie County (Texas) Historical Society and State Survey Committee. 112,113— Courtesy Kansas State Historical Society. 115 — Courtesy Panhandle Plains Historical Museum. 116,117— Courtesy Arthur R. Lawrence, Lawton, Oklahoma. 118— Paulus Leeser, courtesy Panhandle Plains Historical Museum. 120,121— Courtesy Thomas Gilcrease Institute of American History and Art. 121— Inset courtesy U.S. Army Field Artillery and Fort Sill Museum. 122— Courtesy of Smithsonian Institution, NAA. 123— Courtesy of Smithsonian Institution, NAA — courtesy Thomas Gilcrease Institute of American History and Art. 125— Courtesy of the Texas State Archives. 126,127 — Courtesy Thomas Gilcrease Institute of American History and Art. 128— Courtesy of Smithsonian Institution, NAA — Lloyd Rule, courtesy Denver Art Museum. 129— Lloyd Rule, courtesy Denver Art Museum. 130 through 135— Courtesy The Walters Art Gallery. 136 — Frank Lerner, courtesy The American Numismatic Society, New York. 138— Courtesy Western History Department, Denver Public Library. 140,141— Courtesy of The Oakland Museum, Andrew J. Russell Collection. 144,145— Courtesy The Haynes Foundation. 147— Frank Lerner, courtesy National Archives. 148 through 150— Courtesy of Smithsonian Institution, NAA. 151 through 153 — Courtesy Western History Department, Denver Public Library. 155 — Courtesy of Smithsonian Institution, NAA. 157— Courtesy The Huntington Library, San Marino, California. 158,159— Courtesy American History Division, The New York Public Library, Astor, Lenox and Tilden Foundations. 160,161— Courtesy of Smithsonian Institution, NAA. 162,163— Henry Beville, courtesy of Smithsonian Institution, NAA. 164— Courtesy Library of Congress. 167— Herb Orth, Time-Life Picture Agency, from *Wilderness Kingdom: The Journals and Paintings of Nicolas Point, S. J.* Copyright ©1967 by Loyola University Press, Chicago. Translated and introduced by Joseph P. Donnelly, S.J. Reproduced by permission of Holt, Rinehart and Winston, Publishers. 168— Washington State Historical Society, courtesy American Heritage. 170,171— Courtesy of Smithsonian Institution, NAA. 173— From *The Illustrated Wasp*, September 1, 1877, courtesy Bancroft Library. 174— Courtesy Library of Congress. 175— Courtesy of Smithsonian Institution, NAA; courtesy Culver Pictures; courtesy National Archives. 176— Map by Rafael D. Palacios. 178— Courtesy Horner Collection, Enterprise Public Library. 179,182— Courtesy of Smithsonian Institution, NAA. 184,185— Courtesy Montana Historical Society. 186 through 189— Courtesy National Archives. 190— Courtesy National Archives — courtesy American History Division, The New York Public Library, Astor, Lenox and Tilden Foundations. 191— Courtesy American History Division, The New York Public Library, Astor, Lenox and Tilden Foundations. 192,193— Courtesy The Thomas Gilcrease Institute of American History and Art. 194— Courtesy Western History Department, Denver Public Library. 197— Henry Beville, courtesy of Smithsonian Institution, NAA. 198— Lloyd Rule, courtesy Denver Art Museum. 200— Henry Beville, courtesy of Smithsonian Institution. 201— Henry Beville, courtesy of Smithsonian Institution — Frank Lerner, courtesy of Smithsonian Institution. 202— Paulus Leeser, courtesy Robinson Museum, Pierre, S.D. 203— Paulus Leeser, courtesy State Historical Society of North Dakota. 204,205— Courtesy of Smithsonian Institution, NAA. 207— Courtesy Royal Canadian Mounted Police Museum, Regina, Saskatchewan, Canada. 208,209 — Courtesy of Smithsonian Institution, NAA. 210— Paulus Leeser, courtesy State Historical Society of North Dakota. 212,213— Courtesy Map Division, The New York Public Library, Astor, Lenox and Tilden Foundations. 214,215— Courtesy of Smithsonian Institution, NAA. 217— Courtesy Library of Congress. 218,219— Courtesy Museum of the American Indian, Heye Foundation. 221— Courtesy Notman Photographic Archives, McCord Museum, McGill University, Montreal, Quebec, Canada. 222— Paulus Leeser, courtesy State Historical Society of North Dakota. 223,224,225— Courtesy Western History Department, Denver Public Library. 226,227— Courtesy The Huntington Library. 228,229— Courtesy of Smithsonian Institution, NAA. 230, 231— Courtesy Montana Historical Society. 232,233— Charles Phillips, courtesy of Smithsonian Institution, NAA.

ACKNOWLEDGMENTS

The editors wish to give special thanks to the following persons who read and commented on portions of the book: Dr. Raymond J. DeMallie Jr., Department of Anthropology, Indiana University, Bloomington; Francis Haines, Sun City, Arizona; Dr. Mildred Mayhall, Austin, Texas; Dr. Ernest Wallace, Horn Professor of History, Texas Tech University, Lubbock.

The editors also acknowledge the help of: Amon Carter Museum of Western Art, Fort Worth; Manon Atkins, Joe L. Todd, Curator of Collections, Oklahoma Historical Society; James Auchiah, Carnegie, Okla.; Jeremiah D. Brady, Curator of Metals, American Numismatic Society, New York; Margaret Bret Harte, Research Librarian, Loretta Davisson, Asst. Research Librarian, Arizona Historical Society; Andrea Brown, Photo Services, National Collection of Fine Arts, Smithsonian Institution; Richard Conn, Curator of Native Art, Denver Art Museum; Albert B. Elsasser, Assoc. Res. Anthropologist, Robert H. Lowie Museum of Anthropology, Univ. of California, Berkeley; Dr. John C. Ewers, Senior Ethnologist, Dept. of Anthropology, Smithsonian Institution; Eleanor Ferrall, Ref. Librarian, Arizona Collection, Arizona State Univ.; Tracy Forbes, Walters Art Gallery, Baltimore, Md.; Eleanor Gehres, Dept. Head, Opal Harber, Librarian, Agostino Mastrogiuseppe, Curator of Photographs, Western History Dept., Denver Public Library; Philip Gifford, Dept. of Anthropology, American Museum of Natural History, New York; Gillett Griswold, Dir., Walter Jones, Asst. Curator, U.S. Army Field Artillery and Fort Sill Museum, Fort Sill, Okla.; Jack D. Haley, Asst. Curator, Marion Jackson, Bill Mount, Western History Collections, Univ. of Oklahoma; Dr. James A. Hanson, Dir., Claire Kuehn, Archivist-Librarian, The Panhandle-Plains Historical Museum, Canyon, Texas; Villette Harris, Washington, D.C.; David B. Hartley, Museum Curator, Bonnie Gardner, Photos, South Dakota State Historical Society; Isabel M. Haynes, President, The Haynes Foundation, Bozeman, Mont.; Joan Hofmann, Senior Library Specialist, Beinecke Rare Book and Manuscript Library, Yale Univ.; Jerry L. Kearns, Head of Reference, Prints and Photographs, Library of Congress; Gary Kurutz, Photos, Mary Wright, Rare Books, Henry E. Huntington Library, San Marino, Calif.; Robert Kvasnicka, Richard Crawford, Natural Resources Branch, Civil Archives Div., National Archives; Alice Marriott, Oklahoma City; Harriet Meloy, Librarian, Montana Historical Society; John Miller, Chief, and the staff of the American History Div., Maud D. Cole, Rare Books Div., The New York Public Library, New York City; Prof. Morris E. Opler, Norman, Okla.; Norman Paulson, Curator, State Historical Society of North Dakota; Paula Richardson, Museum Specialist, National Anthropological Archives, Smithsonian Institution; R. Henderson Shuffler, Exec. Dir., Univ. of Texas Institute of Texan Cultures at San Antonio; Dan L. Thrapp, Whittier, Calif.; Virginia Cole Trenholm, Cheyenne, Wyo.; Robert M. Utley, Dir., Office of Archeology and Historic Preservation, National Park Service, U.S. Dept. of the Interior; M.J.H. Wake, Dir., Royal Canadian Mounted Police Museum, Regina, Saskatchewan, Canada; Oliver Willcox, Staff Photographer, Thomas Gilcrease Institute of American History and Art, Tulsa, Okla.; Steve Wilson, Dir., Museum of the Great Plains, Lawton, Okla.

BIBLIOGRAPHY

Adams, Alexander B.:
    Geronimo. G. P. Putnam's Sons, 1971.
    Sitting Bull: An Epic of the Plains. Putnam, 1973.
Andrist, Ralph K., *The Long Death: The Last Days of the Plains Indians.* Collier Books, 1964.
Annual Report of the Commissioner of Indian Affairs. 1874, 1881, 1889. U. S. Government Printing Office.
Barrett, S. M., ed., *Geronimo — His Own Story.* Ballantine, 1973.
Beal, Merrill D., *"I Will Fight No More Forever": Chief Joseph and the Nez Perce War.* Univ. of Washington Press, 1963.
Belous, R. E., and R. A. Weinstein, *Will Soule: Indian Photographer at Fort Sill, Oklahoma 1869-74.* Ward Ritchie, 1969.
Betzinez, Jason, with Wilbur Sturtevant Nye, *I Fought with Geronimo.* Stackpole, 1960.
Billington, Ray A., *Westward Expansion: A History of the American Frontier.* Macmillan, 1967.
Bourke, John G.:
    An Apache Campaign in the Sierra Madre. Charles Scribner's Sons, 1958.
    On the Border with Crook. Univ. of Nebraska Press, 1971.
Brown, Dee, *Bury My Heart at Wounded Knee.* Holt, Rinehart & Winston, 1971.
Brown, Mark H., *The Flight of the Nez Perce.* Capricorn, 1967.
Capps, Benjamin, *The Warren Wagontrain Raid.* Dial, 1974.
Carter, Captain Robert G., *On the Border with Mackenzie.* Eynon Printing Company, 1935.
Catlin, George, *North American Indians,* Vols. I and II. Ross & Haines, 1965.
Connor, Seymour V., *Texas: A History.* Thomas Y. Crowell, 1971.
Coues, Elliott, ed., *History of the Expedition under the Command of Lewis and Clark,* Vol. II. Dover Publications, Inc., 1965.
Cremony, J. C., *Life Among the Apaches.* Rio Grande Press, 1970.
Davis, Britton, *The Truth About Geronimo.* R. R. Donnelley & Sons, 1951.
DeVoto, Bernard, ed., *The Journals of Lewis and Clark.* Houghton Mifflin, 1953.
Dodge, Col. R. E., *Our Wild Indians.* A. D. Worthington, 1890.
Dorsey, James Owen, "A Study of Siouan Cults," *11th Annual Report Bur. of American Ethnol.,* Smithsonian Institution, 1889-1890.
Downey, Fairfax, and Jacques Noel Jacobsen Jr., *The Red Bluecoats.* The Old Army Press, 1973.
Ellis, Richard N., *General Pope and U.S. Indian Policy.* Univ. of New Mexico Press, 1970.
Ewers, John C., *Indian Life on the Upper Missouri.* Univ. of Oklahoma Press, 1968.
Faulk, Odie B.:
    Land of Many Frontiers. Oxford Univ. Press, 1968.
    The Last Years of Spanish Texas 1778-1821. Mouton & Co., 1964.
Fehrenbach, T. R., *Comanches: The Destruction of a People.* Alfred A. Knopf, 1974.
Frazer, Robert W., *Forts of the West.* Univ. of Oklahoma Press, 1965.
Fritz, Henry E., *The Movement for Indian Assimilation, 1860-1890.* Univ. of Pennsylvania Press, 1963.
Gard, Wayne, *The Great Buffalo Hunt.* Univ. of Nebraska Press, 1959.

Grinnell, George Bird, *Two Great Scouts and Their Pawnee Battalion.* Univ. of Nebraska Press, 1973.

Haines, Francis, *The Nez Perces.* Univ. of Oklahoma Press, 1955.

Hassrick, Royal B., *The Sioux/The Life and Customs of a Warrior Society.* Univ. of Oklahoma Press, 1967.

Hebard, Grace R., *Washakie.* The Arthur H. Clark Company, 1930.

Hodge, Frederick W., ed., *Handbook of American Indians, North of Mexico,* Vols. I and II. Rowman and Littlefield, 1971.

Howard, Helen A., *Saga of Chief Joseph.* The Caxton Printers, 1965.

Howe, George Frederick, *Chester A. Arthur: A Quarter Century of Machine Politics.* Dodd, Mead, 1934.

Howell, Edgar M., "Hermann Stieffel, Soldier-Artist of the West." U.S. National Museum Bulletin No. 225, Smithsonian Institution, 1960.

Hyde, G. E., *The Pawnee Indians.* Univ. of Oklahoma Press, 1974.

Jackson, Clyde L. and Grace, *Quanah Parker: Last Chief of the Comanches.* Exposition Press, 1963.

Johnson, V. W., *The Unregimented General.* Houghton Mifflin, 1962.

Joseph, Chief, "An Indian's Views of Indian Affairs," *North American Review.* April, 1879.

Josephy, Alvin M., Jr., *The Nez Perce Indians and the Opening of the Northwest.* Yale Univ. Press, 1971.

Kennedy, M. S., ed., *The Red Man's West.* Hastings House, 1965.

Lockwood, Frank C., *The Apache Indians.* Macmillan, 1938.

Mails, Thomas E.:
The Mystic Warriors of the Plains. Doubleday, 1972.
The People Called Apache. Prentice-Hall, 1974.

Mayhall, Mildred P., *The Kiowas.* Univ. of Oklahoma Press, 1962.

McCracken, H., *George Catlin and the Old Frontier.* Dial, 1959.

Mooney, James:
The Ghost-Dance Religion and the Sioux Outbreak of 1890. Univ. of Chicago Press, 1965.
"Calendar History of the Kiowa Indians," *17th Annual Report Bur. of American Ethnol.,* Part I, 1895-1896. Smithsonian Institution.

Newcomb, W. W., *The Indians of Texas.* Univ. of Texas Press, 1961.

Nye, Wilbur Sturtevant, *Carbine and Lance: The Story of Old Fort Sill.* Univ. of Oklahoma Press, 1969.

Ogle, Ralph Hedrick, *Federal Control of the Western Apaches, 1848-1886.* Univ. of New Mexico Press, 1970.

Opler, Morris E., *An Apache Life-Way.* Cooper Square Publ., 1965.

Otis, D. S., *The Dawes Act and the Allotment of Indian Lands.* Univ. of Oklahoma Press, 1973.

Peterson, Karen Daniels, *Plains Indian Art from Fort Marion.* Univ. of Oklahoma Press, 1971.

Pratt, Richard Henry, *Battlefield and Classroom.* Yale Univ. Press, 1964.

Prucha, Francis Paul:
Americanizing the American Indian. Harvard Univ. Press, 1973.
A Guide to the Military Posts of the United States 1789-1895. The State Historical Society of Wisconsin, 1966.
Indian Peace Medals in American History. The State Historical Society of Wisconsin, 1971.

Reynolds, Sidney O., "The Redskin Who Saved The White Man's Hide," *American Heritage,* Vol. XI, Feb. 1960.

Richardson, Rupert N.:
The Comanche Barrier to South Plains Settlement. The Arthur M. Clark Company, 1933.
Editor, "The Death of Nocona and the Recovery of Cynthia Ann Parker," *Southwestern Historical Quarterly,* XLVI, 1942.

Rister, Carl Coke, *The Southwestern Frontier—1865-1881.* The Arthur H. Clark Company, 1928.

Ross, Marvin C., *The West of Alfred Jacob Miller.* Univ. of Oklahoma Press, 1951.

Russell, Don, *The Lives and Legends of Buffalo Bill.* Univ. of Oklahoma Press, 1960.

Scott, Hugh Lenox, "Notes on the Kado, or Sun Dance of the Kiowa," *American Anthropologist,* Vol. XIII, No. 3, 1911.

Stewart, Edgar I., *Custer's Luck.* Univ. of Oklahoma Press, 1955.

Stirling, M. W., *Three Pictographic Autobiographies of Sitting Bull.* Smithsonian Miscellaneous Collections, Vol. 97, No. 5, Smithsonian Institution, 1938.

Tatum, Lawrie, *Our Red Brothers and the Peace Policy of President Ulysses S. Grant.* Univ. of Nebraska Press, 1971.

Thrapp, Dan L.:
The Conquest of Apacheria. Univ. of Oklahoma Press, 1967.
Victorio and The Mimbres Apaches. Univ. of Oklahoma Press, 1974.

Tilden, Freeman, *Following the Frontier With F. Jay Haynes.* Alfred A. Knopf, 1964.

Tilghman, Z. A., *Quanah: The Eagle of the Comanches.* Harlow, 1938.

Trenholm, Virginia Cole, and Maurine Carley, *The Shoshonis, Sentinels of the Rockies.* Univ. of Oklahoma Press, 1964.

Utley, Robert M.:
Custer Battlefield. Office of Publ., National Park Service, U.S. Dept. of the Interior, 1969.
Frontier Regulars, the United States Army and the Indian, 1866-1891. Macmillan, 1973.
The Last Days of the Sioux Nation, Yale Univ. Press, 1973.
"The Bascom Affair: A Reconstruction," *Arizona and the West,* Vol. III, No. I (Spring 1961), 59-68.

Vaughn, J. W., *With Crook at the Rosebud.* Stackpole, 1956.

Vestal, Stanley:
New Sources of Indian History. Univ. of Oklahoma Press, 1934.
Sitting Bull, Champion of the Sioux. Univ. of Oklahoma Press, 1972.

Wagoner, Jay J., *Arizona Territory, 1863-1912, A Political History.* Univ. of Arizona Press, 1970.

Wallace, Edward S., "General Ranald Slidell Mackenzie: Indian Fighting Cavalryman," *Southwestern Historical Quarterly,* XLVI, 1953.

Wallace, Ernest, *Texas in Turmoil.* Steck-Vaughn, 1965.

Wallace, Ernest, and E. Adamson Hoebel, *The Comanches: Lords of the South Plains.* Univ. of Oklahoma Press, 1964.

Wellman, Paul I.:
Death on The Prairie. Macmillan, 1934.
Death In The Desert. Macmillan, 1935.
"Cynthia Ann Parker," *Chronicles of Oklahoma,* XII, 1934.

West, G. Derek, "The Battle of Adobe Walls," *Panhandle-Plains Historical Review,* Vol. 36, 1963.

Wharfield, Col. H. B., *Alchesay.* Arizona Pioneers Hist. Soc., 1969.

Wiltsey, N. B., *Brave Warriors.* The Caxton Printers, 1964.

Wissler, Clark, *Indians of the United States.* Doubleday, 1940.

Wood, Norman B., *Lives of Famous Indian Chiefs.* L. W. Walter Co., 1906.